Benjamin Morgan

Shams

Or, Uncle Ben's Experience with Hypocrites

Benjamin Morgan

Shams
Or, Uncle Ben's Experience with Hypocrites

ISBN/EAN: 9783337141103

Printed in Europe, USA, Canada, Australia, Japan

Cover: Foto ©ninafisch / pixelio.de

More available books at **www.hansebooks.com**

...SHAMS...

....OR....

UNCLE BEN'S EXPERIENCE WITH HYPOCRITES.

A story of simple Country Life giving a Humorous and Entertaining Picture of Every Day Life and Incidents in the Rural Districts, with Uncle Ben's trip to the city of Chicago and to California, and his Experience with the Shams and Sharpers of the Metropolitan World.

BY JOHN S. DRAPER,

OTHERWISE,

UNCLE BEN MORGAN, OF MORGANVILLE, N. Y.

THOMPSON & THOMAS,
PUBLISHERS.
924 DEARBORN STREET, CHICAGO.

COPYRIGHTED BY
JOHN S. DRAPER,
1887.

WITH THE HOPE THAT THE SAME

HONEST SIMPLICITY THAT HAS MARKED HER GIRLHOOD

MAY ADORN HER FUTURE LIFE, THIS WORK IS

DEDICATED

TO HIS DAUGHTER

MABEL,

BY THE AUTHOR.

PREFATORY.

According to the custom of authors my story should be introduced to the public in some befitting manner. How best to make you acquainted with it, so as to save time and words, I know not, unless I divide you into two classes, viz: Plain, honest folks, and hypocrites. The first class have so often formed the acquaintance of the last that the experiences of Uncle Ben will no doubt call to your minds so many incidents of your past life, sad and joyous, pathetic and laughable, sublime and ridiculous, that you will be interested from first to last, and when you have finished the story, you will say, "I am glad I met Uncle Ben Morgan. I have gone over my past, and have brighter glimpses of the future; I have drawn lessons of value from every chapter." The last class will discover their photographs hanging on the walls, houses, barns, fences, telegraph poles, Rocky Mountains' sides, in the hotels, steamboats, cars, private offices, and in the churches, and they can also trace their course through life backward, whether with pleasure or remorse Uncle Ben leaves them to decide. With the hope that the reader will not only be amused, but profited by the time spent in "Uncle Ben's Experience with the Hypocrites,"

I am yours truly,

BENJAMIN MORGAN.

P. S.—Since writing this book I have sat up nights and Mondays, reading Webster's Dictionary through, to correct the bad spelling. I couldn't find a grammar big enough to do me any good, so I have used everybody's everyday grammar.

CONTENTS.

CHAPTER I.
Uncle Ben Meets Clarissa at the Gate—His Attack of Inspiration—Clarissa's Surprise—He Overcomes the Obstacles, and Writes a Book............ 11

CHAPTER II.
Planting Corn vs. Inspiration—A Visit to Jim Teeters—Teeters buys her Butter and Eggs—Teeters a Methodist and I a Baptist—Clarissa and I Discussing Betsy's Coming Visit—Forgetfulness—Mary's Plan........................ 15

CHAPTER III.
Sickness in the Neighborhood—Clarissa in Demand—Nancy's Carelessness—The Doctor's Timely Arrival—A Meeting in the Red Schoolhouse—Ingersoll's Hypocritical Tirade—Clarissa's Comments.................................. 25

CHAPTER IV.
Betsey Teeters' Visit—Teeters as a Schemer—Clarissa on Teeters—The Quilting—The Dinner—Woman's Rights Question—Clarissa Settles it—Sally Tompkins indorses Teeters' Remarks—Sarah Smuggins in no Danger of being Subject............ 29

CHAPTER V.
The Quilting Party Broken Up—Mary's Party—Mary's Organ—Influence of Music —Melanethon Stevens' Musical Tour—Bascom Bigler's Speech—Sarah Smuggins and Bigler—The Party dissolved after an Announcement of a Literary Meeting at the Waddles Corners Schoolhouse—Clarissa Talks in her Sleep.................. 39

CHAPTER VI.
The Waddles Corners Meeting—Speech of Timothy Brown—Organizing a Lyceum —Music—Debate. Question: Which is the Most Beneficial to the People, Lawyers or Doctors—Decision—A Spelling Match—Elder Jonas Danberry's Speech on the Importance of Right Spelling—Julia Spears' Essay—Music..................... 50

CHAPTER VII.
Discussing the Lyceum—Disappointment of Clarissa and Benjamin—Jim and Betsey's Visit—Teeters buys the Hogs—Benjamin Drives the Hogs to the Village—Teet-

CONTENTS.

ers' Scheme Discovered—Benjamin's loss $273.78—Benjamin's Meditation—Confession to Clarissa—Transfer of the Finances... 68

CHAPTER VIII.

Methodist Meeting at the Red Schoolhouse—Elder Danberry's Prayer—Clarissa on Sin—Sermon by Presiding Elder Jones—Relating their Experience—Clarissa's Comments on the Sermon... 74

CHAPTER IX.

Lecture on Phrenology at the Waddles Corners Schoolhouse—Speech of Timothy Brown, introducing Professor Theodocius Leviticus Feeler——The Professor's Lecture —Examination of Clarissa's and Benjamin's Heads—A Strong Contrast—Examination of George Waddles' and B. B. Bigler's Heads—A Strong Similarity—The Phrenologist's Dream.. 86

CHAPTER X.

A Visit to Jim Smuggins, the Infidel—Jim Wants to Examine Ben's Head—Ben's Scorching Reply—The Ferry Boat—Clarissa's Views in Regard to Man's Responsibility and Future Destiny—Benjamin Surprised and Smuggins Astonished—Sarah Criticises the Creator—The Storm Brewing—Clarissa and Benjamin go Home—Ebenezer and Mary in the Front Room—Two is Company, More is Not—How Tedious and Tasteless the Hours... 112

CHAPTER XI.

Zolliver Ramsdell and Nancy Boyles Married—Ebenezer and Mary's Awkward Position at the Wedding—Bigler at the Republican Convention—Defeated—He Enters the Democratic—is Nominated—Tom Conners nominated for Assemblyman by the Republicans against Bigler—Hot Campaign Work—The Election—Bigler Defeated—Sick and Disgusted Bigler decides to go West—Benjamin's Confidence in his Wife—Benjamin on Politics—Ladies' Sewing Society—Mrs. Dave Kirk's Letter of Condolence to Squire Bigler... 124

CHAPTER XII.

George Waddles and Jim Teeters Caught Swindling—Both in Jail—The Methodists meet to Discuss the Advisability of Expelling them from the Church—Disaster to the Church... 136

CHAPTER XIII.

Mrs. Buzzbee's Paper—The Advertisement—Mr. and Mrs. Morgan Decide to go to California—They Start—Two Days in Syracuse—Uncle Ben at the Club House—His Rebuke to the Mayor and Prominent Citizens.. 145

CHAPTER XIV.

He Attends the Temperance Meeting—He buys the Tickets........................ 151

CONTENTS. ix

CHAPTER XV.
PAGE.
Their First Night in the Sleeping Car—They View Buffalo from the Depot in Twenty Minutes—Buys a Paper 155

CHAPTER XVI.
The First Meal in a Dining Car—Gets Acquainted with Four Elegant Gentlemen, Messrs. Smooth, Three, Kard and Monte.. 163

CHAPTER XVII.
They Teach Him how to Play Cards—About to Cash a $500 Check—Timely Interference of Clarissa—She Mends his Coat—He gets into a Crowd at the Cleveland Depot with his New Acquaintances—Goes into Dining Car for Supper—When he looks for Money to Pay he Discovers he is Robbed of every Cent, about $1,500—A Horrible Night in an Attic Berth—The Panorama—Arrival in Chicago............................ 173

CHAPTER XVIII.
They take the Bus for the Palmer House—Arrival at the Great Hotel—Write their names on the Big Book—Take a Balloon Ride—You are still in the Palmer House—His Money is Saved—Clarissa his Guardian Angel—Breakfast in the Grand Dining Room—He Shows Clarissa the Pretty Things with his Fork—What's the Price of hogs, Clover?—How did you know my Name?—She is a Dumb Good Cook Anyhow—The Clerk Directs Clarissa to her Friends—The News Boys on Corner of State and Monroe Streets—A Ride on the Cable Cars—The Home of the Friendless—Battle of Gettysburgh—Douglas Monument—Hahnemann College—Ben on Glory—In Favor of Pensioning the Soldiers and Their Widows—Return to Dinner................................ 187

CHAPTER XIX.
After Dinner Talk—The Anarchists—The Jury—The Brass Band—Going to the Fat Stock Show—On the Wrong Road—Bunions and Corns are Troublesome—Terribly Deceived—Relating his Experience in the Palmer House Office—Meets the Tribune Reporter—Advice to the Town Tattler—Clover is a little too Dusty to Chaw—Palmer House Lobby in the Evening—The Abraham, Solomon and Isaac's Combination Troop—The Evening on the Balcony.. 206

CHAPTER XX.
Uncle Ben and Clarissa call on Mayor Harrison—His Pleasant Reception—The Tribune's Notice of their Arrival in the City—The Mayor on Reporters—Their Departure—Uncle Ben Dumped into a Peanut Cart on the Sidewalk—A Visit to the Dime Museum—Dante's Inferno—The Dinner—Mrs. Langtry the Recipient of Small Bouquets—Clarissa receives Big Bouquets from Big Men—The Comparison—Clarissa Receives Several Letters of Invitation—Benjamin Receives a Letter from Kohl & Middleton with a View to Business—His Reply.. 215

CHAPTER XXI.
They go to Mr. Harrison's House—Interesting Talk of the Mayor—The Prosperity of Chicago under his Reign—A Martyr to the People—At the Theater—Uncle Ben Getting on to the Stage to Whip the Villain...................................... 227

CONTENTS.

CHAPTER XXII.

PAGE:

Sunday Morning in a Strange Room—He Wonders if They will care if He gets into that Coffin—His first Experience in a Bath-Tub—They go to the Central Music Hall to Hear Professor Swing — The Grand Organ — The Eloquent Sermon—The Value of Such Men as Professor Swing in a Community— The Mayor might be Improved by Listening to them Frequently—At the Mayor's House — Another Visit from a Reporter —Bridget at the Door—"I'll Ax the Boss if the Morginses be in"— Clarissa Receives the Reporter in the Library and gives him a Just Rebuke— Harrison has Callers, Dan Wren and Van Pelt —"Coming Events Cast their Shadows Away in Front of Them."— 233

CHAPTER XXIII.

A Ride in the City — A Visit to Mr. Rosster's — At the Opera in the Evening — Librettos and Spy-glasses Confuse Uncle Ben — He goes on the Board of Trade— Thought there was Going to be a Fight—The Game—The Shearers and the Lambs— Who Builds the Magnificent Buildings and Feeds the Pockets of the Rich Operators?— The Unsophisticated Lambs—A Letter from Honest Abe—A Letter from Mary— Ebenezer's Poetry.. 244

CHAPTER XXIV.

Clarissa's Surprise at Mary's Request—Ebenezer Touched her Soft Spot with his Poetry—Clarissa Sends $50 to buy Stockings with—Clarissa's Letter—Clarissa Buys a new Dress Cheap—It Creates Gossip in the Dining-Room—The Hypocrites get a Scoring from Clarissa—Discovers a True Woman—A Visit from John Wentworth— His Graphic Description of the Growth of Chicago — A Trip Around the World in Eighty Days 255

CHAPTER XXV.

A Call on Mr. Harrison— He Gives Clarissa a Book —Good-Bye to Chicago— On Board the Cars on the C. & N. W. Ry.—Delayed at Boone by an Accident—New Methods of Hotel Advertising—Omaha Passengers in the Sleeper—Omaha's Marvelous Boom—Colonel Sellers going to Invest Heavily—The Man that Couldn't Lie—Arrive in Denver—At the St. James—Uncle Ben Receives a Fall—It was Squire Bigler—His Big Schemes—Uncle Ben Knew him as well as Though he had Made Him—Wasn't Born under the Scheming Star... 266

CHAPTER XXVI.

A Carriage Ride in Denver—Visits the Great Reduction Works—Gets Acquainted with Professor Hill—King Pharo in Denver—A Good Thing for Moses that He was Hid—Squire Bigler Takes them to see the Three-eyed Richard in the Evening—Wonderful Chances to make a Fortune—Declines being made Rich on Short Notice—Money, Money, Money, the Absorbing Idea—A Trip through Clear Creek Canyon—The Idaho Springs Bath—Colorado is a High State—Clarissa Gets High Notions—A Visit to the Garden of the Gods—Clarissa Engraves her Cla on the Balanced Rock and Receives a Sudden Fall—Ambition Ruined—Surrounded by a Doctor and Medicine—Departure from Colorado 279

CONTENTS.

CHAPTER XXVII.

Once More on the Main Line — The Skulls — The Highest Railroad Point — Sleeping Car Incidents — Drummers and Newspaper Man — Tall Stories — The Newspaper man Takes the Dutch Oven — Dinner at a Station Compared with a Dining Car — First Railroading in America — Peter Cooper Lost the Race — They were Bound for Honolulu — The Sea Captain After Whales — "We was Barren of Interesting Experiences" — Ben's Dream — Green River — 150 Miles of Railroad Stealing — Trout Dinner Served by the Heathen — "Me No Savee Melican Mannee" — Arrival at Ogden......... 287

CHAPTER XXVIII.

Ten Days among the Mormons — Close Proximity of the Headquarters of the Saints to the Sulphur Works Below — Salt Lake City, the Mecca of the Saints — Interview with Brigham Young, Jr. — A Visit to the Tabernacle — The Z. C. M. I. Store, a marvel of System and Neatness — An Evening with the Irish Bishop — An Exposition of the true Inwardness of Mormonism — Relationship is a Riddle — Human Love............. 297

CHAPTER XXIX.

On Board the C. P. Railroad — Disposition to Exaggerate — Commercial Travelers Noted — It is Catching — All Classes liable to an Attack of it — A Night in Carson City — A Night in Virginia City — Wonderful Stories — A Dream that Hits the Case — Results of a Restless Night — He Ate too many Pancakes................................... 313

CHAPTER XXX.

On Our Last Stretch — Truckee — Mountain Scenery — A Pleasing Change from Winter to Spring — Passengers in a California Train — Tower of Babel — The Lacking Ingredient, Sarah Smuggins — The Largest Ferry boat in the World — Arrival in Oakland — Crossing the Bay — The City of One Hundred Hills — They Pillow their Heads in the Baldwin... 322

CHAPTER XXXI.

Awake in San Francisco — Slander in the Breakfast Room — The Important Hotel Clerk with Bosom Pin that is a Stunner — The Proprietor Directs Them — They Call at the Office of Dodgem, Skipem & Oppenheimer — Dodger Dodged — Skipem skipped — Oppenheimer Sailed for Europe — The Jew Caught — $200 Saved — Signing a Receipt — Return to the Baldwin — Letters from Mary and Abe — Something Wrong at Home — San Francisco — The Persecuted Heathen in California — Don't waste your Brine for them — Advice to them as wants to Marry.................................. 326

CHAPTER XXXII.

On their Way to Los Angeles — The Big Trees — A Horse Railroad around One of Them — Native Passengers on the Train — Orange Groves — Fond of Gossip — Lying an Essential Qualification — Arrival in Los Angeles — Sunset in California — Angels without Wings — The Spaniards made a Mistake — Angels Froze out — A Beauty Spot — St. Paul's Advice to Timothy in Full Force for the Benefit of Hypocrites........... 338

CONTENTS.

CHAPTER XXXIII.

PAGE.

Departure from Los Angeles—Uncle Ben and Clarissa take a Stateroom and are regarded as Millionaires by the Porter—Mistaken for Spreckles—Clarissa interviewed by *World's* Reporter—The Sham Appearance Commands the Sham Respect of the Shams—Clarissa takes her Taffy—Prince Kingokangokoko and other Distinguished Passengers—Stuck on Antique—Mexican Farmer—Adobe 348

CHAPTER XXXIV.

Change of Scenery—The Oldest City in America—Santa Fe, the City of Holy Faith—The Hotel—Dinner—Cannibalism—Mr. Juan Fernandez Maracillo Romeo Martinezo, Our Guide, who had Resided there 117 Years, takes them through the City—Fort Marcy—Bird'seye View of the Town—History of Santa Fe—Possessed of a Chicago Appetite—Bishop Lamy's Garden—The Plaza Palacio-del-Gobernador—Lew Wallace and Ben Hur—Old San Miguel—Las Vegas—Phœnix Hotel—Clarissa's Dream—"We have Got Las Vegas and Gallinas River on our Farm"—Kansas City—Omaha Outdone—A Typical Real Estate Agent—A New Way to Sell Lots—Uncle Ben gets Dizzy—The Tallest Liar of the West 358

CHAPTER XXXV.

Arrival in St. Louis—Hands Off—At the Southern—Meeting the Mayor—They take a Ride over the City with the Mayor—Shaw's Garden—The Bridge—Uncle Ben Makes a Suggestion to the Mayor for the Benefit of St. Louis—Carter Harrison to be Consulted. 386

CHAPTER XXXVI.

Arrival in Chicago—Everything on the Move — The Tribune Reporter with his Gimlet Lights Down on Uncle Ben, but is Rebuffed—A Call at the Mayor's Office — Surprised—They Call On McDonald — Harrison not Elected—The Cranks Run the City — After the Boodlers—Calling on Mr. Harrison — The Great Man's Sorrow for the City—Clarissa Cries with one Eye.. 390

CHAPTER XXXVII.

Farewell to Chicago—At Buzzbee's — Reformation a Dangerous Disease — Benjamin has Improved—The Trip Worth All it Costs—Pardoned by the Mayor of Syracuse — Arrival at the Village—Met by old Neighbors and a Brass Band — Escorted to Ebenezer's Store—Cigars for the Crowd—Squire Bigler's Cattle Scheme—An Hour in the Bank—Waddles' Forgeries—Uncle Ben's Note for $2,000 — They Got the Drop on Him — Conners turn the Tables and Uncle Ben gets the Last Drop on them—The Old-Fashioned Home.. 400

ILLUSTRATIONS FOR "SHAMS."

	PAGE.
UNCLE BEN	*Frontispiece.*
"PRETTIER THAN THE HONEYSUCKLES."	11
UNCLE BEN AND CLARISSA IN TEETERS' STORE	17
"I FORGOT ALL ABOUT IT."	22
WE SAW THE LIGHT FROM TOWZER HILL	24
DR. DICKEY EXTRACTING THE HAIR PIN	26
TEETERS' FIGURING HOW MUCH HE COULD MAKE ON THE HOGS	31
CHOIR AT THE HUDDLE	33
THEY PLAYED ALL KINDS OF PLAYS	40
ZOLLIVER RAMSDELL AND NANCY BOYLES SPARKING	47
DOCTOR'S OFFICE	53
BUZZARDS AND CARCASS	55
A "GARDEN ANGEL."	57
READING THE ESSAY	62
HE KICKED POOR FIDO	64
TEETERS TALKS OVER THE HOG BUSINESS IN THE BARN	69
DRIVING THE PESKY BRUTES BY THE TAVERN	71
ELDER DANBERRY	75
PRESIDING ELDER JONES	77
THE COLLECTION	82
HEADS	87
SOCRATES AND YOUNG AMERICA	91
YOU FORGET THAT I HAVE GOT YOUR KEYS HERE	97
HE WAS GOING TO FIGHT THE PROFESSOR	103
SIZING UP THE STEERS	107
THE PHRENOLOGIST'S DREAM	109
CAPTAIN OF THE FERRY BOAT	113
SARAH SMUGGINS WHEN A GIRL	119
WATCHING MARY AND EBENEZER	121
KISSING THE BRIDE	126
BIGLER STARTS FOR CHICAGO	131
LETTER OF CONDOLENCE	124
WADDLES FAINTED; THEY DOUSED HIM WITH COLD WATER	139
REFUSING TO GO ON TEETERS' BAIL	141

xiv   ILLUSTRATIONS FOR SHAMS.

	PAGE
EXCURSION TRAIN..	145
ARRIVAL AT DEPOT in SYRACUSE..	147
BUYING TICKETS IN SYRACUSE..	151
"HE BROUGHT HIS FOOT DOWN ON BUZBEE'S CORNFIELD."....................	153
UNCLE BEN GOES UP CHAMBER TO BED..	157
"MISTER, WON'T YOU BUY A MORNING PAPER?"...................................	159
"BREAKFAST IS NOW READY IN THE DINING CAR FORWARD."....................	162
THE OLD INQUISITOR...	166
THE "HAND OF PROVIDENCE."..	170
"SHE ACTED VERY COLD, ALMOST FRIGID."..	174
"BENJAMIN MORGAN, WHAT ARE YOU DOING HERE?"............................	176
"I DIDN'T WAIT TO HITCH UP T'OTHER GALLUS"....................................	178
"ALL ABOARD."..	180
"NOT A SIGN OF EITHER POCKETBOOK."...	183
"BENJAMIN, WHAT IS THE MATTER WITH YOU?"....................................	188
PALMER HOUSE...	192
"I SAW ONE OF THOSE THINGS DRESSED IN UNIFORMITY.".....................	197
"WE TOOK A BIG RIDE FOR FIVE CENTS APIECE."..................................	199
BATTLE OF GETTYSBURG...	201
"WHILE I WAS RESTING, CLARISSA WAS READING TO ME."....................	206
"WE WILL JUST FOLLOW UP THIS BRASS BAND."..................................	208
THE TRIBUNE REPORTER..	211
"ABRAHAM, SOLOMON AND ISAAC'S COMBINATION.".............................	213
CARTER'S PRIVATE OFFICE..	219
"LOOK HERE, YOU DUMB SASSY SCAMP"...	221
"CLARISSA WAS DUMBFOUNDED!"...	223
"IS IT A NIGH RELATIVE YOU HAVE LOST?"...	227
"I WAS JUST STEPPING OVER THE BALUSTRADE."..................................	231
"ONE RUN COLD, T'OTHER RUN HOT...	233
CARTER CROSSING THE DESERT...	237
"READY AND ANXIOUS TO BORE A HOLE."..	241
"WE WENT TO MR. LINCOLN'S PARK."..	245
"SOMETIMES THEY'LL SHAKE ONE FINGER AND SOMETIMES TWO."..........	249
EBENEZER PLUNKET...	251
MARY...	253
CLARISSA'S QUEEN ANN DRESS...	257
"BECAUSE IT'S THE ONLY BUILDING I KNOW OF IN THE CITY THAT HAIN'T GOT A MORTGAGE ON IT."..	261
"I HOLLERED, 'SQUIRE BIGLER."..	264
WELLS HOUSE...	269
"UNLESS HE IS IN THE LIQUOR BUSINESS, THEN HE CUSSES IT."..............	271
OMAHA WITH COLONEL SELLERS' ADDITION.....................................	273
THE FELLOW THAT COULDN'T LIE..	274
"UNCLE BEN, HOW ARE YOU?"...	277
"GET IN BACK OF ME, YOU GOLDEN TEMPTER.".................................	281
"SHE WISHED SHE COULD GET UP HIGHER."......................................	285

ILLUSTRATIONS FOR SHAMS.

	PAGE
"A Dollar, If You Please."	290
Strange Visions	293
Brigham Young, Jr., Tells Us Terrible Things	301
Polygamous Mormon	308
"Holiness Unto The Lord."	310
Sandy Bowers, An Uneducated Irishman	314
Sandy Bowers After He Got His Wealth	315
Doing Chores at 4 O'Clock in the Morning	318
The Grand Master of the Fireworks	319
A Regular Old '49er	323
San Francisco in the Evening	325
Moses Oppenheimer	329
"You Vas Proke Us All Up in Peezness."	331
Jack Rabbit	337
The Dead Giant	339
"A Little for Thy Stomach's Sake."	343
A Street Scene in Los Angeles	347
Greaser Plowing	356
Scene on the A. T. & S. F. R. R.	359
Mr. Juan Fernandez-Maracillo-Romeo-Martinezo	363
Head Waters of the Rio Grande	365
Palacio Del Gobernador	373
Blowing Out the Electric Light	375
Sinking a Shaft for Blood	391
Pointing Out with My Fork the Most Interesting Points	393
"Nothing Stronger than Lemonade and Cigars."	402
Bigler Makes a Speech	404
Sarah Smuggins	409

CHAPTER I.

THE showers of April had cleared away and brought in a lovely May, with peace and green grass spread all around. The sweet scent of apple blows was floating through the air, inspiring new life and new ambition. I was getting tired of the hard work that had ever been my lot through life thus far. I had finished the chores and was going into the house for breakfast, when I met Clarissa at the gate with a pail of fresh water she had just brought from the spring down at the foot of the hill. (Clarissa is my wife, and one of the smartest and best wives ever married to a ignorant but honest man.) Says she,

"Ben, breakfast is all ready and steaming hot."

As she looked up through her specs, her face as clean and pretty as a brand-new silver dollar, I could not help kissing her right there. I don't know what made me do it, but there was something in the air that seemed to make me feel young and keen-like, and I thought Clarissa looked a heap prettier with her clean calico dress and white apron on than the morning-glories that were creeping up beside the front door. After we had set down to breakfast, either the smell of the hot biscuits and fresh coffee, and the fragrant breeze that came in through the open window next to the orchard, or something else, seemed all of a sudden to inspire me, and I spoke up in more of a man-like manner than usual (for usually I am quite calm and meek-like; so much so, that folks don't think I know much), and said,

"Clarissa, Clarissa!" Says she,

"What! Ben, have you got a colic?" I suppose my strange look caused her alarm. I replied:

"No, I haven't got the colic, nor anything else that is catching, unless being a author is catching. I am going to surprise you." Says she,

"Are you going to buy me a new dress?"

"Well," says I, "that would be surprising, but that ain't it; I'm going to write a book." Clarissa dropped her cup of coffee on her clean table-cloth, she was so astonished, and exclaimed,

"Benjamin Morgan! have you gone crazy?" Says I,

"I don't know but I have; they say when a fellow is a little off he will generally, and more or less frequently, turn out to be an author."

"Well, if ever I'd thought that of you! Who do you think will be fool enough to read your book if you write one?" she asked. Says I:

"I don't know, but one thing I do know, that if all the fools in the world will read my book, it will be read more than any other book that was ever printed."

"Well, Benjamin, what on earth ever made you get the idea into your head of writing a book?" she said, to which I replied,

"I guess I'd caught an inspiration." Says she,

"More likely you've caught a cold; this is just the kind of weather for that." Says I,

"It's nothing of the sort; I'm in dead earnest. I'm going to write a book. I know I haven't got any education worth speaking about, but I have paid close attention to what few folks I have seen in this world, and I know that a good share of them seem to be one thing, and really are another; and I can see it just as plain as if I'd been born in a Yale or cradled in a Oxford. And if I can't write as pretty words or spell them as correctly as some of these great writers, I can unmask some of the hypocrisy practiced every day around us, and give a hint, at least, to some of the rising generations, as well as to them that's already rose, how to detect the false from the true; and if I can even get, as you say, Clarissa, the fools to read it, I will be satisfied, for I shall then think that a service rendered to them as is called fools, that will enable them to see the deceitful mask of cunning and unscrupulous persons, and help them to avoid danger, will be of some value. So I have concluded, and my mind is set on it, to write a book on my experience with hypocrites."

Clarissa was silent for a few minutes, and then said:

"Benjamin, hadn't you better finish planting that four-acre corn-field before you write your book?"

That is just like a woman, says I to myself. Just let a man get an inspiring spell onto him, and think he is going to do something for his fellow man, and perhaps raise himself onto a high eminence, and his wife, or some one else, will remind him of his duty to his family, and call his special attention to some work that has got to be done.

"Yes, Clarissa," said I, "I know I have got to plant that corn, and I'll do it to-day; but that ain't going to stop me writing the book. I suppose that everybody that has wrote a book, or preached a sermon, or gone to Congress, has had to overcome obstacles. If the Almighty hasn't given a man brains enough to overcome obstacles in order to rise in the world and accomplish some good, he never intended him to rise. All men wasn't created to rise, as that plan would keep everything unsettled; everybody would be rising; but the Almighty designed it otherwise, and when he sees fit to touch a human soul with the finger of inspiration, and bid him tell the people something, he also gives him courage and power to overcome all obstacles, which are purposely put in his way to strengthen him. So, Clarissa, I'll get around that corn-field by just planting it, and at the same time I'll try to think up something."

CHAPTER II.

PLANTING corn in old Blank County, New York, has a tendency to paralyze any inspiration one may have to be an author. The pesky stones and old stumps drives all poetry out of a soul that has to plow among 'em, or plant corn and carry a hoeful of dirt two or three feet to cover it. A person may arise with the bright, radiant sun in the morning, his soul filled with love for nature, his heart happy and in accord with all pleasant thoughts and inspirations, and a determination to write something that will startle the world. But after he has got his planting done, and he comes to the house at sundown, with scarcely strength enough to pull his feet after him, and then have to milk ten cows and do the rest of his chores, he will find his morning inspiration has taken wings and flown, and he feels more like saying "Dumb it" than anything else. Most persons would give up the author idea; but Uncle Ben Morgan ain't going to give it up for any trifles of that kind, for he has got it on his mind to show up some of the mean folks in this world, and if he should fail to make the attempt he would be haunted by a nightmare, and that is the worst kind of a haunt. So I have concluded to make a note now and then on things I have seen in the past, or may come across in the future.

I'd got that corn planting business off my mind, and took Clarissa down to the village to do some trading. She is a very domestic body, but powerful smart. She keeps house in perfect order, and has time to read an awful sight besides. She hadn't been down to the village for three months, and she had considerable trading to do and quite a lot of butter and eggs to sell. The first place we went into was Jim Teeters' new grocery-store. Jim Teeters came from Connecticut, and was a regular Yankee. He married Betsey Coon— she and I used to go to school together, twenty-five years ago—but she went back East to live twenty years ago, and I hadn't seen her since then. He opened a big grocery-store about two months ago, and done lots of advertising in the *Village Blade*, and out on the fences and barns, and he was getting a big trade.

Clarissa thought that we had better go in and try the new store; and I had quite a desire to see Betsey's husband, and a hope that I might see Betsey. We had no sooner entered than a tall, lean fellow, with thin, sandy chin whiskers and blue eyes, and a face all covered with smiles, approached us as if he had known us a lifetime, and put his hand out in a cordial manner and shook hands with Clarissa, and then with me, and said,—

"This is a beautiful day; just step back and have a seat. Let me see, your name is— is— is—"

"Uncle Ben Morgan!" shouted a little red-headed woman of forty, who was coming out from behind the counter, "how do you do?" and the next minute the hand of Betsey Teeters was clasped in mine in a regular, old-fashioned shake. The cordiality with which Betsey met me run close onto affection. Betsey is a marvel in the way of a rapid talker; I think she would take the grist-mill over any woman I ever met, and on this particular occasion we was glad to see each other, and Betsey had to ask me so many questions about our old schoolmates and the old neighbors, and one thing and another, that a whole half-hour went by before I thought a thing about introducing Clarissa, or she thought of introducing Teeters, and as I turned round I noticed Clarissa was looking very considerably carroty-colored; but Teeters was doing the smiling act in good style, and I remarked to Betsey that if she'd just hold on a minute I'd introduce her to the best woman in Blank County—my wife, Clarissa Morgan.

The pause was obtained, and the introduction performed.

UNCLE BEN AND CLARISSA IN TEETERS' STORE.

Clarissa was almost frigid at first, and seemed to feel as though I had used a little too much time; but under Betsey's warm reception and April shower of words, she gradually thawed down to the talkative degree. Betsey introduced me to the gentleman who met us at the door, as her husband. He was very polite and very friendly; but I thought then that I could see policy written on his face. Betsey, no doubt, had told him about the good men and women to work for as customers, and she, of course, mentioned "Uncle Ben Morgan," as it is known all over the county that he prides himself on paying for everything he gets, promptly.

"Mr. Morgan," said Mr. Teeters, "I have heard Betsey speak of you more than any other man in the county, and I feel as though I was already acquainted with you. I was in hopes you would have called before this. Now I just want you and your wife to make my store your headquarters whenever you can come to town, and if you have anything to sell at any time, give me the first chance to buy it, and I'll give you the biggest price for it of any one in town."

"Well," I said, "we'll give you a trial, and so long as you do right by us we'll trade with you."

Clarissa had brought in about one hundred pounds of butter and eighty-two dozen eggs, and six pair of socks she had knit. Teeters wanted me to bring them in, and I done so. He examined the butter closely and said:

"Mrs. Morgan, did you make this butter yourself?" Clarissa told him,—

"Yes."

"Well," said he, "that is the best lot of butter I have seen since I have been in the village; and I want to engage all the butter you make from now on, and I'll give you one cent above the market price for it."

Clarissa is a powerful good butter maker, and she prides herself on it; and this compliment of Teeters' done just what he intended it should; it tickled her, and made her a customer for his store.

Right here let me suggest to any one who intends embarking on the sea of trade and traffic, it matters not what branch of mercantile business you take, if you want to build up a good trade, just compliment every woman that comes into your store—in some way or other see that she receives a compliment at your hand—either for her taste in the selection of goods, her knowledge of the value of goods, her ability to make nice things, or the extreme beauty of her baby, or the bright intelligence of her tow-headed young one that is pulling her dress and crying, "Ma, ma, ma, I want that doll; I want that rocking-horse, or I want some candy." Be sure that you give her to understand that you appreciate her worth in some manner, and never speak ill of a woman under any circumstances, and you can have all the trade you can attend to. The women control more of the trade than the men, every time.

Teeters understood this thoroughly, and he made Clarissa a customer. She asked him how much he would pay her for the butter and eggs, and with a very sweet smile and a rubbing of his hands, he said:

"Butter, just now, is low; the New York market is glutted, and consequently the price has dropped to four and a half cents a pound; I am really only paying four cents; but your butter is so very nice I will give you five and a half cents."

Of course, Clarissa was somewhat disappointed, as she had never sold any butter for less than ten cents; and when she thought how hard I had worked to take care of them twenty cows, and milking, and how awful hard she had worked, with no one to help her except Mary (who was only nineteen), taking care of the milk and churning the butter and working it over, five and a half cents didn't look as if it paid to make it. But of course Mr. Teeters was very kind to give her a cent more for it than he give any one else, so she sold her butter and eggs to him, and made her purchases from him. After she had finished her trading Betsey invited us to dinner with them (they lived up over their store), and we accepted the invitation. Betsey had a splendid dinner, and we used all the spare time we had from talking, in eating.

We found out a good many things during our dinner visit; for instance, and to wit, we found out the following: That Clarissa and I had two children, a girl and a boy. The girl we named Mary, nineteen years ago, after Clarissa's mother, and the boy we named after our President, Abe Lincoln; and he is such an honest boy that we call him Honest Abe. He is fourteen, going on fifteen; that they had two boys, the oldest sixteen, named Jay Gould, because J. Gould was Teeters' idea of a great man. The second boy Betsey had named after me—Ben M. Teeters. Both the boys was at the dinner table, and the oldest one looked as though he could skin a whole church and not get caught at it; but the other fellow didn't look as if he knew enough to eat a hotel beefsteak without a receipt.

I told Betsey I thought she exhibited great knowledge of human nature when she named her boys, and that tickled Betsey. I just felt then that I wished I was running a drygoods store so as to get Betsey for a customer—I'd have her sure.

We also found out that Teeters had joined the Methodist Church (although he had not belonged to any church before he moved into the village), and that he was one of the class-leaders; also, that I was a Baptist, but not powerfully stuck on them, although I liked them, and that Clarissa didn't belong to any visible church, but I believed then, and have since been fully convinced that she was and is a better Christian than any of the church members I was acquainted with, not excepting myself. I have weaknesses that she hasn't got, notwithstanding women are considered the weaker vessels. We found out that Teeters and one of our neighbors, George Waddles, was well acquainted; that George was a customer of Teeters'; that in fact, it was through Waddles that Teeters moved from Connecticut to the village.

By this time we found it was getting late and time for us to be going home. Clarissa and Betsey parted the best of friends, and

EXPERIENCE WITH HYPOCRITES. 21

Clarissa urged them to come out and make us a visit some day next week, which they agreed to do.

It was quite late when we got started for home, and we had got to drive twelve miles, some of the way pretty hilly, and the old gray mare was lame in both front feet, and had one bad hind leg, and I felt it would be long after dark before I got the chores done. We had got about half way home when Clarissa said,—

"Benjamin, I forgot that dress I bought for Mary, in Brown's, where I traded my socks. I'm awful sorry, as Mary is expecting it, and she has worked so hard helping me this spring; and she narrowed off the toes of all them socks, besides."

"Well, Clarissa," I said, "why don't you think of these things and take care of 'em; it's just like a woman, always forgetting something or other." After I had scolded more than I ought to, Clarissa spoke, in a calm mood, while her complexion showed rebuke in every wrinkle:

"Benjamin, we are all of us liable to forget something sometime or other, and I don't think it is any worse for me to forget to put that dress in the wagon than it was for you to forget that you had built a fire in the kitchen stove and then set down on top of it to pull your boots on." I said:

"I forgot all about that."

"Well," she replied, "I haven't forgot that I had to spend a whole day to build over them satinet breeches." With a sort o' cowed expression on my front face, I said,—

"Clarissa, I didn't intend to injure your feelings." She spoke quick, but firm-like, and said:

"Benjamin, my feelings aint spoiled a bit, and I didn't mean anything wrong when I referred to the cook stove misunderstanding, although it is a tender subject to reflect upon, but I merely wish to show that we are all poor human creatures after all, and liable to forget a great many things it would be better for us to remember; we are not only liable to forget some of our errands, and to do things we should not do, but we are sometimes liable to forget to appear to be just what we really are. Too many folks in this world that are not honest, either by training or by nature, forget to appear what they are, and so go through the world appearing to be honest and upright, and trying to make others believe they are. There are lots of wolves that forget where they take off their clothes at night, and get up in the morning and put on the clothing that belongs to the sheep; and they'll wear them all day. There are farmers that will

"I FORGOT ALL ABOUT THAT."

haul load after load of wood to town and sell it for so many cords, and forget where their measuring stick is; and there are merchants who forget to balance their scales. There are lawyers that forget that truth is an essential element in trying a case, and ministers that forget that the eye of the Lord is upon them when they are stealing their sermons as well as the eye of the critic, when they are delivering them from the sacred desk. The office seeker forgets, after his election, every promise he made before it, and what is worse than all else, the husband and the wife too frequently forget those pledges of love and faithfulness and sobriety. Of all sad things in this world, the saddest is when memory between plighted mates for life is lost to the extent that not only is duty neglected, but affection chilled forever, hearts crushed and bleeding, to rise no more. The strength of a government rests upon the strength of its homes. Every home is a foundation stone upon which the superstructure rests. If the individual homes throughout the country fall to ruin by forgetfulness, the government will surely follow; and I have read in some of my books about a once flourishing republic, I believe it was Rome, falling to pieces from this very cause—forgetfulness; forgetting to be true, honest and square."

Clarissa got into one of her inspiring spells, and preached a better sermon on forgetfulness than Elder Chapin preaches upon fore-ordination.

Says I to Clarissa, "It must be catching."

"What must be catching?" she asked.

"Oh," said I, "this is the time of year for it."

"The time of year for what?" she exclaimed, somewhat puzzled by my remark.

"Inspiration," says I.

"Oh, pshaw," she said, "there's no inspiration about that; it is just plain, common sense, and real facts."

"Well, then! I have come to the conclusion that plain common sense is a scarcer article than uncommon sense."

"Benjamin, now I've asked Betsey out to see us next week, and she is coming. What am I to do with her? She is such an everlasting talker my nervous system can't stand it," said Clarissa. I thought it over considerable while the old mare was climbing the big Towzer hill, from the top of which I could see a light in our front window, and I told Clarissa that I would manage it. I would take Betsey around the farm with me and show her the cows and pigs and geese, etc., and then I would take her down to see Aunt Pollie Clark who used to know her when she was a Coon; and in that way I would keep her out of the house till supper was ready, and she could get along with her the rest of the time. By this time we had reached home and it was some time after dark.

Mary and Abe had got the chores all done and had a good hot supper on the table. After supper Clarissa told Mary how she had forgot her dress, but promised to send Honest Abe after it the next day, and then she told her about Betsey and Jim Teeters coming out to visit us next week. Mary said she would fix it all right. She

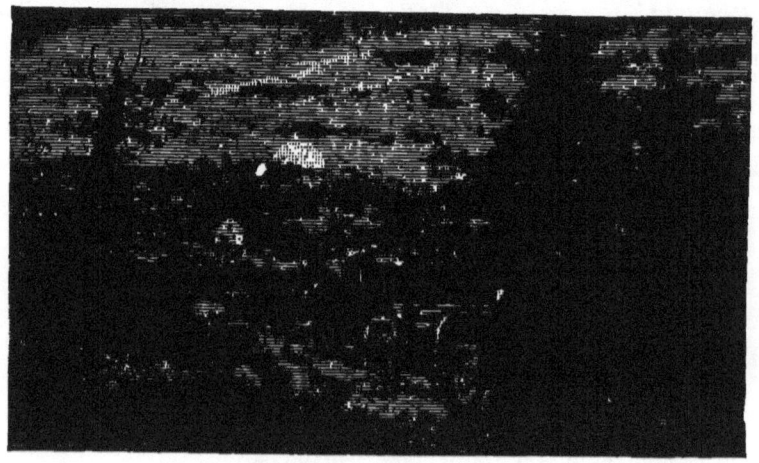

WE SAW THE LIGHT FROM TOWZER HILL.

would go down to Giddingses and borrow their quilting frames, get a quilt on and invite the neighbors, and she would send a special invitation to Sarah Smuggins, the woman's rights old maid, and Betsey would find her match.

Mary's project seemed to meet Clarissa's approval, and I am sure it did mine, and we retired to rest

>Amid thoughts of Teeters,
>And the hum of 'skeeters
>In regular meters.

CHAPTER III.

SICKNESS in the neighborhood, a meeting in the schoolhouse, and getting ready for Betsey Teeters' visit, has kept Clarissa awful busy for the past week. There isn't a family within five miles of our house that doesn't expect Clarissa to help take care of 'em, or come in and say a cheering word when they get sick, for she has such an even disposition, and kind and amicable ways with her, that she is a regular angel in a sick room. Old Mrs. Boyles was taken very sudden with a powerful fit of weakness in her body, and a terrible sharp pain in her throat. Clarissa was sent for in great haste, and so was Dr. Dickey. When Clarissa got there she inquired all about how she was taken, and the youngest girl, Nancy, told her that her mother was as well as usual before supper; that she eat supper with the rest of 'em, and right after supper she complained of an awful sharp pain in her throat. Nancy said she had made some soda biscuits for supper, as her mother was real fond of 'em, and that she eat four or five.

Now Clarissa begun to reason it out (and I want to remark right here, that whenever Clarissa begins to reason on anything, she is mighty sure to come out at the right end, for she is not only a powerful reader and good scholar, but she is a regular philosopher). She reasoned in this way: Nancy is young and pretty, and thinks she is prettier than she is. She is in love with a smart young man down to the village by the name of Zolliver Ramsdell, who pays her steady company. She was expecting him out to see her that night, and she had her hair all twisted up in papers and fastened with invisible hairpins; and just as likely as not, and a good deal more so one of them hair-pins fell in to the biscuit dough when Nancy was working it, and had got into one of the biscuits that old Mrs. Boyles eat and it had got into the old lady's windpipe.

When the doctor came Clarissa suggested her theory to him. He acted upon her philosophy of the case, and put an instrument they called a speculator down her throat so he could examine it, and sure enough, there he found the hairpin sticking right in her windpipe. He took a pair of small tongs he had in his pocket and pulled it out, and the old lady got well in a day or two after. She feels so grateful that she prays for the blessing of Heaven to come down on to Clarissa.

DR. DICKEY EXTRACTING THE HAIRPIN.

The next night after the Boyles' disaster there was a meeting in the red schoolhouse. Clarissa and I went over to the meeting, expecting we would hear a good sermon, although we didn't know who was going to preach. As a general rule Clarissa leads in the singing at all the meetings, as she is a good singer and very independent; and she most always pitches the tune, where most of 'em can sing. The schoolhouse was well filled when the preacher came in. He was a stranger to all of us—a powerful big man with a bald head and face. He was a different man from what the folks expected, and talked altogether different from what they supposed he would.

Clarissa said if she had knowed what stuff he was going to preach, she'd a never sung the first piece—" Come, Holy Spirit, Heavenly Dove;" and she was so mad when he got through, she wouldn't sing the last song.

He just made all sorts of fun of Abe and Ike and Jake, and said they did not belong to our class of people. He said they was of a race called pawnbrokers, and their principal business was receiving stolen goods and cheating their neighbors; that Moses was a regular old impostor; that he went up on top of a mountain and claimed that God had handed him some stone plates, with his law written on them, and commanded him to take them down and read them to his people and make them obey the law; that while he was coming down the mountain he stumbled over the root of an old tree and fell down and broke the stone plates into a thousand pieces. Then he *told* the people what was written on them, and ever since then they called him the law-giver, and strange to say, thousands and thousands of people that don't belong to that race, to this day, believe that yarn of old Moses.

Then he went on to show what a lot of mistakes Moses had made; and he made all sorts of ridicule of the Bible, and done everything in his power to spoil that sweet peace of mind and confidence that the Christian men and women had by a simple faith in the Saviour and his word. And after he showed what a sham he was, by trying to make out that he didn't come from any thing bigger than he was himself, and that there was no God, and no hereafter, he made a fool of himself by repeating as his motto in life, The Golden Rule, as he called it, which he stole out of God's own book. He wasn't satisfied by using some of the best part of God's work, but the dumb hypocrite denied the author. So he went on for nigh two hours, saying something to hurt some one's feelings, and then, like a clown in a circus, laughed at his own foolishness.

Clarissa says that he is as big a hypocrite as she ever saw, for all the things he said that he wanted the folks to understand as his original ideas had been said and written by Voltaire and Tom Paine and others long ago, and he was parading them as his ideas. She said, although she didn't believe everything about the Bible as others did, and while she didn't believe the representations of Bible doctrines and theories as presented by a good many well meaning ministers, yet she didn't believe it was right to say anything to destroy the confidence that professed Christians had in their beliefs.

He is a sham, and I've got him on the list.

CHAPTER IV.

MARY had completed all her arrangements for her quilting bee, and about half-past 10 o'clock, Friday morning, Betsey and Jim Teeters drove up to the front gate, and Clarissa and I went out to welcome them. Betsey begun, "Clarissa, dear me! I am so glad to see you; what a handsome place you've got here; what a beautiful door-yard, and what beautiful flowers. Why, I've been telling Jim all the way out here how I wished he'd sell out and buy a farm, and get a lot of pigs and cows and hens and geese, and other cattle, and go to raising something, and be independent, like Ben Morgan." And so she went on, a regular blue streak, observing everything she took notice of, until we got to the house. Clarissa introduced her to Mary, who met her in a most cordial spirit.

In about an hour the neighbor women began to come in, and a few minutes later Sarah Smuggins arrived, with her mouth as full of words as a hive is of bees. Mary introduced Betsey to the company, and especially to Sarah, and then the fun begun. If you had gone by our house you'd a thought that a woman's rights convention was going on inside, or that something had broke loose. Betsey talked a perfect stream to Sarah, and Sarah just let a river of words flow back to Betsey, and neither one knew a single word the other had said. It was just the thing for Clarissa, who took advantage of the occasion to slip out into the kitchen, away from the noise, and get dinner ready, while Teeters and I took a walk over the farm. Teeters seemed to enjoy the walk, and took particular interest in the hogs and cattle. I soon found that Jim Teeters was like a singed cat—a good deal smarter than he looked, and I could see that he had an eye on the main chance all the time. Some day I believe he will make an Astor (as Clarissa calls that rich man in New York), for he is bound to be powerful rich, if he don't die too soon. He's got more schemes in his head than Deacon Long has got words in his Sunday night prayers, and he'll make some of 'em win some of these days.

One of his schemes is to go to Chicago and work a job through the city council to buy the whole of the Chicago River, and then put stone walls across it every hundred feet, and put a roof over it and divide it off into private bath ponds, and then rent them out by the season to the wealthy folks. He says there is a fortune in it, and he thinks he can make a cool million in five years. I never thought on it before, but Clarissa says she has no doubt of it, for she says she knows lots of folks in Chicago that would give a good deal to have a private bath; but she believed if Teeters could put some ingredient into the water that could cleanse 'em from sin, that he could make more than two millions in less than a year. But that is impossible. While she believes that Teeters is a smart man, he ain't smart enough for that. There never was but one man on this earth that had that ingredient, and that was a Jew, and lived here over 1,800 years ago. He never sold it to any one, but he gave it to any and every one that would take it and use it. This fact seems incredible, for the Jews are not inclined that way; but he offered the ingredient free to every one that would believe in him, and use it as he told them. And every human being that has believed in him and taken his gift since then, have got themselves cleaner a'washin' in his blood than they could in any other way. "He was despised because he was a poor Nazarene, and that's the way," she says, "that the world looks on poor people now. It don't know enough, or else it don't care, to look through their rags and see an honest heart that works hard to keep the wolf from the door, and praise its Creator; that ain't all the while a-figuring to get a posi-

TEETERS FIGURING HOW MUCH HE COULD MAKE ON THE HOGS.

tion in a bank and then build a big house in Canada, where there are no extradition treaties; but that's a-figuring how it can get a pry under the front wheel of his neighbor's wagon that has got down, and give it a lift out of the ditch, and secure a mansion in the sky."

So Clarissa went on moralizing, and said if Teeters didn't get that ingredient, he would make a failure of all his schemes.

I find I am digressing from what I was going to say about the folks in the house. Just as sure as I get to thinking about some of Clarissa's remarks and reasonings, I get to wandering from my subject. So I'll digress back again, and take Teeters from the hog-pen where I left him figuring on how much he could make on sixty-one hogs that he guessed would weigh 240 pounds apiece by killing them, if he bought them at my price, three and one-fourth cents a pound. and go in to dinner, for Clarissa rung the bell five minutes ago.

We went into the side door of the sitting-room, where Clarissa had the table set, and if you ever put your head beside a bee-hive, you never heard a bigger humming. They had got the big extension-table and the kitchen-table hitched together, and it was loaded down with victuals. Nearly all the women in the neighborhood was there. After reconnoitering, we come to the conclusion that Jim Teeters and Ben Morgan was the only two male persons present.

Mary managed the table affairs, and she showed her true sagacity in seating the company. She put Betsey at one end of the table, and Sarah Smuggins at the other end. Clarissa was put in the middle of one side, and Teeters and me on each side of her. The rest of the company was distributed among the other seats.

Clarissa invited Mr. Teeters to ask the blessing, which was done in regular class-leader style. Right opposite to me sat 'Squire Bigler's wife, she that was Maria Tifft, who used to sing in the choir up to the Huddle before she got acquainted with young Bas-

EXPERIENCE WITH HYPOCRITES. 33

com B. Bigler, who had been off to college, and was powerful smart, and after he married her he went to farming on old man Tifft's farm, and mixing in politics, and got elected to the 'Squire's office. After he got elected he signed his name with three big B's. She is a pretty smart kind of a woman, and tolerably well educated. There was Sally Tomkins, Peleg Tomkins' wife, one of the pillows of the Baptist Church, Mehitable Green, wife of Bill Green, the blacksmith, and Jane Kirk, whose husband, David Kirk, is a worthless coot, with unsettled principles, and Mrs. Melancthon Stevens, whose husband teaches singin'-school, and Mrs. Jim Smuggins, and Miss Lilly Doolittle, an innocent, but somewhat soft maid

CHOIR AT THE HUDDLE.

of uncertain age, and George Waddles' wife (Waddles is a big farmer, and makes a specialty of religion, and short-horns and hogs; he buys and sells from 700 to 800 head of cattle every year, and leads in prayer-meetings down to the Methodist Church at the village). There was Abby Standish, the relict of the late Morton Standish, and also Dollesky Baker, a well-meaning but simple-minded woman, who was always on hand at funerals and revivals.

The usual table talk went on, that one might expect on such an occasion, until Sarah Smuggins lit out on her favorite topic of woman's rights. Now it don't look very well in me to be writing about this old worn out subject, and I wouldn't be surprised if the readers would pull their chestnut bells when they come to this; but as shams and hypocrisy is my theme, I want to show how women's shams impose upon society as well as others. She declared that the men was all a pack of self-conceited, cold blooded and selfish things, and she wanted to see the time come when women would be the rulers of this country. If the women had to be the mothers of all mankind, they certainly ought to be the ones to have the say in the government of them. This idea that a woman had got to crawl after the dictates and commands of a puffed up, conceited man, was abominable.

Clarissa had been silent up to this time, but now she broke in. I knew well enough what was coming, for I haint lived with Clarissa Morgan (she that was a Snodgrass) for twenty odd years and better without knowing her sentiments on that question, and I knew that Sarah Smuggins just opened a subject that she couldn't close with very much satisfaction to herself.

Clarissa said, "Sarah Smuggins, you're takin' a credit to yourself that you haint entitled to when you claim as a reason why you should set in Congress and become one of the rulers of the great United States, that the women are the mothers of the race. If you was called upon this minute to show your credentials you couldn't produce 'em; and as for your being so afraid of being dictated to by the men, everybody knows that you was running after them every chance you got, twenty-five or thirty years ago, and it ain't very becoming for you to abuse 'em when they haven't done anything against you. While there may be plenty of women that have a clear knowledge of the requirements and needs of the country, and a keen perception of the right way of doing things in the various official positions of government, yet, as a class, they certainly are not fitted to fill official positions. They should never set in Congress if the country is in need of any laws, for they could never agree upon any. They could not endure the fatigue of setting upon the judicial bench a lifetime. Why, it nearly kills me to set on them hard pews in the Baptist Church an hour. To set in the Presidential chair and have to be told what to do by seven other women that she might pick out for that purpose, there aint a woman in America that would stand it a month, and you know it, too, Sarah Smuggins, if you know anything about your sex. About all the women that want your idea of things is a few that have arrived at the noon-mark in life, or are on the shady side of the hill; that have traveled life's uneven journey single-handed, and have nursed a hatred to mankind, and seem to have a spite against the men in general, combined with a few that have started on the journey in double harness, and because they could not pull even with their mates they would nip at them and put their ears back, and kick and squeal, and act ugly (instead of being kind), and then jump out of the harness altogether. Now, if the first class referred to should be law-makers, we would have a government of spite. Of the second class, if they couldn't control one man, how could they control thirty millions?

"Now, Sarah Smuggins, I don't believe in any such sentimental bosh, nor do I believe that women have no rights that men are bound to respect. I do know this: That women has a right that every man that wants to get married is bound to respect; that is the right, when their hand and heart is asked for in marriage, to say *yes*, or *no*, and that right is respected. They also have a right to say who shall and who shall not be admitted to their society ; to say whether young men who dress well and cut a swell, regardless of their moral principles, can enter their society to the exclusion of true moral worth, or not. The women of the United States carry in their hands the keys to society, and if they choose to lock out young men who are profligates, and intemperate, who hold virtue in light esteem, and whose principal commodity is cheek, and open the door to honest, virtuous, hard-working and industrious men, men whose morals are elevating, it is a right they have, and which all men observe according as it is used,

"This, in my opinion, is the most important right and privilege that lies at the very foundation of our government; and until the women of America will prize honesty above dishonesty, virtue above vice, sobriety above intemperance, and will make the distinction in society so that its effects can be seen in the country, they have no right to ask greater privileges.

"Now I am contented to try my hand in government affairs at home, haint I, Benjamin," said she.

With due deliberation I replied, "Yes."

"And I manage to have you think just about as I do, don't I, Benjamin?" she said.

I replied, "Well, Clarissa, because you always *think right*, I can truthfully say, yes."

(It wouldn't do for me to say yes, without explaining before all them women, for if I did, they would misconstrue my position in the neighborhood.)

Clarissa continued, "I stand as firm as the stone of Gibraltar on the right that women have to mould the thoughts, socially and politically, of the world. They can make our country better and purer, just as they appreciate their grand and noble rights; and the very fact that the country is no better, that there is so much corruption in our government, is an evidence in my mind that if the women can't show better results of their influence in society, they are a long way from being competent to fill official positions.

"I am in favor of women's rights—in their rights to rise up in the majesty of the nature their Creator give 'em, and emancipate themselves from the foolish fashions and sentiments and female dudeism of the age, that carries them down, and soar aloft to the high pinnacle they ought to set on; and when they do that they will be more respected by all mankind than all the rulers of the earth from Adam down to the present day."

As soon as Clarissa had finished her remarks (which seemed to command the attention of every one present) Betsey Teeters said:

"That's just what I believe, and I've thought that way a good many years; but I never could express my opinions as you can, Clarissa Morgan; if I could, I'd get right onto a stump, or stage, or wagon, or any kind of a elevating place, and make the world feel my eloquence." Teeters interrupted further remarks of Betsey's by saying: "There's a big difference between talk and eloquence. Some folks will talk all day, and all the time, and not say anything, either; while others will say a good deal in a few words, and when such persons talk it is generally eloquent. Now Mrs. Morgan has spoken a whole volume in a few words, and if some big man like Lord Salisbury had written a book of 500 pages, and borrowed all he could from Bill Shakspere and others on this same subject, and expressed no more thought than Clarissa has just given us, we'd all say, 'That's a powerful good book.' I believe in giving honor to them it's due to. If we find a rose in the shade of a rock giving off as sweet a scent as one that sits in the bay window of a palace, we should pay just as good respects to it as if it was in a palace. However, that isn't the way of the world. Some poet has said something about a good many gems of serene rays being born to get red in the face and throw away all their sweet scents in the airy desert, or words to that effect. Clarissa may be one of them gems, and she may not be. I believe she will some day make her sentiments known to the world." "James Quincy Teeters," said Betsey, "what ails you? I never heard you talk so much good sense in my life before." "Nothing ails me, Betsey," said Jim; "I never had a chance before since you knew me, to get out so much. I've got lots more if I get the opportunity to tell it sometime." "Well," said Betsey, "I don't see what you mean, Jim Teeters; I'm sure I don't talk much." "I beg pardon, my dear, I never said you did; but you know some persons that do, I presume," replied Jim.

Sally Tomkins spoke up and said she "felt as Mr. Teeters had remarked, that some folks talk a awful sight and say nothing, while others talk but little but say a powerful sight. And that puts me in mind of something I read in a book about a man named Solomon, saying that a greenhorn was known by his much racket, but a wise man was troubled with the lockjaw considerably, or words that conveyed a similar meaning, I don't exactly remember the phraseology. I've heard Peleg say, when I was reading from that passage out loud, that he knew whole families, not far from this neigh r hood, either, that didn't stand in the least mite of danger of ever having the lockjaw," and as she spoke she cast a sort o' wise glance over the top of her gold-plated spectacles toward Sarah Smuggins.

Whether or not Sarah caught her in this act, I don't know; but Sarah spoke right up and said,—

"Anybody that will believe what is writ in that book aint very strong-minded."

Sally asked, "What book do you think I've been referring to?"

"You've been readin' that old, worn-out book, the Bible. It goes on to tell about God, and how He made the world, and man and woman, and a whole pack of lies it can't prove; and then it tells the women folks to be subject to their husbands, and such a book as that aint fit to have in a house," and Sarah looked as if she had made a center shot.

Clarissa remarked in her cool way, "Sarah, I don't believe your folks have had a Bible in the house for fifty years; at any rate, since you was born, and I don't believe you know much about it except what you've heard your father tell. So far as it tells about wives being subject to their husbands, that ought not to worry you any, for you'll never be called on to be subject."

They all laughed except Sarah, who got a swallow of hot tea down her windpipe which nearly choked her, and she had to be excused from the table.

I could plainly see that my prediction was correct—that Sarah had opened a subject she couldn't close with much satisfaction to herself.

CHAPTER V.

WHEN Mary went around the neighborhood to invite the women to the quilting, she also invited the young folks to come in the evening to a party. Some of the young married folks was invited with the rest. Of course Ebenezer Plunket was on the list, and I guess Mary had his name at the head, as she thinks immensely of him, and he pays her steady company when he gets a opportunity.

After tea the quiltin' party broke up, and Betsey and Jim expressed themselves as wonderfully pleased with their visit, and after we had exchanged mutual invitations to visit one another often and frequent, we bade them adieu (which in French is au river).

Again we got our chores all done up it was lamplightin' time and the young folks begun to come in. Mary had got the big front room slicked up, and the new hanging lamp that we bought when we was out to Syracuse on a visit last winter, lit up; in about a half hour the house was pretty well filled up. They begun to have fun and a good time immediately. I was glad on't, for if there is one thing that I enjoy more than another, it is in seeing others have a good time; and if they are going to have a happy time, the sooner they begin and the longer they keep it up the better it pleases me. Life is altogether too short to spend three-fourths of it under a cloud and one-fourth in the sunshine. I believe we ought to spend it all in sunshine, and if we would all be frank and honest, and not assume to be what we are not, and resort to all kinds of devices and schemes to palm off our counterfeit instead of letting ourselves go for what we are actually worth, there would be lots more of sunshine for the human family than what they receive. The world is full of shams, and one sham helps to make another sham, and the hard work too many folks have in keeping up the shams, causes a heavy bank of dark clouds to shut out the sunshine. A desire to have the world think they are wealthy and doing well in the world, causes more people to live beyond their means, to do things they know they cannot afford to do, than anything else, and consequently they have a

THEY PLAYED ALL KINDS OF PLAYS.

sham exterior, but a dark, gloomy and cloudy interior. A nice bedspread and finely embroidered pillow shams too frequently covers up sham bedding. "What will society say?" is one of the biggest shams of all, and keeps too many people in a chilly, unpleasant and unwholesome atmosphere. I want to see folks have sufficient moral courage to appear natural and enjoy the blessed sunshine of life; and if a cloud of sorrow passes over them now and then it is but temporary, and joy is more keen after it passes by.

They played all kinds of plays that was becomin' to their age, sex and condition, and some that wasn't. Mary's new organ helped a powerful sight in entertaining the folks. Clarissa and I talked the matter over considerable before we concluded to buy the organ. I felt too poor to put $250 into a wind box when I needed a windmill out in the barnyard more; but after Clarissa entered into the merits of the case, and said it was as much our Christian duty to do all that was in our power to elevate and improve our children as to go to church and prayer-meetin'; that she believed the Almighty would stuff cotton in his ears, if he had any, when folks prayed to him that was stingy and mean to their own children and wives and husbands, that he might not hear their hypocritical prayers. She said an organ or a piano in the house would of itself educate the finer qualities of the mind and heart, and would assist in blending the intellectual with the sentimental and would aid in unfolding and developing the beauty of their natures; that pictures, musical instruments, pretty decorated walls and handsomely carpeted floors, a nice library of well-selected books, would educate and elevate the dwellers in such homes more than all things else combined. Clarissa is a very economical and judicious wife, and looks onto both sides of a dollar before she lets it go, and when it does go it generally brings back value equivalent. She said with a firm and decided tone that she was in favor of buying the organ; that cattle wasn't anything but cattle and never would be in this world nor the world to come, that they wasn't made in the image of their Creator, and they could do just as they had done in the past—go down to the creek to drink. But our children was the very image of our Heavenly Father, for the good book says so, and if we do our duty by 'em, and bring 'em up in the right way, they was liable to turn into brighter beings in the "sweet by and by," and if that is true, as the Bible says it is, and they are going to sing all the time and play on harps, then it is our duty to do all we can to fit them so they won't make horrible discords up there. (However, I don't believe much in the idea of being transformed into angels, and singing and playing, etc.; but some folks seem to get that idea from the way the Bible is explained to them.) She said she was fully satisfied that $250 put into a fine Estey Organ would be the best investment I ever made. I like to argue pretty well, especially when I think I've got a good fair chance to beat; but when Clarissa takes the floor and ends her side of the case, I haint got much to say in general, and nothing in particular. On this occasion I hadn't a word to offer, for I knew she was level, and so she and I looked into organs considerable and decided to buy an Estey. Mary said they was the best according to her teacher's judgment—and right there comes in another sham. Somehow or other, if you ask for the unbiased judgment of a music teacher in regard to the quality and merits of an instrument you may wish to purchase, ninety-nine times out of one hundred, a 10-per cent. commission decides their judgment, and they put on a sham face and act so completely disinterested that you think they are honest about it when they are perfect hypocrites. The bigger the commission the stronger is their recommendation, and the real merit of the instrument cuts no figure.

Well, we have been well pleased with our organ, but if we had never said a word to Mary's teacher about it we could have got it for $25 less than we paid. *Shams* are terrible mean things, but they seem a sight meaner when you have to pay a good price for 'em.

Mary has learned a powerful sight of music since we give her the organ, and when Clarissa and I get real tired and fatigued from hard work, we go into the square room and I lay down on the lounge, while Clarissa sets in her big cane-seat rocker. Mary sets down to the organ, and with her sweet voice, accompanied by the harmonious wind she turns out of the organ, lulls us to repose and seems to waft our souls to fairer lands, and we feel completely rested; and a hundred times I've felt that the money I put into that wind-box had been paid back to us in the pleasure we have received from it. Mary is considered the best player in ten miles of us.

I find I have slipped away from what I was going to say about the party, so I'll go back to the front room at once.

Melancthon Stevens, being the singing-school teacher, was invited to favor the company with a song, which he very promptly accepted upon condition that Mary would manipulate the organ, and she and Ebenezer Plunket assist on the chorus.

Mary began in the same way that most young ladies do when asked to play, after their parents have spent a good deal of money on their education, "Why, really, Mr. Stevens, you'll have to excuse me, I'm all out of practice." Clarissa spoke up in a sharp tone and said :

"Mary, you know better than to make a fool of yourself by such ridiculous excuses just because they are fashionable. You do the best you can, and then you will have done your duty."

"Yes, mother," said Mary, "I just wanted to see how it would sound if I done as Amelia Curtis does down to the village, whenever she is asked to play the piano. I will cheerfully comply with Mr. Stevens' request."

Mary was trying the silly sham that too many girls make use of for the purpose of being urged. It is an innocent sham that hurts nobody but themselves. It is a good deal like a lace sham—very easily seen through.

At it they went. Mr. Stevens was in good trim. He took a regular tour, commencing, "Down by the Sad Sea Waves," "Where the Sea-gulls Moan," then traveled over to "Old Virginny," and staid all night in "The Old Log Cabin in the Lane," and while under its protecting roof he exhibited his nature by trying to "Steal away softly" with "My Grandfather's Clock;" but fortunately for the old gentleman's heirs, "It was taller by half than the young man himself," so he left it for "Ninety years on the floor," and concluded he had better make himself scarce before the folks woke up, and said to himself, "I'll Speed Away, Speed Away, on my errand of love" where I can "Listen to the Mocking-bird" in the "Sweet

By and-By." After "Roaming over Mountains" and crossing the "Raging Canawl," he felt "Tired Now and Sleepy, too," and bought a return ticket from a scalper in 'Frisco for "Home, Sweet Home."

Ebenezer and Mary kept him company the whole trip, and occasionally, when a familiar strain was struck, we all got on board. We all seemed to enjoy Melancthon's efforts to please us, and at the same time do a little advertising for himself. We concluded he could execute most everything he could get his hands on.

After the music had died away, and Melancthon and Ebenezer and Mary had retired from the organ amid applause and perspiration, there was a lull, each one waiting for the other to speak.

Presently, some one called for a speech from Bascom Bigler, who was for short called "Square Big." After a general and promiscuous call, frequently repeated, the young 'Squire arose and said:

"Ladies and Gentlemen, I did not know it was in order at a social party to have a speech."

Bill Green spoke up and said that this was an exception.

"Well, then, ladies and gentlemen," continued the 'Squire, "as this is an exception to the general rule, I thank you for the honor you have conferred upon me in calling me to the floor on this special occasion. I do not feel myself competent to the task thus imposed upon me, as I have not made a speech since I left college without taking time to consider the subject of the remarks I was to make. However, as it seems to be the unanimous desire of those present, I will try to say a few words. What I have already said, ladies and gentlemen, are prefacing remarks. Now, to what I will say:

"Ladies and Gentlemen, we have met on this occasion to discuss the great political question of the day, labor and capital—the downtrodden and horny-handed sons of toil on the one hand, and the over-fed and bloated capitalist on the other. Excuse me, ladies and gentlemen, I forgot; that is part of a speech I made last fall before I was elected J. P., at a meeting of the Knights of Labor.

"Ladies and Gentlemen: The one great purpose of our lives is to secure the greatest amount of happiness we can at the least expense to ourselves, and the greatest expense to somebody else. In order to do this we must use a great amount of policy sometimes. A person to be successful in this course must be very polite to every one, never giving an insult and never taking one, and especially must he be very sweet to all the children. The dirtier they are the more attention must they receive, for through the children he will reach the heart of the mother, and when he has once captured that fortress he can bombard the rest of the family with soft-soap bubbles— they are cheap things to use in such an attack, as the principal ingredient in 'em is wind. When he has got all the families in the neighborhood to say, ' He is such a nice man,' ' He is a perfect gentleman,' and the young ladies to say, ' He is too sweet for anything,' he has succeeded in placing himself in a position where he can command all the happiness he desires with scarcely any expense to himself, but almost entirely at the expense of his many friends. If he wants to borrow money they are ready to lend it to him. If he has any big scheme on foot whereby he has nothing to lose, but everything to gain, he has but to spin out his web and make it look very fine and very secure, and then say, ' Come into my parlor,' and they will just as surely walk in, as he invites 'em. So if, as I said, the object in life is to secure the greatest amount of happiness at the least expense, I have hinted to you a plan which any of you can act upon with sure results.

"Ladies and Gentlemen: Again I have forgot the occasion upon which we have met, and I humbly beg your pardon. This is a part of a speech I delivered at a society meeting when I was in college, known as the Phi Kappa Society ; none but gentlemen were members.

"The fact is, ladies and gentlemen, it's rather embarrassing to make a speech without any previous preparation ; a fellow is so apt to run right into something he has said on another occasion. I will, however, try once more, and if possible, avoid the switches and keep the main track.

"Ladies and Gentlemen: We have met upon a most solemn occasion. That monster, who is everywhere and by all men, in all nations and climes, and under all circumstances most dreaded, who goes through the land principally riding a pale horse, and carries a sickle in his right hand, has passed through our peaceful land, and taken from us the man most dear to our country, without whom we never would have been a country, as he was the father of it—George Washington—and our temples throb with pain and our hearts sink within us as the teardrops fill our eyes "—At this point in his speech some one said, " Rats! rats!" 'Square Big says, " Excuse me, ladies and gentlemen, where are they? I didn't see 'em.

"Ladies and Gentlemen: Please pardon me again for such a fearful break. I got to thinking of my early school days, and was giving one of J. Q. Adams' favorite speeches on the death of our noble George. I will avoid further departure from what I ought to say.

"Ladies and Gentlemen: We have met in this pleasant parlor by special invitation of one of the fairest young ladies of this county, Miss Mary Morgan, to enjoy ourselves in a social capacity, and each one present, I have no doubt, can say with me, 'I am glad I come.' These social gatherings are good things to bind us together as friends and neighbors, to cheer each other, and there is no place in this part of the country where we are more heartily welcomed than right here—right in this big, square room where Benjamin Morgan lost his first wife with the measles, and where he brought his present wife, the best woman in the State of New York, Clarissa Snodgrass Morgan, to be his consort through life.

"The hospitality of this house is known as far as they are known, and this evening will always be remembered as the happiest of my whole life."

"Look here, Bascom Bigler," said Mariah, "you've told that same story about being the happiest time in your life a dozen times, and at every place we've been to You told it to me when you courted me, and the day we was married you told it again; and I think it's pretty nigh time to quit telling such lies '

Clarissa said, "Mariah, you mustn't mind that, although I don't blame you a mite for condemning deceitfulness. I believe it is the wickedest thing one can practice; but he is only giving us a novel —pretty words to hear, but nothing but a story after all."

ZOLLIVER RAMSDELL AND NANCY BOYLES SPARKING.

Yes, 'Squire Big's speech was only a little speech, but he pursued a line of policy in it that shadowed his future course in life. We will see what his sham led him to, and its results.

All the while we was being entertained with music, speeches, plays, etc., Nancy Boyles and Zolliver Ramsdell got into a corner behind the big, tall stove and sparked the whole evening. I guess they had as happy a time as any one of the party. There was one little black-eyed lady that cast curious glances toward the stove frequently, and that was Lily Doolittle. Poor Lily is a awful good little soul, and as nice as anybody can be; but somehow, everybody that wants to go with her she rejects, and everybody she wants to have accompany her, rejects her, and she is gradually, if not with greater speed, sliding down on the shady side of the matrimonial pyramid.

Sarah Smuggins was trying to look pretty and agreeable; but I don't remember of only one gentleman who had the disposition and courage to enter into a conversation with her, and that was Bigler. After he delivered his speech she told him all the men was acting on his line of policy. She knew 'em, and they was all alike, just like bees; they'd buzz around the clover blossom till it was a little faded, and then fly off to some other new blossom. There was no dependence to be placed upon 'em.

I overheard the 'Squire say to her, "Miss Smuggins, that is perfectly natural; when the bee has extracted all the honey from the flower, and begins to taste the bitter, it can't stand it, and must leave for sweeter blows. There are some flowers the bees light on that haven't a mite of honey in 'em, and the bees don't dwell long enough to argue the case, while there are other flowers that the bees linger around long after they are faded, and seem loth to give 'em up, even after the flower is dead. It ain't very good logic for the bitter blossoms to condemn the bee, when one sip from its cup of life would be death to the bee," and the 'Squire excused himself in his smiling manner, and sought the company of Clarissa.

I noticed Sarah seemed to be in a meditating mood. Perhaps she may change her ideas of things yet; stranger things than that have happened.

It was time for the company to go home, and while they were getting on their things and passing around the good-byes, Ebenezer Plunket said he was requested to give notice that there would be literary exercises at the Waddles Corners schoolhouse next Friday evening, and the new teacher, Timothy Brown, would like to have all come that took an interest in intellectual advancement. The exercises would be of a promiscuous character, and the teacher designed to organize a permanent lyceum in order to promote and stimulate mental culture, not only among the children, but the parents and citizens of that vicinity. The exercises would commence precisely at 8 o'clock.

After the company had all gone, and peace and quiet was again restored, and the lights blew out, Clarissa and I went to bed. We got to talking about the affair to take place at the schoolhouse, and wondered what it would be. Clarissa said, "I wonder if they will spell down? If they do, Ben, I suppose you and I will be the champions; for you know, you and I used to spell anything and everything down twenty years ago. Now, if they should do that, and we should be the last ones standing, one of us had better miss a word on purpose, so as not to tire them out waiting for us." I agreed I'd miss a word for her benefit, and we went to sleep.

Along in the night I heard Clarissa talking out loud in her sleep, and it waked me up. She very frequently talks in her sleep, especially if anything is weighing on her mind. In accents that would wring pity from a stone, these feeling lines poured forth from her lips:

"For in my heart I felt
If Benjamin had misspelt
That word on which he dwelt,
I would have won the belt."

CHAPTER VI.

CLARISSA and I went down to the Waddles Corners school-house, Friday evening, in pretty good season, so as to be sure of a seat, for, as a general rule, when there's any doings in the country school-houses, they are packed full.

We wasn't a mite too early this time, for in less than fifteen minutes after we got there the house was just crowded full, and there was a good many that could not get in at all.

Mr. Brown called them to order by a few taps of the bell, and then said in a very polite and gentlemanly manner:

"Ladies and Gentlemen: My purpose in calling you together this evening is two-fold. First, that I might become acquainted with you. Second, and this is the principal reason, to organize in your community a literary society or lyceum, for the purpose of stimulating a desire for study and self-culture. An institution of this kind will be of incalculable benefit to the young people, and also to you older ones, to come together once a week and discuss questions of more or less importance, prepare essays, deliver original speeches, and enliven the exercises with music; it will serve to develop and strengthen the mental powers, make you more independent and give you something to think of during the week, and withal, furnish a proper amusement.

"I think you will all readily agree with me that it is a good thing for us to do. Some of you may feel a little timid at first about taking an active part in it, for fear you can't say things as you would like to, and think some one will laugh at you. Well, this is just the place for us to learn how to speak freely and express our views, and it matters not if we do get laughed at; it won't hurt us a particle. It is always our turn next, and we can laugh at those that laugh at us; and by doing the best we can after a while they won't laugh at us, and we will be able to command the respect of people when we engage in the discussion of any question

"The person who educates himself to properly argue a question, arranges his proofs so as to have them at his command like so many well-drilled soldiers, can use them as he desires, and always has the advantage over one who has not had that training and education. All through life we will find plenty of occasions to use just what all of us can learn in a lyceum such as I desire you to enter into here, and keep up.

"Now before we proceed further I am going to put it to a vote, and I don't want any one to vote 'Yes' unless you are willing to take hold and work in it. Now, all that are in favor of organizing a lyceum here, to be known as the Waddles Corners Lyceum, please manifest it by saying 'Yes.'"

There was a tremendous response of "Yes" all over the house.

"All that are opposed to it will say 'No.'" But there was not a response.

"The question being carried by a unanimous vote, I will suggest one week from to-night as the time to meet in this house and organize, elect officers, and adopt a constitution and by-laws.

"Now, ladies and gentlemen, we will have a sort of a variety entertainment to-night. I have arranged a programme as follows:

"First, Music.

"Second, Debate. Question: Which is the most beneficial to people, the lawyers or the doctors? Limited to half an hour.

"Third, A spelling match, to last twenty minutes.

"Fourth, Speech by Rev. Jonas Danberry.

"Fifth, Essay by Miss Julia Spear, and lastly,

"Music."

It had been arranged to have Melancthon Stevens, Ebenezer and Mary, and Mrs. Lucas supply the music, and an organ was got for the occasion.

They proceeded at once to sing and play, " What are the Wild Waves Saying," and "Tit-willow." The last piece Ebenezer sung alone.

Mr. Brown selected as principal disputants in the debate, George Waddles and Tom Clark. (Tom Clark is a young man that's been away to a medical school studying to be a doctor, and was at home on a vacation.) The question was stated as follows: *Resolved*, That lawyers are more beneficial to the people at large than doctors. George Waddles took the affirmative, and Tom Clark the negative side. George chose 'Squire Bigler as his assistant, and Clark selected Ebenezer Plunket as his. I was appointed as judge.

Waddles aint much of a speaker, but he done his best at it. He begun, and said:

"Mr. Chairman, and Fellow Citizens; Lawyers is necessary to preserve the rights of the people. Everybody knows we have laws, lots of laws; but there aint one in a hundred that knows what the laws be, nor what rights they have got under 'em, and they haint got time to study 'em, and wouldn't know much more about 'em after they'd studied 'em than before, and it is necessary that some one should make it their special business and be able to tell the people what rights they had, and what they haint, in order to keep 'em from doing wrong and getting into trouble. Lawyers is the ones to do that business, and they stand as garden angels, so to speak, of the rights and liberties of the people. But the doctors is a regular set of humbugs, and most of 'em is quacks. Them as aint regular quacks go off to some school and raise Old Harry a cutting up all sorts of tricks, and steal some dead bodies and carry them off in some attic, and cut 'em all up and find out how they are made; and then they'll get some recipes for curing some diseases, and then they'll manage one way and another to get the teachers in the school to give 'em a certificate and then they'll go out into some town or village, or city, and hire a room up stairs over some drugstore, or as nigh to it as they can, and get some bones and an old skull, and a lot of books and spread 'em around the room and call it an office, and stick out a sign and call themselves doctors. They look wonderful wise, and by-and-by some one gets sick and sends in a hurry after a doctor. The messenger runs into his office and says:

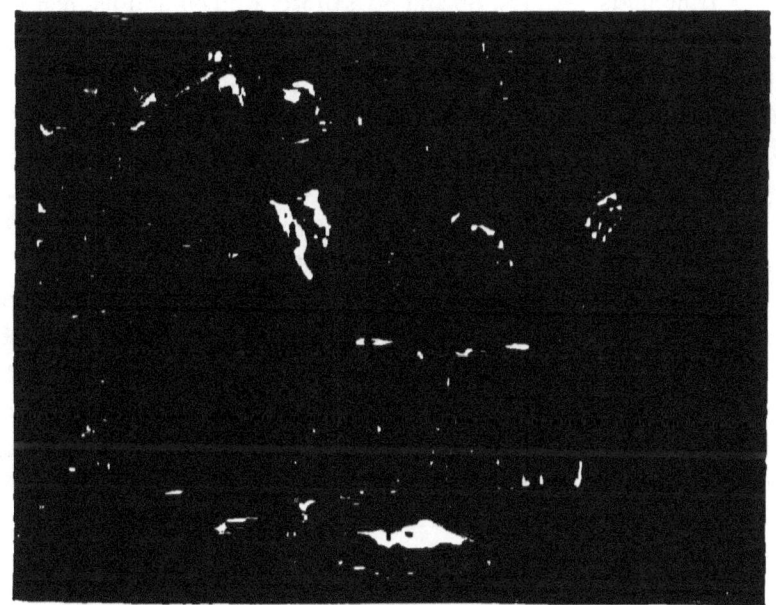

DOCTOR'S OFFICE.

"'Mrs. So-and-so wants you to come right out to her house quick; she's powerful sick.'

"The doctor hitches up his horse and puts his bag of medicine in his gig and drives out at a terrible speed to the house. He goes in as though he owned the place; is shown into the sick-room. He takes a chair very deliberately, sets down by the bedside and looks wonderful wise, and says to the woman, 'Are you sick?' and she will say, 'Yes, doctor, I am terrible sick; can't you do something for me right away, I'm in such pain.'

"'Let me see your tongue,' he'll say, 'and let me feel your pulse.' And then he'll ask her all kinds of questions; and then he ll guess what ails her, and give her a lot of medicine, and go back to his office and put down in his ledger, 'Mrs. So-and-so, debtor, to one visit, $10.'

"If he finds out Mrs. So-and-So is pretty well off, and has considerable influence in the community, he will use harmless medicines, so far as he knows about them, and manage to get out to see her at least once a day, as long as he thinks he can keep her along, out of danger and out of recovery. Every day he makes a new guess as to what ails her, and tries a new remedy. And so he goes along with her and all the rest of his patients, a' guessing what ails 'em, and a' guessing when and where he'll get his pay.

"The fact is, they are a lot of guessers, a' speculating on people's misfortunes. More persons that get sick and, from some cause or other, have to go without a doctor, get well than them that gets doctors. And that fact proves beyond any question of doubt that doctors is shams and humbugs, and is not beneficial to the people, while everybody knows that we couldn't live in safety and happiness twenty-four hours without lawyers; and, therefore, Mr. Judge, you'll have to decide this question in favor of the affirmative."

George took his seat amid cheers. This was the greatest effort of his life, and evidently he felt that he had achieved a victory, before the other side was heard from.

Young Tom Clark arose, and in a calm and pleasing manner said: "Honorable Judge, Ladies and Gentlemen: The gentleman who has been addressing you evidently is better acquainted with agricultural pursuits than either the legal or medical professions, otherwise he would never have made such erroneous statements, or jumped at such rash conclusions. It is a plain fact that lawyers, instead of being the preservers of the rights of the people, are the great disturbers of their rights. They make it their special business to counsel men to all kinds of quarrels and fusses, so they can charge an exorbitant fee for defending persons from a difficulty they have got them into by their advice.

"It isn't safe nowadays for a man of property to make a will and die, or die without one, for, as sure as he does, a lot of lawyers will buzz around some of his heirs and get them to bust up the will. They will gather around that estate like so many hungry buzzards

BUZZARDS AND CARCASS.

around a carcass, and they'll linger around it until every dollar is consumed, and then the poverty-stricken heirs can go to the Devil, for all they care. They are grand preservers of the people's rights, aint they? Show me a single right that some of them have not trampled upon. I will admit there are a good many things a lawyer can do that will benefit some, once in a while, and also that there are some very honorable lawyers, but not many. The great run of them are figuring all the time how they can thrive upon the misfortunes and errors of others. You go to a lawyer and state your case to him plainly, he will turn his hawkeye on you in a minute, and, by inquiries or other means, see right down through you into the bottom of your pockets, and if he finds them lean and no backing visible, he will tell you that your case is a hopeless one, and will advise you to drop it or settle it, as the case may be; or, if he thought he had a good show to get the other side of the case, he will send you to some other poor lawyer. But, if he sees your pockets are full and fat with the world's inspiration, *money*, right or wrong, it matters not to him, he will tell you that you have got a strong case; that you can win, and will advise you by all means to push it. And so the sham will urge you to do what he knows you have no right to do, and then talk about being the preservers of the people's rights! Call 'em 'garden angels!' I think I can imagine one of 'em flying around us now, with a large bald head and heavy, drooping eyelids, a ponderous stomach, and spoons sticking out from under his wings and around his neck, suspended by a white ribbon (the emblem of purity), a gold medal, with engraven thereon the monogram B. F. B. If we had one lawyer where we now have 2,000, the people would feel comparatively happy. There wouldn't be half so many fusses, and those who are wrongfully inclined wouldn't feel that they had a good legal rascal to help 'em out.

"Our friend Waddles may be better acquainted with them in the future. He may find some of them, if not a good many, haven't got their wings yet. He shows equal amount of ignorance in regard to the medical fraternity. That there are some quacks, I'm willing to admit; but a counterfeit dollar always gives evidence that there are genuine dollars. So, a quack doctor is a standing witness that there are genuine physicians. I have but to cite you to one to prove my point conclusively, namely: That the doctors are more beneficial to the human race than lawyers, and that is, the Saviour himself. He went about as the great physician, curing the deaf and the blind, healing the sick, cleansing the leper, and causing the lame to walk; and from that day to this, all along the way, history tells us of the millions that have been cured, or have been made easy, and whose lives have been prolonged by the aid of the physician.

"The class Mr. Waddles has been referring to, I think, must be quacks, for the thoroughly educated doctor knows what he is doing, and doesn't have to guess. There is no class of people in the wide world whose mission is so directly to benefit the people, while they are indirectly benefited themselves, as the doctors.

A "GARDEN ANGEL."

"Honorable Judge, Ladies and Gentlemen, with this plain statement of the case, I am willing to leave the decision in your hands."

The thirty minutes allowed for the debate had already expired, therefore Bigler and Plunket didn't get a opportunity to discuss the question, but the teacher appointed them as captains to choose sides for the spelling, which was to take place immediately. Ebenezer had the first choice, and Bigler the second. Ebenezer chose on his side—me, Sarah Smuggins, George Waddles, Tom Clark, Zolliver

Ramsdell, Mary Morgan, and a lot more. Bigler had on his side—Clarissa, Peleg Tomkins, Mehitable Green, Abby Standish, Nancy Boyles, and a lot more. When all was ready, the teacher put out the words. The first word was *Plough*, a verb, and 'Squire Bigler spelled P-l-o-u-g-h, plow. The next was "*rough*," and Ebenezer spelled r-o-u-g-h, ruf. The next was "cow," and Clarissa thought that if 'Squire Bigler was right in spelling "*plow*," she thought she would be correct in spelling it "*c-o-u-g-h, cow;*" and the teacher bawled out—

"Next."

I don't think I ever saw Clarissa's face more carroty-colored in my life; and she sat down with a visible surprise in her complexion. While Clarissa was sitting down, Ebenezer whispered to me:

"C-o-w;" and I spake up loud and said—

"Well, my opinion is that that animal ought to be spelled with a 'k;' but the way is C-O W, *cow;*" and for once I felt proud to think I had beaten Clarissa, as she always conveys the idea that I am honest but not very smart.

Several words went around, till it came to my turn, when the teacher called out *Chicago;* and I asked him if we had got that far from home so soon—there was such a humming and noise that I didn't know but that we was on a lightning express train.

"No, Mr. Morgan," he said; "if you can't spell the word, sit down."

He spoke so mighty smart it made me mad; and I said, "Any fool can spell that word. I spell it, s-h-e-c-a-w-g-o;" and he yelled out:

"Next," with a broad grin on his face; and I sat down. Peleg Tomkins spelled it " C-h-i-c-a-g-o;" and the teacher said *Correct*, and looked at me with a grin.

It made me mad; and I said, "Didn't I say any fool could spell it; I didn't try to spell it right; for I wanted to see what fool would spell it." That made Peleg hot, and he said,—

"If it wa'n't for the respect I have for Clarissa Morgan I'd show these folks what a smart husband she had."

Clarissa spoke up and said, "La me, Peleg, don't mind Benjamin; that's the way he always does when he gets in a tight place and don't know how to get out. He couldn't spell Chicago right more'n he could play music out of that organ;" and Clarissa seemed to glory in my downfall; and her remarks just caused a perfect uproar of laughter; but I didn't feel a mite like laughing. I was fighting mad; but I concluded to keep cool and not show it. Things didn't pan out just exactly as Clarissa and I had figured they would in case we had a spelling match; and the teacher kind o' nettled me.

George Waddles spelled *cattle*, *Durham*, *Holstein* and *money* all right; but when they gave him the word *religion* he sat down; he couldn't spell it right, although the teacher gave him two chances on it. I concluded that a man could spell any word right that his whole heart is interested in; but that he is liable to miss words that doesn't so particularly interest him, but which may represent a sideshow to his main attraction.

Now, I couldn't no more miss-spell Clarissa Snodgrass Morgan than I could go to heaven on the tail of a kite, for the reason that she is my main attraction in life and my whole heart is interested in her. So, in my mind, it was perfectly natural for George Waddles to spell these words correctly; but when it came to his side-show, the thing he uses to advertise himself as honest, so he can make a good haul out of the people, and especially the Methodists, *religion*, it wasn't so familiar to him and he went down on it as quick as I did on Chicago.

'Squire Bigler went down on the very next word after "religion," *honesty*. He spelled *policy* all right, but honesty was too much for him, and he slipped down on it.

Zolliver Ramsdell was the last man standing, and bore off the victor's palm. He stood up for some time after the rest were all down. He spelled "Boyles" without any visible pain, but when it come to hairpin he went down quicker'n lightning. It was too much for him, and he wilted amid roars of laughter; and I laugned this time.

The teacher asked the choir to favor us with a song—something familiar—and all to join in. So they sung "America."

If "America" was never properly executed before, it certainly was this time. Clarissa said (and she is a remarkably good singer), "If America survives she needn't fear any foreign foe." She has survived, I am happy to state, and as one of her family, I bid defiance to every power except the Almighty, to extinguish her.

After peace and reason was once more regained, and the house had come to order, Mr. Brown introduced the Rev. Jonas Danberry, pastor of the Methodist Church down to the village (he was up visiting Waddles), who, he said, could give us a short speech on the importance of spelling.

The Reverend D. took the platform by the teacher's desk, and said:

"Ladies and Gentlemen, the subject of spelling is a very important one, and one in which every one was more or less interested. Ahem! ahem! as I remarked, spelling is a very important subject. Ever since the spell when the Creator said, 'Let there be light;' ever since the spell when he said, 'Let there be a firmament;' ever since the spell when he said, 'Let the waters be divided and the dry land appear;' ever since the spell when he nailed the sun and moon and stars up against the walls of the sky; ever since the spell when he made all the animals on the earth, and in the waters, and in the sky; ever since the spell when he made man and woman in his own blessed image, down to the time when Grant said, 'Let us have a spell of peace,' spelling has been of great importance. Ahem! ahem! Had the spell that the immortal Grant suggested been adopted before Satan rebelled in heaven; had that spell been adopted before the Babylonians and Assyrians had their falling out with one another; had Alexander the Great adopted that spell before he invaded Egypt; had that spell been adopted by all the rulers of the world, from its first springing into existence down to the present time, the world would have been comparatively peaceful; and blessed be God, millions on millions of people would have been saved, to die a natural death.

"My friends, you can all see the importance of having right spells; but how are we to have right spells without right spelling?

"There are spells in every one's life when they would give a great deal to know how to spell right. There are so many that can't spell right that the wrong spells seem to control their actions through life, and when such persons come down to the spell of death, they tremble as they realize, when it is too late, that they have got a spell of powerful hot weather before them that will last through all eternity.

"Therefore, brethren and sisters, and friends and others, see to this very important subject of spelling, and learn to spell right, that you may spend the spell of eternity in heaven with the blood-washed throng that have spelled their titles clear to mansions in the skies, and gone home to glory, to sing praises to the Lamb, and where spelling is no more.

"I thank you, ladies and gentlemen, for your kind attention, and bid you all good-night."

As soon as the reverend had finished his brief spell of remarks, George Waddles moved a vote of thanks to the minister for his very able address, which was carried by a great majority, as nobody voted against it. Clarissa and I, however, didn't vote for it, for we couldn't see where he threw any light on correct spelling, nor did he even so much as touch on the *shams* in spelling, or explain why *cow* and *plough* should be spelled so different, as c-o-w for one, and p-l-o-u-g-h for the other, and why muff and rough and tough and cuff shouldn't be spelled alike, except the first letter, and a great many other words spelled one way and pronounced entirely different. I'd like to have some one show up the shams of English spelling.

The teacher announced that Miss Julia Spear would read an essay. Miss Spear stepped onto the platform and made a very low "bough," and smiled a sort of a store smile, such as clerks behind the counters have when you go into the store, ready-made for the occasion. She had a sort of cinnamon-rose blush on her cheeks; but I am inclined to think it was a *sham* blush, as it was permanent,

READING THE ESSAY.

and was a little nearer her off ear than her nigh one. She tremblingly held her paper in front of her, and begun:

"I've been asked to write a essay, but I don't know what to write about. I've thought of a good many things, but I don't know what to write about any of them, so I guess I'll write a little about all of them.

"Spring is a lovely season of the year. Everything dresses up in its best bib and tucker. The trees and meadows put on new robes of fashionable green, and trim themselves up with flowers. The posy-beds put on airs, and come out like a cheap millinery window in full blow. The cows change their coats and pants this season of the year, and the girls and boys all get on new clothes and look fresh and green, while all nature and the rest of the folks smile. The church is crowded in the evening this season of the year with all kinds of girls, who go to show off their pretty, new things, and make the other girls envious of 'em, and also to get a beau to take them home.

"The dudes are unusually thick around the church doors in spring. They seem to know 'when the robins nest again,' and are on hand for cherries.

"This is a favorable season of the year for dudes to start a new moustache, and have a lawn-mower run over their heads, and get themselves up in shape, regardless; and a row of 'em at the front door of the church, and on the street corner, look as pretty as a string of fresh trout, and just about as speckled. Speaking of dudes, I asked Judge Seavers, of Iowa, whom I met when I was visiting my cousin, in Des Moines, last winter, what a dude was (as I had heard my cousin say that the city was full of them, and I didn't know then what she meant, as I never was in a city before). He said they were substitutes for dummies used by clothing merchants in front of their stores; the merchants found them much cheaper than the dummies, as they were living, and could walk around town by the aid of a cane; that when they put their dressed dummies out in front of their stores, they had to chain them down to keep the folks from carrying them off, but there wasn't the least mite of danger of any one carrying off a dude, as they would have no use for 'em. Joseph Cook says they are physical, mental and moral shams. What awful things they must be! It's no wonder the girls fall in love with them, for the young and innocent girls are such sympathizing creatures that they always take pity on the poor things that others condemn and despise. I remember we had a real pretty dog once.

He would play around the house, and get hold of mother's ball of yarn when she was knitting, and he would have lots of fun with it; but father tried to make him go and drive some cows out of the cornfield one day, and he couldn't get him away from the door-yard, so he got mad and kicked him, and it just made me awful sorry for poor little Fido, and I went and got him in the house and rubbed some cream on him where father kicked him, and so I know how natural it is for girls to love dudes.

"*Fashion.*—Fashion is the art of doing all you can for the benefit of the dry goods dealer, the milliner and the dressmaker, regard-

POOR FIDO!

less of your own comfort, or the condition of your father's pocket-book or credit. To be extremely fashionable, is to be either a fool or a martyr—generally the latter. Very few women have got good enough constitutions to be fashionable more'n ten years. At the end of that time they are in the hospital, or asylum, or a fashionable grave.

"*Music.*—Music is a charming sensation when it is properly made, but if it lacks a chord, or has too many chords, it makes you feel as if a drag was being hauled over you, and has a tendency to strain your nervous system. Young ladies are supposed to be lacking if they are not accomplished in music. Three-fourths of their time should be devoted to it, whether they can tell a chord from a clothes-pin. They are not supposed to utilize their knowledge for any purpose unless their folks are very poor and they are obliged to do something for themselves.

"*Manners.*—Manners is to know how to behave decent. When you go into a stranger's house you should scrape your feet on the edge of the porch floor; either before or after you go in, remove your hat or bonnet, make a pretty bow and smile sweet, and shake hands with the person that greets you at the door, unless it should be the hired girl, at which time you are not expected to act decent. If you should call during house-cleaning time, and meet the lady of the house dressed in a faded calico dress, with a red handkerchief pinned around her head and some crock and dirt on her nose, you can treat her just as if she was the hired girl, and after you have found out your mistake you can take your time in studying real manners and sham manners.

"*Money.*—Money is the most powerful lever in the world. With it you can do anything. You can say to yonder mountain, 'Be ye cast into this valley,' and your command will be obeyed. You can build railroads, tunnel rivers, speak to distant countries by lightning power, and erect palaces. You can control governments and manipulate the courts just as you desire, and control elections. You can command the attention of all the sycophants of the country. You can buy the average minister to pass you off as a Christian, and at your funeral send you into the fair kingdom. In fact, you can get anything you want except *one* thing, which money can't possibly buy—it is a jewel that is more sparkling and radiant than the most brilliant diamond, but you can't get it with any kind of a price. However, you and all of us can have it; it is a true, honest and upright CHARACTER. A true character can command money.

"*Politics.*—Politics is a fine art, and one that requires a good deal of shrewdness and studying. It consists of a thorough knowledge of how to bamboozle the people, or, in other and more comprehensive language, how to pull the wool over the eyes of the people so they can only see the outside of you. The bold outlines in this art is to work all the points to insure the candidate's election. The deep shades and dark background is the principal work done after he is elected.

"The United States has got within its borders an innumerable host of proficient scholars and old masters in the school of politics. For hypocrisy and sham they excel any equal number to be found in the world.

"I think I have wrote about as long a essay as I ought to for the first one in my life. It is all original except the last article on politics; that was contributed by Gen. J. B. Weaver, who once upon a time had his name printed on some tickets for President of the United States. But I don't suppose any of you remember of seeing any of the tickets. Pa says he is a great deal better than some folks think he is; but pa says the trouble is, they haint anybody found it out.

"*Time.*—Time is a thing most people want more of 'especially if they are short on a deal,' as Uncle John says (he is a dealer in grain in Chicago). It is like charity; it covers all differences, all sorrows and disappointments, all failures in life, as well as all life's joys, in oblivion. Time flies, and it is time for me to close."

She closed amidst tremendous applause. The exercises closed with music from the four musicians I mentioned in the early part of this chapter. Just before we was dismissed, the teacher announced a course of lectures to be given in this schoolhouse, commencing one week from next Monday night, on Phrenology, by Professor Theodocius Leviticus Feeler, of Boston. The first lecture would be free. He would like to have all come.

Mr. Brown also announced a meeting over to the red schoolhouse (which is about a mile from our house) next Wednesday night, at which time the presiding elder of the Methodist Church would preach. There would be a prayer and conference meeting after preaching.

> To spend our leisure hours
> In intellectual bowers,
> And strengthen our mental powers,
>   We firmly resolved,
> With the aid of Timothy Brown,
> Who came from Utica town,
> We surely could not go down
>   Unless we dissolved.

CHAPTER VII.

THE exercises at the schoolhouse last Friday night has been the subject of conversation between Clarissa and me frequently, and especially the spelling part. Things didn't turn out just as we had calculated on before we went there, and both of us was a little disappointed. She says, "The more she thinks of Danberry's speech, the more dumbfounded foolish it seems." She says, "There isn't a mite of philosophy in it, for some of the best spellers in the world are the meanest kind of folks that ever lived, and some of the best folks can't spell their own names right. I know I mean to do my duty all the time, and I up and spelled cow wrong; but I think my chances for heaven are just as good as his are. I believe that education is a good thing—and what we all ought to encourage—yet it haint going to make angels of us, nor take us to heaven, unless it is the education of the heart. The Bible says, 'From the abundance of the heart the mouth speaketh.' If the heart is full of love and kindness and charity and patience, the mouth will talk all right, the hands will do all right, and the feet will carry you straight on the road to heaven; but if the heart is full of hypocrisy and meanness, and all kinds of cussedness, and the head full of right spelling and good grammar, when its owner comes down to the door of death, he will be very apt to realize that the atmosphere in the next room he is about to enter, is uncomfortably hot, if there is any such condition of things to await the soul in the next world, about which I have my serious doubts."

While Clarissa was thus philosophizing on Rev. Danberry's remarks, some one knocked on the front door. I opened the door, and who was there but Jim Teeters and Betsey. We was glad to see them, and had them come right in and take off their things.

Betsey said, "Jim came out to see Benjamin about his hogs, and she thought she'd come along for a ride, and have a little visit with Mrs. Morgan while the men talked business."

Teeters and I went out to the barn and put his horse out and fed it. Then Teeters says to me:

TEETERS TALKS OVER THE HOG BUSINESS IN THE BARN.

"Mr. Morgan, I thought I'd come out and see if you still wanted to sell your hogs."

I told him "that was what I raised them for, and I intended to sell 'em, but I hadn't been down to the village since Clarissa and I was at his house to dinner, and so I hadn't sold 'em."

"Well," says he, "do you still want three and a quarter cents for 'em?"

I said, "Yes."

"Says he, "Let's go out and look 'em over."

After looking them over pretty carefully he said, "I am going to load a couple of cars to-morrow night to ship to Albany, and if you'll drive 'em down to the village to-morrow so as to get there before four o'clock in the afternoon I'll take 'em at your price and give you the cash for 'em as soon as they are weighed."

I told him I'd try to get there by that time, that I'd start early in the morning with 'em. He gave me sixty-one dollars to bind the bargain. And then we went into the house. Dinner was ready. We had a good visit and talked over neighborhood and village affairs, and Betsey was as chipper as ever.

After they went home, Clarissa asked me if I'd sold the hogs to Teeters.

I told her I had.

How much for, she wanted to know.

I told her just what I asked him when they were out here before, three and a quarter cents a pound.

"Well," said Clarissa. "If Jim Teeters isn't a sharp one I'll miss my guess; he haint driv out here for nothing, and when you get down to the village with the hogs, I wouldn't be surprised if they wasn't worth a great deal more, and he has figured it out that you haint very sharp (which is too true, Ben), and probably didn't know what hogs was worth, and he'd make a good speck out of you."

The next morning I and Abe and the hired man started down with the hogs; we got into the village about three o'clock P. M. As we was turning the corner at the top of the hill going down into the village we met Teeters, who came to help us get 'em through the town to the railroad depot. We had a pesky time getting the contrary brutes past Totman's old tavern. (It is hard work getting a hog by a tavern, anyhow.)

Before I got to the depot three different men came up to me and said: "Hello there, have you sold them ar hogs?" I told them yes.

"How much did you git?" they asked.

"How much will you give?" said I. Each one of 'em told me

they'd give me five cents a pound. Then I found out Jim Teeters' scheme. My hogs weighed just 15,616 pounds, and Teeters paid me for them just $507.52, and they was worth at the regular market value $780.80. I lost $273.28 by Teeters' base hypocrisy. I had made a bargain with Teeters, and I wouldn't back out for two reasons: one was, I couldn't if I wanted to, and tother was, I was honest, and always mean to be as long as I can. I hate the aw-

DRIVING THE PESKY BRUTES BY THE TAVERN.

fullest kind to be swindled and robbed by a condemned hypocrite, but come to think it over, I don't see how I could be swindled by any body else.

On my way home I meditated considerable, and was uneasy in my mind. I thought of that passage in the Bible where it says: "Unto them that knows something shall be given something more, and from them that knows nothing shall be taken what little bit they do know and given to them that knows something," or words that give the reader to understand that that is the intention of the Almighty in his law to the human family. I felt that the law was unjust, but nevertheless inevitable, and I had—not for the first time in my life either, but about the hundredth time—obeyed the law. I didn't know scarcely anything, and Jim Teeters was mighty smart and knowing, and what really belonged to me, $273.78 worth, had been transferred from me to him. I felt that I was every day losing what little sense I had, and now I was losing my money, too.

I didn't want to tell Clarissa one mite, for I knew she'd show me what a fool I was getting to be every day, and then I hated to be taken the advantage of by one we had used so well, on such a short acquaintance.

When I got home Clarissa asked me how I got along with the hogs. I just told her all about it, and give her every cent I got for 'em. I told her I was such a dumb fool that it wasn't safe for me to have the money, for I was liable to lose it any minute, and I knew it was safe in her hands.

Clarissa saw my dejected look, and she was real sorry for me. She spoke in a tender and soothing manner, and said:

" Benjamin, I'm awful sorry, for I know how hard you've worked a-raising them hogs, but I hain't a-goin' to blame you, for I know you are a honest and well-meanin' man, and you are a good husband to me, but I think Jim Teeters would do anything that's mean, if he could make anything by it, and I knew well enough he had some scheme to cheat you when he come up here yesterday. Now, if you'll let me make the bargains for you hereafter, I believe we'll make more money."

I fully agreed with her, and have turned the financial part of our business over to her, and have once more obeyed that inevitable law. I think I will be much happier in the future, to have the care of getting swindled off my mind. I am more'n ever persuaded to believe that Clarissa is a true philosopher, and when she said " Jim Teeters, with all his smartness, hadn't got that necessary ingredient to wash his soul from sin," she spoke the truth.

Of all men that are mean—the meanest is the one that will steal from you under the clothes of friendship. I will drop Teeters for the present, but will, no doubt, pick him up again somewhere in the future.

CHAPTER VIII.

WEDNESDAY night I hitched up the old mare and took Clarissa over to the red schoolhouse to meeting. Mary got a chance to ride with Ebenezer Plunket. We was in time to get a good seat pretty well up in front. The house was packed full again the Presiding Elder came; Elder Danberry and Geo Waddles came along with him.

Elder Danberry give out the hymn: "Come thou fount of every blessing." Clarissa haint a Methodist, but they all expected her to start the tune. She did it, and it sounded real good, for you could hear her voice above all the other women, and she has got a powerful sweet voice, when it's in tune. She took along a pocketful of peppermint drops to keep it tuned up to concert pitch and make her breath smell sweet.

After the singing was done and Father Emmons over in the corner had rubbed his hands and groaned and shouted: "*Amen! blessed fountain!*" Elder Danberry prayed.

Now I don't believe in making light of religion, for to me when it is properly understood, it is the most important subject that can interest the human soul, but I don't believe because a man *professes* to be very religious, and has the clothes of a minister onto him, that he should presume so much upon a very limited acquaintance with the Almighty as to ask Him, as Elder Danberry did in his prayer, to come right down that minute, bust a hole right through the roof of this house and come right in here and take every sinner here by the hair of their heads and convince 'em of sin and wickedness, and make 'em be born again. And a whole lot more stuff that I think would look very foolish to the Lord. In the first place I don't think the Lord goes around this world, bustin' holes in the roofs of houses because some ignoramus asks Him to, however earnest the ignoramus may be. In the second place I don't believe the Lord has to take sinners

ELDER DANBERRY.

or any one else by the hair of their heads and rattle 'em up in order to convince them of sin. In the third place I don't believe the Lord has anything to do with convincing people of sin in any sudden and startlin' manner. If I have lied about anything to anybody, or been dishonest or mean, low and wicked, I know it before anybody else does, and the Lord haint got to tell me of it in order for me to find it out. If I have fallen from virtue and put a dark stain upon my life, I am the very first person that will be aware of the fact. And if I want to be forgiven, I must go to them that I have sinned against for forgiveness. I must go to them and not expect them to come to me. Every sin that a man commits is against the divine law of God, therefore, if we want full pardon, we must go to Him and ask it, and the good book says it will be freely granted.

Elder Danberry in his prayer wanted the Lord to do all the hard and dirty work of running around to all the mean, low and degraded cusses in the country and gather them up in His tender arms and hug 'em. He wasn't even satisfied with that request, but presumed the Lord didn't know how to do His work. He went on telling Him how to do it, and advised Him to destroy property in order to get inside of that schoolhouse.

Now that may be the kind of religion the Lord taught while on earth. If it is I can't read the Bible straight.

I believe that kind of stuff comes nearer blasphemy than anything else; greater reverence for the Almighty is manifested by the poor Hindoo widow that casts herself upon the funeral fire of her dead husband, than is shown in such impudent dictations to Him in the prayers of those who even make praying part of their regular business for a living.

Clarissa said, when she heard me criticising Danberry's prayer, that I was too severe; that the minister used them expressions in his prayer paregorically.

"Very well," I replied, "too much paregoric will kill the patient, or even the oldest inhabitant, and too much of this ministerial shamming on the part of honest ignoramuses or cunning hypocrites would kill their work."

I started to tell you about this meeting, and here I've been chasing off after one of them ideas that comes up in front of me once in a while.

After Elder Danberry was through praying he said, " Brethren and sisters, our Presiding Elder, Brother Jones, will preach to you this evening, and after the sermon we will take up a collection to he.p pay the brother his quarterly dues. Remember, 'the Lord loveth a cheerful giver.' 'Cast thy bread upon the waters, and after many days it shall return to thee.'"

Elder Jones is a portly old gentleman with silver hair and long gray beard that mark well into threescore and ten years. He has a brindle complexion and a very important air onto him. He rose up with the majesty of a city mayor, and after carefully looking the audience over, said:

PRESIDING ELDER JONES.

"Ahem! Ahem! My brothers and sisters, you'll find the words of my text recorded in the blessed good book that was given to us that we might know the way of life and salvation. Yes, blessed be the Lord, you'll find my text in the holy writ. Yes, praise his name, you'll find my text in the word of the Almighty, glory be to his great name. You'll find the words of my text in the Bible, 'book divine; precious treasure, thou art mine.' And when you find 'em they'll read in this wise: 'As in Adam all die, even so in Christ shall all be made alive.'"

"Amen! Amen!" is shouted by Father Emmons in the corner.

"These, brethren and sisters, are the words of the Apostle Paul, spoken unto the Corinthians, and they are spoken unto us also, and we should take heed unto them lest at any time we should let 'em slip.

"We are here taught that the first man was Adam. Yes, my brethren and sisters, the first man was Adam—the very first man the Almighty created was Adam. Let us remember that important fact. His name wasn't Charlie, nor John, nor Timothy, nor Teeters, nor Grover, nor James, nor Peleg, nor Ebenezer, nor even Benjamin, nor a thousand other names that I might mention did time permit, but it was Adam—plain, simple Adam. Why the Almighty called him Adam is a mystery he hasn't seen fit to tell us, and blessed be God, he don't have to tell us his reasons for doing things as he is a-mind to; he simply gives us the plain facts, and it's none of our business why he does this or that.

"The book says he called him, Adam and the good book don't mention any other man that the Creator made, and it is to be inferred by that, that we are all the sons and daughters of Adam, born in the regular way.

"Now, it says, Adam died, and I believe it"—again from the corner, comes the shout—"Amen!" "If Adam hasn't died, let some of the world's smart infidels show him up—yes, show him up,—he would be the greatest curiosity ever known. They can't do it, for he is dead; yes, blessed be God, he is dead as a door-nail, and the fact that Adam is dead, establishes beyond dispute that the Bible is true.

"In the fourth place, the text says: 'As in Adam all die;' the inference is very plain and unmistakable, that we are all, from Adam's time down to this present moment, dead or *dying*. It doesn't mean that all men died when Adam died; that wouldn't be possible, for the facts stare us in the face, that there are millions and millions of men and women alive now, but it means that the seeds of death was planted in our nature. Yes, blessed be the Lamb that taketh away the sins of the world. By the death of Adam it was, according to an all-wise and divine purpose, made possible for all men to die; not only possible, but probable that all men would die; and not only probable, brethren and sisters, but a dead sure thing that they'd got to die, every one of 'em, and that includes us, saints and sinners alike. God proves by this very act that he has the upper hand of us, and it wont do us any good to kick—we've got to die. And oh, my brethren and sisters, what a awful thing it is to die. Just think of it; to lay down dead, some time very unexpectedly; and how necessary it is for us to be prepared when our turn comes, so we can die in peace. I beseech of you to make preparation for that time, for you don't know what will become of you after that terrible event. Where Adam went to, we know not, for history don't give us any light upon his whereabouts after he passed over that dark and dismal river we have all got to cross, and some of us, very soon.

"Now brethren and sisters, we come to the second part of our discourse, viz., 'Even so in Christ shall all be made alive.' Yes, glory be unto him, he will bring every one of us to life again. Then we will know where Adam is, we will know where all our relations are, and it will undoubtedly be a lively time for some of us to get around and see our friends before court sets, for we are informed that court will set very soon after, and this same Christ is going to be the judge, and he will then settle with every one of us; and if we haint made our peace with him and got our names registered in the book of life we'll be sorry. Yes, you young sinner that's a settin' in that back seat a pinchin' that girl to make her laugh in this meetin', if you don't repent and get your name on that book, the Devil will give you a pinchin' that will last you through eternity. And you young woman that's been a gigglin' at everything that's been said here, and that spends your time a dancin' and playin' cards, and scoffin' at religion, if you don't make your peace with the Lord and see that your title is clear in that book of life, you'll find yourself a dancin' on the Devil's fire. You'll be playin' a game and not hold a trump in your hands; the Devil will hold all the trumps and big suit cards, and you wont be able to take a single trick; then the scoffin' will be on the other side.

"I want to say to all unconverted persons in this house, pause, and think what you're doing, and do not longer persist in your sinful course, but come to Christ and believe on him. And while we sing the familiar hymn, 'We're going home to die no more,' come right forward to these front seats. Come now, brethren, sing."

"Amen!" shouts Father Emmons—and all begin to sing.

Elder Jones was pressing the invitation. The shouts from the corner and singing was simultaneous. Some went forward.

After the singing there was a general season of prayer, three or four praying at a time, while the Elder was talking to the sinners that went forward.

There are not many persons that could remain long under the cross-fire of two ministers and a half dozen others, without confessing they was the biggest sinners on earth. David Kirk, one of them that went forward, confessed that he was a dreadful sinner, and wanted 'em to pray for him. We all knew he was just what he confessed to be, and we haint much confidence in his conversion, for he does that same thing at every revival at the schoolhouse, and in less than a month after the meetings are over, he is just as mean and low as ever.

Clarissa says, "The only way Dave Kirk can be properly converted, so he will stay so, is for the Lord to knock all of his brains out of his head and put some new ones in, for them old brains of his is a bad lot, and they can't be worked over worth a cent. Where you haint got any true metal to work on, nothing but the basest kind of metal, the work aint going to last very long. It will break down mighty soon."

I believe she is about right. It is all well enough for a person that's got a good head on him to be born again, and the right thing too, so far as the heart is concerned, but a person that naturally has got a mean, dishonest head onto his shoulders, may be born over and over again, a hundred times or more, and it won't make him a bit better, for with him his meanness is like the small-pox, sure to break out.

After prayers was offered a good many told their experience. Old Mrs. Smith said, "It's nigh onto forty years since I found the Lord precious to my soul, and I've been trying in my weak way to follow in his footsteps ever since;" and the tears begun to fall, and her nose run like rain, so she had to use her big calico handkerchief while she continued: "And brethren and sisteren, I want you to forgive all my shortcomings, and don't let 'em be as stumbling blocks in your way, for I shall soon pass away ah! from these mortal scenes, ah!"

"Amen, bless God for that," shouted Father Emmons, and Elder Jones groaned out:

"Yes, dear Lord."

"Once, ah! I was a dreadful sinner, ah!"

And Elder Danberry said:

"Bless God for that."

"And I got no peace in my heart until I surrendered and give myself to God—and over since then I have been as peaceful as a lamb, ah!"

As soon as the old lady set down, old Uncle Nat Baker arose. He was never looked upon as being very bright; he is very tall and has a small head, and from the end of his long, sharp nose to the back upper corner of his head, it is a straight line. And his chin tapers back to his throat in a corresponding manner. The old man has helped his good, honest wife in raising quite a family, six boys and seven girls. One of the boys who has always been called Bub, is quite a tinker; he has put up a little shop near the schoolhouse, and got some tools for mending boots and shoes, and wagons, and sleds, and plows and such things, and he has got a little hand cider press, in all worth, I should think, about seventy-five dollars. As the old gentleman rose, he said:

"I bless God for this glorious religion that happifies the soul. It's the pearl of great price. It's worth more'n all other pearls in the world, and you can have it if you want it, without money and without price. Oh, sinner, come and secure this pearl of great

THE COLLECTION.

price, now, before it is too late. You'll have to make haste to get it, or it will be forever gone."

"*Yes, praise the Lord,*" remarked Elder Danberry.

Immediately after the old man sat down, his daughter, Dollesky Baker, got up and said:

"My young friends, I'm glad I've come. I feel it's good for my soul to be here, and I thank father that he ever showed me how to secure this pearl of great price, and I devise you to come and get it now; it's worth more'n everything else in the world. It's worth more'n all of Bub's machinery. Pray for me that I may hold on to it."

After Dollesky was seated they took up a collection. Clarissa always believes in giving to a good cause, and she put in fifty cents. I put in twenty cents and George Waddles, who sat right in front of me put in a copper, while the old man Baker who set right next to me, left his pocketbook at home, so he didn't give a cent, although he had the pearl of great price. After they got through and counted up all the money they got, Elder Danberry arose and said:

"Brethren and sisters, I am somewhat disappointed in the amount of the collection. I expected we would raise at least ten dollars, but I find on carefully counting it over the second time that there is just one dollar and thirty-nine cents, and that is about one-half a cent a head for those present. Now, brethren, supposing that the pearl of great price that has been referred to by Brother Baker, was to be sold for money, how much of a chance do you think any of you would stand in getting it? Why, brethren and sisters, if this collection would be a proper indication of the bid you'd make for it, about as near as you'd come of getting it, would be to catch one glimpse of its brightness as the light of God's holy countenance would flash upon it, and then it would be forever out of your sight. But, thanks to our all wise and good God, this pearl was sold to mankind for a costly price, and we can freely have it if we will only take it.

"I think when we consider the wonderful price paid for this precious pearl, that it is a mean man or woman that won't give more'n one cent to support those whose business it is to carry this costly pearl around on a platter to each and every one, and persuade you to take it and wear it on your bosoms so it will shine and give light to others to see how to walk, for without a light men are constantly stepping into the mud and mire holes in this world."

"Amen! Amen! Thank God for that," comes from the corner.

"And now Brother Jones who devotes his whole life to this blessed cause, comes here once in three months and he only gets one dollar and thirty-nine cents. Well, we are thankful for that much, and hope God will cause the light of his countenance to shine upon you, and make you more liberal to his cause. We will close by singing the Doxology."

While we was driving home Clarissa said: "Benjamin, what do you think of the sermon?'

I told her I didn't think much of it, and asked her opinion of it. She replied:

" I think his philosophy is powerful weak. He took one of the most beautiful texts in the whole Bible, and made it appear as if Paul, who wrote those beautiful words, was a idiot. If Elder Jones had just quoted the text and stopped right there, he would have given us something more comforting and more sublime to think of than what he said. Why, Benjamin, now just think for a moment what this text means, 'As in Adam all die.' The meaning of Adam is earth-born, or earthly. The Bible tells us that the first man was of the earth, earthy, but the second man was the Lord Jesus Christ, or the heavenly. Now, the first man called Adam, was the earth man, which is the human body, made of material in common with the earth, and destined to return again to its original condition, to the elements from which it is composed. The second man is the spirit that dwells in these earthly bodies and animates them. The first man, Adam, must die, must dissolve and return to earth, in the very nature of things. While the second, the Spirit which is from God, must, by the same natural law return to its author, God, and must live as long as he lives, which is forever. So the meaning Paul intended to convey is, as the human race must taste death by the destruction of their bodies, they will also by the same law, in spirit live forever, and being free from this earth body, will the more rapidly develop into what the Creator chooses to have us."

"That glorious old man, Paul, put that text right into that good book on purpose to settle any and all disputes in regard to the resurrection."

She then asked me what I thought of Elder Danberry's remarks.

I told her I thought he was about like the average of 'em; he measures a man's chances for heaven by the amount of money he gives, and said I: "Clarissa, you and I are all right, according to his idea, for we give seventy cents of the one dollar and thirty-nine cents, and that gives the balance of the scales in our favor. And probably according to his views, we would be the only two in the audience that are on the road to brighter skies."

I wonder where George Waddles will go with his copper, or if old man Baker will lose his pearl of great price after all by constitutionally leaving his pocketbook at home.

Clarissa said: "Well, Benjamin, this world is made up of strange incongruities. It takes all kind of folks to make people, and of course they will have various notions about things. If they are only honest in it, it is all right so far as I'm concerned, but I can't bear hypocrisy."

> Oh, priceless pearl that's freely given
> To us to wear from earth to heaven,
> Guide us on earth to do our part,
> With a warm and cheerful heart.

CHAPTER IX.

FRIDAY evening Clarissa and I took an early start for the Waddles Corners schoolhouse, so as to make sure of a seat. We knew the house would be crowded, for a free lecture in a country schoolhouse, on any subject, will draw a full house every time, and especially a lecture on Phrenology would surely pack the house. There is something about that subject—it makes no odds how old and threadbare it is—that will attract most people. There is something in the nature of men and women that they like to hear something said about heads and bumps, that they know is true, and especially about their neighbors—and about themselves if it can be done privately.

We was in time to secure a good seat; we wasn't a mite too soon, for in less than ten minutes there wasn't standing room left in the house.

The room was well lighted with about thirty lamps. The walls were covered with pictures of men and women noted for their great ability as authors, or statesmen, or generals, or inventors, or men of great wealth or of great kindness and benevolence, or stinginess, or great idiots, and also some heads of animals. It was a regular panorama of heads, and was very interesting to look at.

The remarks of our simple country people about the pictures, before the Professor came in, was highly instructive. For instance, old Jim Smuggins pointed his finger up to John the Baptist and said to his wife and Sarah :

EXPERIENCE WITH HYPOCRITES.

"That's George Washington."

Sarah said: "Well, I can't see what made such a smart man as he was part his hair in the middle."

Another person, pointing his finger at a picture, said, "Say, Tom, haint that a bully good-looking fellow? Do you know who it is? He is the man that can lick any man in this house. That's John Sullivan."

Tom replied: "No, it haint Sullivan—that's President Cleveland."

"Well, then, they must be relatives, for they look a heap alike."

Bill Green pointed to the picture of a plain-looking woman, and said: "I wonder who she be."

I said, "I guess it's Joan of Arc."

Clarissa said, "Why, Benjamin, don't you know better than that? That is Susan B. Anthony."

"Well," said I, "I never met either one of 'em, or corresponded with 'em, but I thought she looked savage enough to lead the whole world to war."

Sarah Smuggins spoke up, "Well, Ben Morgan, I don't want your judgment for me. I think she looks like an angel without wings."

And so the remarks went on about the pictures for about twenty minutes, when Timothy Brown walked in with a small, red-headed and red-whiskered man, dressed up very slick, and set down behind the teacher's desk in a chair that had been kept empty on purpose for him.

In a few minutes Mr. Brown got up and said:

"Ladies and Gentlemen: We all realize the benefits derived from education, and we ought to welcome any and every means for obtaining it; and one of the best things for us to know, is to know our own capabilities; that is, to know what we are the best fitted for in the nature of things, so we can more properly educate ourselves for the particular place we can most advantageously occupy, and thus save much valuable time and labor, that without such knowledge would be lost.

"We have with us this evening Professor Theodocius Leviticus Feeler, from Boston, the most renowned lecturer on Phrenology in America. He delivers this lecture free, but will deliver four more lectures after this evening, for which there will be an admission fee charged of fifteen cents, except to school children, who will be admitted for five cents a head. I would like to have you be as quiet as possible, considering your crowded condition.

"Ladies and Gentlemen, I now have the pleasure of introducing to you Professor Theodocius Leviticus Feeler."

The Professor made a pretty bow, and said:

"Ladies and Gentlemen: The greatest duty man should perform is to his God, and the next is the duty he owes to himself. Whenever he properly performs these two duties he will, in the nature of things, have done his duty to his fellow men. He cannot possibly do his whole duty to his God without doing his duty to his fellow men. In order to do his duty to himself properly, he should know himself. Therefore, this great fundamental law, KNOW THYSELF, should be our first and constant study, in order that we may fit ourselves for the positions the All-wise Creator designed us to occupy.

"It will be my object to show you how you can know yourselves and give you such instructions, which if you will follow them out you will know how to manage yourselves.

"Gentlemen will, by the study of this greatest of all sciences, know what course of business to pursue in order to be successful. They will know what kind of women to marry that they may have happy and prosperous lives.

"Ladies, by the application of the laws of Phrenology, will know who to accept or reject, in offers of marriage. Young ladies will know who it's best to let court 'em, and young men will know who to court.

"Parents will know how to bring up their children, that they may be ornaments to society and a blessing to the world; and all of us will know how to get along right with other folks.

"When the Creator went to work and got up a man, do you suppose he didn't know enough to label him in a right manner? If you do, you suppose wrong. When he made man, he knew that there would be a great many men and women in the course of time, and in order to preserve order and peace among them, he made them all with different looking faces, so they wouldn't get mixed up, and not know themselves from their neighbors; and when he made them with distinguishing features, he made them with a corresponding difference in temperament and heart, and he gave his children the peculiar features and shape of the head, as a key to unlock the heart and brain, and know what the motives are that actuate its possessor. This *Key* we call Phrenology. We will proceed to unlock a few heads to-night and see if the Almighty has made a mistake.

"The first picture on our right, is a correct representation of Adam.

"You will observe that he is very narrow between the temples. This shows that he was deficient in Time and Tune. Now, who ever heard of Adam singing a tune? No one. He was never known to sing a note in his whole life.

"It is plainly evident that his Time was poor, or he could have got away from the Devil, when the old feller was tryin' to catch him in the garden.

"You will notice his sloping forehead, which shows that his Intellectual faculties was very small, and as a proof of it, he never left the scratch of the pen to show to the world that he ever had a thought. It also shows that he was lacking in Benevolence. He was never known to give away a single thing, but on the contrary, he took all he could get. When his devoted and generous wife, Eve, passed the first dish of fruit to him in the garden, he grabbed the biggest apple on the plate, and hogged it down, and never even thanked her for it.

"You will notice right here (pointing with a stick to a hollow in Adam's head), where the organ of Inventiveness is located, that he is deficient. He didn't know enough to make any clothes for himself, but had to wait 'till good, kind Eve sewed some fig leaves together and made him a dress, and then she had to show him how to put it on. You will further observe, right here behind the ears, he is very full; he is very broad through the ears; this denotes great Combativeness, and meanness in general.

"To prove that the key is right, in this instance: The very first thing he done that we have any account of, after hoggin' down the apple, was to raise Cain.

"This picture on our left is said to be a very correct likeness of the great philosopher, Socrates. It was painted from an original photograph, taken by Sarony's great-grandfather, who was at that time engaged in the business of catching shadows in the city of Athens. Socrates is here represented in full figure, as he was standing in the market-place, bare-footed and bare-headed, with an old shawl over his shoulders, that he used to wear summer and winter.

"You will notice a very marked difference between him and Adam. He has a large, high forehead which denotes great Benevolence. He was never known to save a cent, and had it not been for his faithful friend, Crito, who was with him to the last moment of his life, and who, by his own request, gave him the bitter cup of hemlock poison, his family would have suffered. He was not a spendthrift, but his great benevolent nature caused him to give freely from his scanty resources to alleviate human suffering.

EXPERIENCE WITH HYPOCRITES.   91

"You will notice his large, round, full eyes, and those heavy pouches under the eyes. They denote Language, and he had a wonderful command of language. Not only was he gifted with wonderful oratorical powers, but he was the greatest logician in all of Athens that city of learned scholars. You will notice all these or-

SOCRATES AND YOUNG AMERICA.

gans in the regions of the eye are very large. Everything about his head and body shows that he was a powerful man mentally and physically, possessed of great power of endurance. He was, in all respects, the most remarkable man of his age, and could he have lived until now, he would be the most remarkable man ever created.

"This picture right above Mr. Socrates, represents the result of a union of two common flowers, the calla lily and sunflower. It is named Oscar Wilde. You will notice that his smooth, beardless face is broad in the region of the eyes, and tapering down to a very narrow and slightly drooping chin; the balance of the head corresponding with the face, is richly ornamented with a profuse growth of mer-maiden hair, and the whole supported by a delicate and slender neck, the lower extremity of which is surrounded by a faultless white linen collar and huge necktie of green satin, presenting a striking resemblance to the calla lily. Sunflowers is his hobby, and these characteristics predominate in his nature.

"You will see here, where the bump of Approbativeness is located, he is very full indeed. It is the largest bump on his head. You make him think he is one of the smartest men in the world, and you touch his tender spot. Public opinion has branded him as a soft-headed dude, a good sign to put up in front of a milliner's shop.

"Right here allow me to remark, that public opinion is not always correct; it is once in a while mistaken, as it doesn't always see through the mask.

"This one at our right, is a marked character. You'll observe that the head is very large, very full in the back part where all the animal and social organs are located, broad through the region of the eyes, a low forehead, and the top of the head is very flat; the lines of the face very positive, the mouth large and firmly compressed, indicating firmness, strong will-power and determination; full over the eyes, showing that he is a quick reader of human nature; his perceptive faculties are very keen. You notice he is very full back of the ears; Combativeness is very largely developed. It is one of the controlling organs in his make-up; he can argue well, as far as his limited education allows him to go, and when he gets that far, if he is still opposed, he is ready to fight. The most prominent bumps on the back head, are Amativeness and Philoprogenitiveness. He is powerful fond of children; the more of them he can have around him, the happier he is. He is remarkably fond of a wife; he thinks so much of that article, that during his life he had more than a score of 'em at the same time, and, not being fully satisfied with that number, he was courting about a dozen girls with a view to making them all Young in a short time. The consummation of his wishes in that direction was only prevented by the timely arrival of that grim messenger, death.

"You observe the top of his head is very flat. The bump of Veneration was swept off deck at a very early period of his existence, and consequently, he had very little respect for the Deity. His god was his ambition and passion—ambition to rule others, and accumulate wealth, and a passion to control a harem of well-selected, obedient and submissive wives.

"The loss of his bump of Veneration involved the partial or complete destruction of several other organs, consequently he was unscrupulous. To carry his point was his determination, regardless of the method. He had perfect Order, and the way he systematized the organization of the Mormon Church and carried out his plans in life, proves that the head we are describing properly belonged to no other than its owner, BRIGHAM YOUNG.

"This lady that hangs next to Brigham is, in many respects, the direct opposite to him. You can see her head is narrow through the temples, and very high on top, like a church steeple. The greater part of her head is in front of her ears; the back part is in a straight line with her neck, and where the bump of Philoprogenitiveness and Amativeness should be, there are hollows. Consequently, she is by nature a regular man-hater. She had rather see forty cats in the house than one sweet, innocent baby, and she could no more tolerate a man in the house than she could convince the people of America that she is an angel. She is fully developed in the organ of Combativeness. She can argue from morning till night, and not feel a mite like giving up then. Naturally she has a large amount of Veneration, and would be a very devoted religionist if it wasn't for her hatred of the first part of God's creation of the human race. She cannot conceive of the wisdom of the Almighty in making such a useless and bothersome thing as a man, and especially in making him before he made woman, therefore it is hard for her to worship such a Creator. She is quite deficient in knowledge of human nature, and her perceptive faculties are very small. She has but one predominant idea, and that excludes from her mind all other subjects requiring much thought. I need not tell you her name, for I presume there is not one in this vast and intelligent audience that does not recognize in her Susan B. Anthony.

"This good-looking man that hangs on the stovepipe has given more real fun and amusement to the millions of book-readers in America and Europe than any or all of American authors. His keen sense of the ludicrous side of human nature enables him to strip things of their fictitious robes and let folks see facts undressed. His power to present to the human mind things in nearly their true light causes laughter and amusement. You will notice his perceptive organs are extremely large, while his deep-seated eye is as keen and piercing as a hawk's. He can smell a joke as far as a Dutchman can Limburger cheese, and if it's *stale* he can ring the bell on it before it arrives. He can see more curious and funny things in a bag of dried peas than ninety-nine in a hundred can out of a bottle of champagne, even if it is labeled '*Extra Dry*.'

"With him the sacredness of antiquity is destroyed, and mummies twenty thousand years old are treated with no more, if as much, respect than Mrs. Jarley's wax works; and the wonderful descriptions given by others of the works of the 'old masters' drop to a par with a pair of fifty-cent oil-painted window-shades. The monk ceases to be of much more value than the pile of old bones and skulls he watches. American speculation, with its glitter and show, instead of having millions in it, hasn't got a cent to bank on, and has to borrow its chew of tobacco from any one that happens to have it in their pockets.

"The only real scientific work he has dropped onto is piloting a boat down the Mississippi, and putting wit and humor on paper in good shape. This man is a *benefactor* to his race, for he drives away the blues, and lights up the face with smiles. I wish we had more like him, and in passing to our next, I will say, long live Samuel L. Clemens.

"Ladies and Gentlemen, I will introduce but one more character this evening, and then I will devote a half an hour in examining the heads of half-a-dozen persons, to be selected from the audience by yourselves, which will close this evening's entertainment.

"I take pride in showing you this picture, as it is a very good representation of one of God's own noblemen, and the United States' best friend, Abraham Lincoln."

(At this point there was tremendous applause.) "His head is very large in all the organs that develop the highest and noblest traits of character in man, and is deficient in those organs which develop the evil nature of the race.

"You will notice the face beams with a bright, intelligent and kind expression, which indicates an honest, warm, tender and sympathizing heart. There is no deception, malice, or low, mean and treacherous disposition there, nor can such traits hide behind such a countenance. The large, full eye denotes Language large, the fullness above the eye denotes perception, judgment, calculation and forethought. He was a ready and correct reader of human nature, and few persons ever approached him upon business that he did not perceive their purposes before they even disclosed them, consequently he was able to meet them upon the most advantageous grounds. While Combativeness in him was only moderate, his clear insight and powerful logic gave him success in debate.

"His social qualities were very strongly developed, mirthfulness being very large; he was a man well calculated to make friends, and society was always more cheerful by his presence. His devotion to truth and honesty was not an acquired art, but the very essence of his nature. It was this that endeared him to the people, and it is this trait of his character that will cause his name to live as long as that of his country. When the names of many illustrious men shall have been forgotten, that of Abraham Lincoln will be fresh and green, and will always be coupled with the epithet of *Honest Old Abe.*"

Clarissa nudged me with her off elbow and whispered,—

"Say, Ben, Jim Teeters' head haint a mite like Lincoln's, is it?"

With the hog trade fresh and green in my memory, I could not say it was, and so I spoke very emphatic like and said, "No! by thunder, nor it never will be;" I wouldn't wonder if I spoke a little louder than I intended to, for a good many who set near us, turned round and looked at us real sharp.

Professor Feeler said: "Now, if any lady or gentleman will come to the platform, I will give them a full and complete examination, free of cost. Will some one be kind enough to call for some lady and gentleman that is pretty generally known."

There was more'n a dozen hollered out for Clarissa and Uncle Ben Morgan; we declined to go, for the reason that we don't like to make ourselves conspicuous; we are both of us very retiring in our natures. Clarissa is more retiringer than I am. Our declining didn't work worth a cent, for the whole house kept a hollerin' for us until we concluded to go. We worked our way to the platform amid applause, and occupied the two chairs that was made vacant for our accommodation.

The Professor run his fingers all over my head, then took a good square look right into my face, then he went to Clarissa and pulled her back hair down and fumbled her head all over, and then looked her in the face as if he intended to know her the next time he met her, and then he said: "This gentleman and lady ought to be married, if they are not already, for the reason that there is just enough in their nature of the opposite to make them well adapted for a happy union, their general temperaments are opposite, but in some respects they are similar. This lady would rather manage their business affairs, and look after the finances than to trust it to him, and he would rather she would."

I spoke up before I thought and asked him who had been telling him about us.

He said, "Nobody but yourselves."

Said I, "I never spoke a word to you before."

"Well," said he, "You forget that I have got your keys here," putting his hands on our heads at the same time, and he went on:

"YOU FORGET THAT I HAVE GOT YOUR KEYS HERE."

"This gentleman has a negative temperament, while the lady has a positive. She is not obstinate nor quarrelsome at all, but she is very firm. She is governed by her convictions of right and wrong, and when she has decided a thing is right, you might as well try to move one of the pyramids in Egypt as to move her. You couldn't no more persuade her to do a thing she thought wasn't right than you could get Bob Ingersoll to join the Baptist Church in the regular way. She is domestic in her habits, peaceful in mind, wouldn't quarrel with any one, except forced to in self-defense, or in defense of her family, and then she would stop the moment she won the victory.

"She likes fun as well as anybody, but it must not be at the expense of principle. If this man is her husband, she keeps a close eye on him, and (giving a sharp glance at me, and a cunning wink to the audience) I think he deserves it. She wants to know where he is nights if he isn't at home in good season. Of course I don't mean to say she is jealous, but—but—she doesn't believe in other folks meddling with her property. She wants to be her own insurance company, and as long as she assumes all the risk, she will naturally keep a sharp eye on what belongs to her.

"She is quite accommodating, likes to be neighborly, is willing to borrow when she is in need of something she is out of, and is equally willing to lend. But she will lend any other animal she has got on her premises quicker than her husband. She is a good judge of human nature, her perceptive organs is very full, she doesn't have to wait until you knock her down in order to understand that you mean to hit her. She will see the blow in your intention before you make it, and will dodge your aim. She has good order and calculation, is naturally very tidy and economical. She can get up a good meal out of what many women throw away. She is a good talker and can keep up her end of a conversation or an argument, especially the latter, and her philosophy is largely original, abundant and sound, and she generally carries her point. She is inclined to see the ludicrous point in anything. If she was in Washington, she would be very apt to express her opinions on the way the women dress there. She would not be one of the admirers of Helen Potter either; Miss Cleveland would rather suit her style.

"This lady has a great deal of Veneration, and is naturally inclined to be worshipful. She holds her God as next to her firm principles, which she is set on.

"She likes to go to meeting and wants to do her share of the singing, and I think she can do that part well, as the organs of time and tune are very prominent. She is fond of society, likes to receive company as well as to go a visiting. But to her, home is the dearest spot, and to beautify and ornament it is her delight and pride.

"Take this lady's head all through, and it is remarkable. She is well balanced on all subjects except her Benjamin; on that point she is inclined to be a little cranky.

> "Take her head all through and through—
> Hair of a rich auburn hue,
> Eyes of an enchanting blue,
> That speak as they look at you.
>
> "Strong in her Veneration,
> Keen in her Observation,
> Full in her Approbation,
> Ready in Accumulation.
>
> "With very strong Ambition
> To rise to great distinction,
> And with her Determination
> She will prove to this nation
>
> "By her continuation
> In careful calculation
> And due consideration
> Of men in every station,
>
> "That she is of high degree,
> With a noble pedigree;
> To which you will all agree,
> According to Phrenologee."

So far I stood the examination first-rate. I was rather amused some of the time when he was describing my other half. Clarissa didn't wince a mite as he drove the nails of truth into her head. Most all of them he hit right square on the head, too, except when he referred to her keeping a eye on me. She didn't like to have that told, for she knew 'twas just so. She watches me like a old hen does her one chicken when all the rest but one have died. I haven't been away from home without her with me but once in the last two years, and that was when I drove them hogs down to Jim Teeters', and I don't expect she'll ever trust me to go again without her for twenty years to come.

The crowd enjoyed the examination, and laughed frequently;

and when the Professor made the hit on her jealousy, they gave considerable applause.

I didn't exactly like to have him come at me before all that crowd, specially after he made her out so all-fired smart. I just expected he'd make out I was a fool. The Professor, coming up against my head, said:

"We have a very different individual here from the one I have just examined. This gentleman is naturally very kind, does not want to quarrel with anybody, but if he is cornered and has got to fight or run, he will fight, and he will fight hard, but it will be a case of necessity with him. He is not as firm as this lady. In fact, he is not firm enough to keep from being imposed upon by sharp and designing persons. He is strictly honest, unless he sees a splendid opportunity for making a bargain and not get caught at it; and he naturally thinks everybody else is honest. He is not much inclined to roam around, for two reasons: First, he is not very familiar with the country far away from home, and is a little too timid to go alone; and second, he is afraid to go away to be gone over night unless his wife gives her full consent, which is not very probable, especially if this lady is his wife. I'll take it for granted she is. He is not very devotional or religious, but his wife being strong-minded, and possessing a strong positive temperament, can mold his belief. If she entertains any religious sentiment he will simply second the motion and join the same church she does, and will, no doubt, see things in about the same light as she does.

"In politics he is not very firm, though naturally inclined to be on the right side.

"He is very fond of company, and the more ladies in the company the better it suits him, unless his wife watches him too closely. But if he gets into conversation with some pretty woman and his wife drops her eye on him, it kinder frustrates him, and he forgets what he is talking about, and is just as apt to ask the lady he is talking to how much she is paying for *hogs*, as to ask who made her dress. In fact, he can't stand watching by his wife and enjoy it. Left to his company without the feeling that he is being squinted at by his wife, he could keep up quite a conversation, providing the other party could stand it.

"Alimentiveness is full. He is a good eater and likes pie. Accumulativeness is very full. He has a strong desire to make money, and as a farmer he would be successful in that direction, for he is industrious and economical; but he would be a poor merchant. He ought to have a wife that is a good financier, and this lady has got a good head for that. Nature has calculated these persons for each other; they can pull in double harness well, and never have any serious difficulty. Hitch him with some women, he would balk and kick, but this lady can hold him level and keep him cool.

"I would advise him to never attempt to sing if he has any regard for the peace and quiet of his neighbors, for it would prove a calamity, and cause him to be covered with ridicule; not but what he is fond of music, but he wasn't built for a canary bird.

"Let me suggest to you, to cultivate firmness and independence; learn to rely on yourself more. Try to make others subservient to your will rather than act as a servant to theirs.

"Let your constant aim be higher;
Be led by ambition's fire
To firmness, and each day aspire
To get nigher and nigher
To the full stature of a man.

"And when you have accomplished in life what it is your privilege to, and you step down the rapid decline, at the foot of which is the open grave, you may be able to say, as did that noble and good man, Judge William Wilkins, of Pennsylvania, when about to part with mortal scenes:

"'Stronger by weakness, wiser men become,
As they draw near to their eternal home,
Leaving the old, both worlds at once they view,
They stand upon the threshold of the new.'"

With this he dismissed me from the platform. Evidently he was pleased with the impression he made upon the audience, for there was tremendous applause as he finished me off; but I assure you I wasn't a mite pleased, for he might just as well said I was a dumfounded relative of Balaam's beast, as to tell me what he did, and I said to him,—

"You think you are darned smart, don't you? If you'll just set down in that ar chair and let Clarissa tell this crowd what's in your little head, she'll show 'em that you are a dumbed sight bigger fool than I am."

Then the crowd just applauded me. But he replied, "I ain't big enough fool to let her have the chance."

Then they all laughed like fury, and I concluded I had better keep my mouth shut. Clarissa and I took our seats. The Professor then asked the audience to name two others to come forward and be examined. I wanted some one else shown up as well as me and Clarissa, so I yelled out, "'Squire Bigler and George Waddles," and the whole house called for them until they went up to the platform.

The Professor took the 'Squire first, and after feeling all over his head carefully, and looking him out of countenance two or three times, he said:

"This gentleman is a very ambitious man. He has a great deal of pride; he has more pride and ambition than honest principle. He has good calculation and keen perception, is a good reader of human nature, has good command of language, and is a good easy talker; somewhat magnetic, and can make himself very agreeable when he wants to. He would make a very good public speaker. He has a good deal of the fox in his nature; can be very sly and conceal his real motives. I think he is governed very largely by policy.

"He studies policy in all his dealings with men. He can make friends easily, but most of his friends, or those he seeks to make his

HE WAS GOING TO FIGHT THE PROFESSOR.

friends, he intends to use for his own purpose, and it's only a question of how much he can make out of them, or how far he can gain his points by them, that he measures the strength and duration of that friendship.

"In the true sense of the word, I don't believe it is in his nature to know what real true friendship is, but his affable manner, coupled with his command of language, knowledge of human nature, and shrewdness, will win him many friends, who will in turn, be duped and made ashamed by their disappointment in him."

Bigler got hopping mad and jumped up and said, "I didn't come here to be insulted, and I don't propose to submit to any more abuse." He was going to fight the professor, but the professor very coolly replied, "Hold on, my young friend; I mean no insult. You are a stranger to me, and I am only telling you what your head indicates, phrenologically. When I examine a person, I must tell what I find, and not lie about it; I must tell the truth as I find it. If you can't stand the examination, I will willingly excuse you."

The 'Squire got so awful mad that he left the platform, while some cheered and more hissed. I am afraid it will hurt the 'Squire, as those who are not acquainted with him, will think the Professor told the truth, and all those who know him, know the Professor hit him square on the head every time.

I pitied George Waddles and at the same time I was glad to have him get a dose of the same medicine I had to take. I said I pitied him, and so I did, for after young Bigler got such a scoring, he must have felt as if he was about to be put into the chemist's crucible, and thoroughly analyzed, and with his peculiar nature, analyzation before the public, would be about as bad as annihilation.

As the Professor walked up to George, I could see George's face turn red, and he trembled slightly. We had seen enough of the Professor to know that he could handle his subjects as well as his subject, without gloves. He proceeded as follows:

"Ladies and Gentlemen: I wish you would please bear in mind, that I do not wish, nor intend to say anything to hurt any one's feelings, but as phrenology is the key the Almighty has given me to unlock the heads and hearts of the people, I am going to tell what I find in them, truthfully, and if any one who may pass under my examination during my stay with you, should find their heads or their hearts out of order, the best thing for them to do, instead of becoming angry at me, is to change the wrong things for right ones, to cultivate those points of character that seem to be deficient, and suppress the excessively strong points that lead in the wrong direction.

"If you will see phrenology in the right light, you will strive to understand it, and will bless God for this wonderful key that unlocks the chambers of the soul."

Advancing to Waddles, he said, "I find, upon close examination of this gentleman, some very marked and prominent organs, while others are quite deficient. He has a very good memory; his perceptive faculties are large; his judgment of men is quick, and generally correct, although once in a while he misses it. He thoroughly understands that sugar will catch more flies than vinegar, and also that it is a human weakness to like taffy, and he always has a good supply of that article on hand to deal out to men, women, and children in just such doses as he thinks they can swallow without making them sick.

"Flattery is the most potent sugar to use in dealing with the human race. Much as we may pretend to the contrary, the real fact is, we are all more or less subject to it. Sweet words, sweet smiles, pleasant things said to us about ourselves, please us much more than sour faces and bitter words.

"This gentleman thoroughly understands this principle, and, if I am not very much mistaken, he makes use of his knowledge of this fact as a prime factor in his business operations. He has excellent calculation, is shrewd, and possesses the cunning of a fox; he covers up his shrewd tricks and plays, so that most of the people cannot discern them; but men with good perception and penetration, can see through his mask, and understand his motive as well as he can see into others'. He is very avaricious; his great ambition is to become wealthy.

"He doesn't want any one to think he is shrewd, and therefore frequently pretends to be very dull. To illustrate: If I had a dozen steers to sell, and he wanted them (provided he could buy them to suit him), he would *happen* by my house on his way to prayer-meeting, or somewhere else; he would *happen* along just as I was milking, and he would in a careless manner say:

SIZING UP THE STEERS.

"'Got some nice-looking steers there, h'ain't you? How much will they weigh, do you think?'

"I would probably give him my idea in regard to their heft. He would then say:

"'What are fat steers worth nowadays?'

"I would tell him the last price I had learned. His quick judgment of weight would tell him in an instant whether I had over or under-estimated them, and being thoroughly posted on the market values, he would readily know whether or not there was money in them if he could buy at my estimate; if there was, he would close a bargain with me if possible, and let his prayer-meeting, or other engagement, go to the winds, and in less than a hour he would be home, figuring out how much he had made out of the prayer-meeting speculation.

"This gentleman is liable to make a cloak of great moral rectitude and religion, to cover up a cold, selfish, remorseless and avaricious disposition. He always counts the cost and considers the investment before he puts his name down on paper. He is deficient in veneration. With him, serving God means to serve himself best, and whatever he contributes to the religious cause is merely incidental, the same as the merchant pays the printer for advertising his business; but he will be very careful to allow no impression of insincerity to prevail.

"His powers of invention are large, enabling him to readily assume any role he desires, and he can therefore act the part of a zealous Christian so well as to deceive the average man.

"He is naturally rather cowardly, and shrinks from any argument or quarrel. He does not believe it pays to combat any one; he can't see that it does any good, and frequently costs a man some money and loss of friends. He is domestic in his tastes and habits; thinks a great deal of his home and family; is naturally socially inclined, and, were it not for the expense, would like to go into society a considerable. He is very cautious, and ventures nothing, unless he is well satisfied of success in the outcome.

"My advice to him is, to be more frank and honest, and use less policy; be more considerate of what will pay the best at the end of life's career, than what will yield the most money in the passing bargains he may make.

"A life of honesty and truthfulness, with less lucre, makes the closing hours of life's race more serene and glorious than a large fortune gained at the expense of principle and honor, and the legacy left to the heirs more valuable in every sense of the word."

The Professor said, as the time had passed so rapidly, he would make no further examinations, but would conclude his lecture by reciting an original poem, entitled:

"THE PHRENOLOGIST'S DREAM.

" Wearied by the labors of the day,
The professor sought to rest his clay.
His couch invited him with its charms
To seek seclusion in Morpheus' arms ;
While the busy world faded from sight
Behind the sable curtains of night,
A bright spirit, beautiful and fair,
Winged its way through the soft balmy air

To his bedside, and folding its wings,
Talked to him of the wonderful things
That God had for his own glory made.
And all these things, the light and the shade,
The pale moon, and the glittering stars,
The bright sun with his radiant bars,
The silver stream, and broad, restless sea,
The peaceful meadows, and charming lea,
The granite mountains that pierce the sky
Proclaiming a Creator on high;
The carpet of verdure o'er earth spread,
The fragrant flower that lifts its head
To bless and kiss a Creator's hand,
And give joy and brightness to the land;
The cattle that graze on mead or hill,
Or slake their thirst in the running rill;
The beasts of the forest, strong, untame,
Various in nature and in name;
The many-hued birds that fill the air,
And in song proclaim that God is there;
The fishes that plow the mighty deep,
And say the Creator knows no sleep;
All these, and all things else he hath made,
To Him honor, praise and glory paid,
Except the last of creation—man;
Who deliberately laid the plan
In Eden's fair and lovely bower,
To defy his Creator's power,
To show the world that man would not die
If he ate the fruit that pleased the eye;
Adam took from the tempter's hand
The apple fair, that cursed the land,
And by disobedience fell
From Eden fair to Orthodox hell.

"Now go with me to history's tower—
Man's record of weakness and power
While tossed upon the ocean of time;
And there you will trace in every line,
The motive that inspires his action
To be his own, and not other's good.
From its lofty height where prophets stood,
And with mystic vision foretold the strife
Of selfish man on the field of life,
I'll show you a mighty, boundless sea
Of struggling, restless humanity,
With rocky shoals and fathomless deep,
Whose surging billows in motion keep.

"The masses ebb and flow with the tide,
While a few souls on the breakers ride
Like nauticals in a ship of state,
Controlled by ambition, love or hate.
Their glory is for a single day,
Then, like butterflies, they pass away,
And into deep oblivion sink,
While passers by stop only to think
Of their deeds, both for good and evil,
And wonder if with God or Devil
Their poor souls found an abiding place,
After they had run their earthly race.

"A glorious few, a few indeed,
Were ever born to take the lead,
To hold the sway in mind's dominion,
To form and shape public opinion,
Their names are written on these pages old,
Where also their life's story is told.

"Then taking my hand, the spirit bright,
Led me unto a wonderful sight,
A large room on whose walls were displayed
The heads of all these great men arrayed
In their glory. Then said, Would you know
The secret by which these great men show
Their strength and power? Then take this key,
Unlock their heads, and then you will see,
The mystery—it is PHRENOLOGY."

CHAPTER X.

THE chief topic of conversation in our neighborhood for the past week has been the lecture of Professor Feeler. And I daren't go into a neighbor's house for fear they'll want to feel of my head, just to see if am such an all-fired fool as that professor tried to make out I was.

Even old Jim Smuggins, who doesn't know enough to pack down a hog in butchering time to keep it from spoiling before spring, said to me t'other night, when Clarissa and 1 was up to his house spending the evening: "Uncle Ben, just let me examine that ar top-knot of your'n, and see if I can't find more in it than Feeler did."

Said I, "Look here, you infernal old infidel, if a man is such a ignorant old fool, and low, mean cuss as to not know there is a God, who created all things, and who engineers the whole universe, he is too mean and ignorant to run his fingers through my scatterin' locks, hunting for bumps that the Almighty put there. If I haint got as large a crop of bumps on my head as some of our great men have got, I haint to blame for it. The Almighty knows pretty well what kind of soil is best adapted to raising intellectual and etcetera, bumps on, and if there haint rich enough soil in my head to develop as many and as big bumps as Clarissa, or Horace Greeley, or Daniel Webster, and a few others I could mention, had I time, it's no fault of mine, for I had nothing to do in getting myself up, but I'll take just as good care of what few I have got as I know how to, and see they don't grow less; and what time I am allowed on this earth I'll use in doing the best I can with 'em, and when the ferry-boat whistles for me to get on board for the other shore of that stream that we've all got to cross, and the Captain calls for the fare, I'll just point to the few bumps I have and say to him, ' Here is all I've got; you loaned 'em to me; I've done the best I knew how to with 'em, and now take 'em, they're yours, it's all I've got; what little I've done with 'em is left back there. You can judge whether it's good or bad work, and deal with me accordingly.'

"Now, Jim Smuggins, what will you say to the Captain? You'll have to say something to him. I know what you will say. You'll look up at him like a whipped cur, and say, 'I haint got nothin' to give you. I didn't know I had got to cross this stream before; I didn't believe there was any ferry-boat to cross it on, even if there was such a stream: and I didn't know, nor I didn't believe there was any Captain on the boat, even if there was a boat, and I didn't believe the Captain

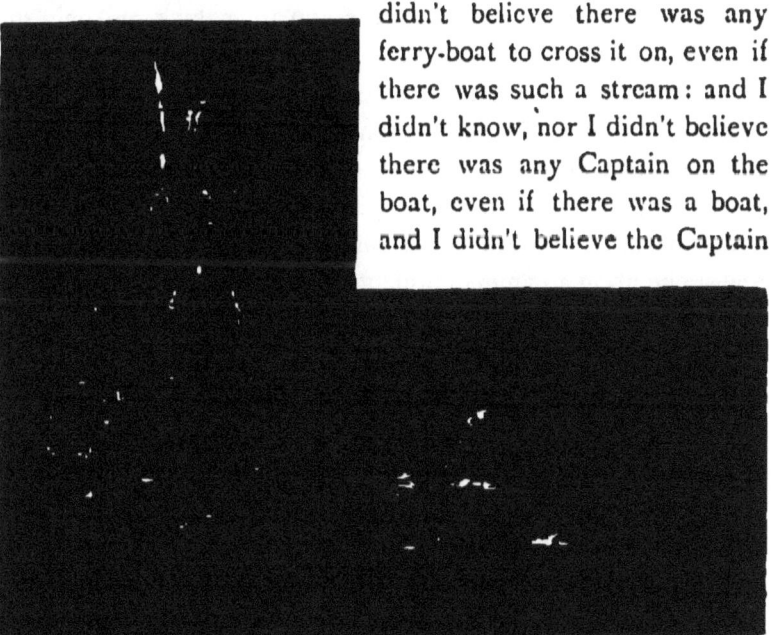

CAPTAIN OF THE FERRY BOAT.

would exact any fare from me, even if there was a Captain, and so I haint prepared to give you anything.'

"That's the same story that all you infidels will have for the Captain. You have been all your lives trying to hatch up some infernal lie to give the Captain on this last trip, that you know well enough you've got to take; but you mark what I tell you, Jim Smuggins, the *gang-plank* will be barely hauled in, and the boat will have just left the dock, when the Captain will cast every one of you dead beat unbelievers overboard; and you'll wallow around in the dark and murky waters of despond and despair, without any light to show you the way out, and you will never get out.

"You may think it's wonderful smart to make all sorts of fun and ridicule of everybody's religious opinions, and try to make out the Bible is a lie, and God is a myth, a creation of the imagination, and all such stuff; but it's a mistake you are making, and only shows to thinking, reflecting and intelligent minds what a idiot you are."

Clarissa and the other women had been listening to our conversation closely. She couldn't hold in any longer, and she began on a new idea, at least it was new to me, although I have known for a long time that she had philosophized a different theory than most folks entertain in regard to the human soul and its future destiny. She spoke up in an animated manner, and said:

"Now, in my humble opinion, you are both talking on a subject that you don't know anything about. Mr. Smuggins, you certainly don't know much, if anything, about the Bible; if you did, you wouldn't make such false statements as you do in regard to it, and you are equally as ignorant in regard to nature—at any rate, you don't exhibit any knowledge of either in your everlasting pratin' of your infidel opinions. If you will study the operations of nature, and take the results of investigations of men who have devoted their lives to study, and who by nature are endowed with mental power that towers as much above yours and mine as the Alps do above the ant-hill in the meadow, and then compare them with a careful analysis of the Bible, you will both see that you are wonderfully in the dark, especially you, Mr. Smuggins. Benjamin is honest in his convictions, and tries to do his duty in the light of 'em, while you are not honest in what you talk on this subject. You have no well-defined convictions, and consequently have nothing to teach you duty, except a kind of instinct common to animals in general. I don't mean to be disrespectful, but I do mean that by your continual harping upon the subject of atheism and unbelief, you have crushed out of your heart whatever convictions of a moral nature you may have had in a younger and tenderer age.

"I was reading Dr. Draper's recently published book, this morning, and there was one thing that impressed me as being similar to what I have for a long time believed in regard to the human soul. I've got the book in my pocket, and I want to read it to you. Here it is, 'Tracing a Drop of Water:'

"'A particle of water arising from the sea may ascend invisibly through the air, it may float above us in the cloud, it may fall in the raindrop, sink into the earth, gush forth in the fountain, enter the roots of a plant, rise up with the sap to the leaves, be there decomposed by the sun into its constituent elements, its oxygen and hydrogen. Of these and other elements, acids and oils and various organic compounds may be made; in these, or its own undecomposed state, it may be received into the food of animals, circulated in the blood, be essentially concerned in the acts of intellection executed by the brain; it may be expired in the breath. Though shed in the tear, in moments of despair, it may give birth to the rainbow, the emblem of hope. Whatever the course through which it has passed, whatever the mutations it has undergone, whatever the forces it has submitted to, its elementary constituents endure. Not only have they not been annihilated, they have not even been changed, and in a period of time, long or short, they find their way, as water, back again to the sea, from whence they came.'

"Now, there is given in a few sentences the result of deep study and investigation, not of Dr. Draper alone, but a great many scientific men who have preceded him. What is true in regard to the drop of water, is also true in regard to all the elements of the material universe; none of them are lost, or even changed, although they are continually changing positions, parting with old and forming new associates. They are brought into activity by the invisible influence of the sun. All this is done in a regular order, everything in the material world working under the system of natural law.

"Now my opinion is, that we have in the material nature a type of the spiritual, and I think the Bible, when rightly understood, conveys the same idea. God is the great spirit power that animates everything; that is the life of all things that exist. While this power animates the human clay for a few moments of time, and then leaves it, it as certainly returns to Himself, the Great Spirit fountain, as does the drop of water return to the sea. It may, perchance, energize a mortal that is so frail as to fall into all sorts of vice, wallow around in mire and filth, for a time, but it will certainly emerge from its poor association and return to itself, its author, a pure, free spirit, pure by being freed from its material association.

"If this thought—which is clearly taught us by all of nature's operations, is true—then it follows that the doctrine of eternal future punishment of the wicked and the eternal future happiness of the righteous, or of the eternal separation of the two classes, falls to the ground. The doctrine of rewards and punishments, in fact, has no ground. It is the invention of man—man governed by feelings not in accord with natural or divine laws. So also is the doctrine false, perniciously false, that there is no God; for He is the Great, Supreme Spirit power, the All in All by which we all exist, and to whom we must yield this vital spark, this spirit He has by His own law placed in our clay."

Said I; "Clarissa, if your idea is true, then what's the use of being good? You haint no better off than if you was as mean as pussly."

She replied, "That is all foolishness. Should it for one moment lessen our moral responsibility because we have no heaven to gain for doing what we ought to do, and no hell to scare us away from doing what we ought not to do? The fact that man is endowed with an intellect capable of evolving thought (the divine image in man) is sufficient reason for us to do right and shun wrong. That our own highest happiness and the happiness of our fellow men in this life is only secured by doing right, is the great lever that should move us to act in harmony with the moral law.

"Any man that will serve God because he expects to get a crown of jewels and a seat in the kingdom, and to walk the golden streets of the New Jerusalem, is an avaricious and selfish being, expecting large pay for doing nothing but what he ought to do, and is unworthy to receive any such reward; and any man that is such a coward that it requires a hell to make him do his duty to himself, his family and his fellow men, deserves punishment for his cowardice instead of reward for being scared into doing right, and that punishment he will receive in life, for not being true, but wearing a mask that illy becomes him.

"Christ was a type of a perfect man, and the spirit manifested in his life was pure and not contaminated with its earthly tabernacle, and shows to the world what man ought to be, and what he can be by strict obedience of the moral law. He neither held in one hand a ticket to heaven to buy man to do his duty, nor a whip in the other to drive him to hell for not doing it; but He taught men the moral law by precept and example, and showed them that they had it in their power to make their own happiness or misery. And he who obeys the moral law while on earth receives the just reward, not as a gift for obedience, but as a result that cannot be denied; and the reverse is equally true. In my opinion this is the idea intended to be conveyed to men in the great volume that is ever open to us."

I was surprised at the way Clarissa handled the subject. Smuggins looked astonished at her, but couldn't say a word in reply. Sarah Smuggins looked up to her father after a few moments of silence that followed the remarks of Clarissa, and said to him:

"Pa, what have you got to say to that?"

He looked red in the face, then took a cud of tobacco out of his mouth, threw it on the stove hearth, and squirted a lot of tobacco juice after it, wiped his mouth on his coat sleeve, and replied:

"Nuthin'!"

Says I, "Jim, don't you want to examine Clarissa's top-knot and see if you can't find more in it than the Professor did?"

Said he, "No. She's got more in it than I ever dreamed of, and she has said more for you and me both to think of than I ever heard any one say before on that point. I guess I'll look it up, and if she is right I'll change my ideas."

I said, "You can't look it up any too soon."

"Well," says he, "you haint got much to brag about, for she has taken the starch out of your biled linen."

Sarah had been quiet as long as she could stand it, and finally broke out:

"Well, perhaps Mrs. Morgan is right, and perhaps she isn't; but there wouldn't be any necessity for any moral law or anything of the sort if things was done right in the first place. All this comes because old Adam was created before Eve was, and just like the men have always been ever since that performance—claimed the right to boss everything just because he was on the ground first. If Eve had been made first things would have all been different. She would have made the bigoted thing stand around and do what was right. And the women of the world would have managed the affairs and made the men do right. They would make the men respect them, and we wouldn't have such a state of affairs as there is now. We wouldn't have any rum and rows, and fighting and murder, and all sorts of wickedness.

"But as woman wasn't made first, and things are as they be, it is the duty of the women to reverse the order of things, and take the lead and management of things throughout the world."

Said I, "Sarah, what a pity it is you wasn't born before the

Creator was, so you could have shown Him how to commence business."

Clarissa spoke in a sarcastic sort of way and said, "If we are to believe what sacred history tells us, the woman took the reins of government out of the man's hands the first day she met him in the garden, and told him what to do, and he minded her; and also that she was the first to transgress the law."

I spoke, and said, "And she has kept the lines in her hands ever

SARAH SMUGGINS WHEN A GIRL.

since, I think; the only women that I know of that does much kickin', is them that can't find some poor feller to hitch onto."

At this remark Sarah flew mad, and said, "Well! for her part she never had seen a man yet she would tie her lines to, and she pitied any woman that was fool enough to do such a thing."

"Why, la sake, Sarah, how you talk," said old Mrs. Smuggins. "You have forgot what a powerful sight of trouble you made your father and me, when you was determined to marry that rattle-headed Dugood that the Smith gal married; you'd ride the front gate a watchin' for him to come along 'till you broke seven pairs of hinges, and you wouldn't sleep nights, and would go round the house daytime a dreamin', and would put sugar in the butter for salt, and put salt in the coffee for sugar, and write notes and send to him; and almost went crazy when you found he was goin' to marry the Smith gal. Perhaps you've forgot it, but I haint."

"Well, mother," said Sarah, "I think it's real mean for you to tell everything I done when I was a foolish girl, right before these folks."

We saw there was a storm coming up sudden-like, and if there is one thing on earth that Clarissa dislikes more than another it is a row, especially a regular family storm, so with a calm and dignified complexion onto her face, in a tender tone she said, "Well, Ben, it's getting late and we must go home; we left Mary all alone in the house with no one but Ebenezer Plunket, and she'll be lonesome, and like as not half scared to death, and we must go right away;" and suiting her actions to her words, she rose majestically and pinned her shawl and bonnet on. After extending the customary invitations to come over and spend an evening with us, we bid them good-night, and walked out into the starlight night, and started homeward.

Arm in arm we walked along, commenting upon our visit and what was said. I said, "I hope what you said will cause Jim to think, and change his mind. I believe you are right."

"Yes," replied Clarissa, "I hope Mr. Smuggins and every other man will study the great question of what is right and wrong for them to do, and will strive to do right at all times and under all circumstances. If we will all do our duty here it matters not what theory we may have in regard to that unknown future, when the last night closes in upon us; it will be one of delightful rest; soft breezes to cool the lifeworn and tired body; while deeds of kindness, charity, truth and love, and devotion to principle, will shine above and around us, as do these glorious stars in the heaven, all seeming to say, 'Well done, thou art entitled to a blissful repose; thy life has not been a blank, but one of benefit to the world.'"

When we arrived home we noticed a dim light in the front room. Clarissa thought she would go up kind o' cat-like

WATCHING MARY AND EBENEZER.

and peek into the window, and see if Mary was there. When she got to the window she saw Ebenezer a' settin' in the big rocking-chair, and Mary settin' in his lap comfortable-like, and she didn't look a mite scared nor lonesome. Then we both stepped onto the front porch floor, heavy-like, and scraped our feet, then opened the door and walked right into the room. The light was turned up real high, and Mary was setting on one side of the stand, doing some needle-work, and Ebenezer was on t'other side, reading out loud from Logan's "Great Conspiracy." They was both the very picture of dignified innocence. I said, "Mary, have you been scared any since we went away?"

"Not a mite," she said; "what made you think I would be?"

"Oh, nothing," said I, "only your mother thought you might be, so we came home early."

"Well," she replied, "I'm sorry you hurried on my account." Ebenezer looked a little carroty-colored in the face, and confused-like.

We set down and talked about neighborhood affairs and about the lecture. Eb said young Bigler was bilin' mad at the Professor; it was a little more than he could stand to have the truth told on him. He has had the idea that he was a little smarter than any man in this part of the country, and has been expecting to run the political machine, and get elected to the Legislature; but the Professor's examination kind o' tore the mask off of him, and give the people a chance to see what kind of a feller he really was, and he is afraid it will hurt his chance for the office he is anxious to have. I told him that Bigler was foolish to get mad about that; the Professor was only an ordinary man, and guessed at one-half he said about anybody's head. Ebenezer said that might be so, but he hit Bigler and Waddles right square every time, and didn't miss them a mite. They are both as dishonest as they could be; one is all policy with the voters, and t'other is all policy with the church folks, and everybody else, where he thinks he can make a dollar. They are both infernal hypocrites and shams. I told him I guessed there was no room for any argument on that point.

The clock struck ten, which was one hour later than we was in the habit of settin' up, and we thought, by the way Mary fidgeted, and the hard work Eb had in thinking what to talk about, that our room was more desirable than our company, and so we went to bed and left them in possession of the square room once more. Both of them seemed to be relieved of a load of something when we bid them good-night.

> How tedious and tasteless the hours,
> When kindred souls are kept apart;

When Cupid cannot use his powers
   To draw his bow and shoot his dart.

Dear parents are good in their sphere;
   Their sphere is large in Mary's eyes,
But when her Ebenezer comes here,
   He is her all, her only prize.

It's hard work for Ebenezer
   To talk of rascals and their mask,
When Mary wants him to squeeze her,
   And he is dying for the task.

So we had better go to bed,
   And leave them to their glory,
And not listen to what is said,
   When love is telling its story.

    Them is Clarissa's and my sentiments, and we advise everybody to let lovers alone when they want to talk, for it's the only time in their whole lives they will have to find out whether they want each other for life, or whether they can get each other. So we want all our friends to join us in saying good-night to Ebenezer and Mary, whether they be our Mary and Eb, or some one else's.

CHAPTER XI.

THINGS have been running in the usual way in our neighborhood for the past two months. Threshing, husking corn, digging potatoes, gathering apples, making cider, et cetera and et cetera. And to keep the social engine moving, and give the young folks an opportunity to unload their accumulating burden of love and moonshine, there have been a number of paring bees and huskings, and a few picnic parties down to the lake.

Zolliver Ramsdell and Nancy Boyles concluded they had endured the anticipation of future bliss about as long as they could stand it, and decided they would enter upon the realization of what joys belong to the marriage state. By the assistance of Rev. Jonas Danberry they placed their names on the roll of independent families, as Mr. and Mrs. Ramsdell. The affair took place down to Mrs. Boyles' house on the 15th of September. Nearly all the neighbors was there; Ebenezer and Mary stood up with them when they was married, and they become so interested in the proceeding, that when Rev. Danberry said, "Let the parties join hands," Ebenezer and Mary grabbed each other's hands, and stood blushing at the minister, not really thinking what they was doing until the minister asked in a peculiar manner, which couple he was to unite. Then they came to consciousness as quick as a flash of lightning. Mary felt as if she had received a shock. The smile that was visible on the faces of the assembled neighbors and others, found an audible expression, to the discomfort of both Eb and Mary, who retired from their position on an Eb tide. They were not seen again until they was brought into the supper room by a searching party, who found them in the northwest corner of the orchard. Aside from this little mistake, Zolliver and Nancy completed their part of the ceremony in good shape amid the applause and congratulations of their numerous friends and the rest of the folks that was waiting with pent-up appetites, to devour the fatted calf and other delicacies to be served up in the supper-room.

At the table Ebenezer and Mary received a good many jokes and rubs, until Eb finally mustered up courage like a giant, and spoke right out and said: " Well, if we did make a little mistake, I don't see that it's very much to laugh at; the next time we do it we won't run away, but will stand there and let the minister guess who it is that wants to be married; won't we, Mary?" And Mary blushingly replied, "I suppose it will be just as you say, Eb."

Rev. Danberry promptly suggested the present occasion as a fitting time for the re-occurrence of the accident, but Ebenezer said, " Not just now, but when there was a minister handy by who could tell, without asking, who wanted to get married," and so Danberry's prospect of another five dollar job vanished, while a calm settled down around the table like a pall, disturbed only by the rattle of dishes and the oscillating motion of the under jaws of thirty-five hungry mouths, until Clarissa remarked,—

"Mrs. Boyles, what excellent biscuits these are; I never tasted of any better."

"Yes," said Mrs. Boyles, " Nancy made them ; she's a splendid bread-maker."

Another short calm ensued, when Lily Doolittle spoke up in her innocent manner and said, "I am so glad the fashion for women to wear short hair has come around ; it is such a bother to take care of long hair, and then, hairpins are not only extremely bothersome, but they are positively dangerous."

I made no comments on the whole of this occasion. I do not just now remember of opening my mouth but once except at the table, while I was there, and that was when I kissed the bride with the rest of the procession that passed by her, but I could not help thinking then, and I haint stopped thinking yet, why it is that some folks instinctively (as it were), spring a conversation upon the most disagreeable topic, just at a time when both peace of mind and tranquility of stomach demand the choicest language and upon the most agreeable topic. If ever there is a time when pleasant sub-

KISSING THE BRIDE.

jects of conversation should be selected and choice, pleasing language used, it is at the table, when that organ, the stomach, which is very sensitive, can be stimulated to increased powers of digestion by delicate and pleasant conversation, or nauseated, if not completely paralyzed, by unpleasant words associated with unpleasant memories. Now the remark of the innocent Miss Doolittle called up the narrow escape the old lady Boyles had from Nancy's hair-pin in the biscuit, and the entire party had their sufficiency of a delicious meal, carefully prepared and nicely served. Lily's remark was like ipecac thrown into the soup.

Thoughtless and needless unpleasant remarks similar to those of Lily's, made in the sick room, arrest the progress of the patient's recovery, put a damper upon the doctor's success and frequently supply the undertaker with work he ought not to have. In society it sends the raven croaking from house to house, destroys the peace and happiness of home, keeps the lawyer busy, fills the public press with sensational matter and is the daily diet of tattlers and mischief-makers. Prospects are blighted and the honey of life frequently turned to wormwood and gall by ignorant thoughtlessness in conversation.

I did not intend on this occasion, to indulge in criticisms on the frailties of human nature. My own frailty should forbid any such criticism.

After supper the young folks had a dance, and Zolliver and Nancy was made the recipients of some nice presents. A host of jokes was freely passed around at the expense of Zolliver and Nancy, and Eb and Mary.

There has been considerable excitement throughout our county for the last month on account of the election that has just passed off. This being an off-year in politics, as they call it, there wasn't so much interest taken in the State ticket as the county ticket. The people got more excited in the contest for assembly-man than any of the other candidates. They had a lively time at the caucus down to the village in electing delegates to the county convention, but there was a good deal more excitement at the convention than at the caucus. Young Bigler was at the Republican convention and working as hard as he could to get the nomination for member of the Assembly on the Republican ticket, but it was no go; they didn't want him, and they gave him the grand snub, by nominating Thomas Conners, a smart young lawyer at the village. Disappointed in his failure, young Bigler immediately deserted the Republican party and became a rabid Democrat. The Democrats held their convention a week after the Republicans. Young Bigler succeeded in getting the nomination at this convention. He promised to work faithfully for them. The county is very strongly Republican, so his prospects was not very bright, but he went to work making speeches all over the county, speaking in the schoolhouses every night until election day.

He attempted to show up the rascality of the Republicans, and the necessity of a reform, and worked in all the claptrap that political stump speakers use for fillin' in their wind puddings; but where he spread himself in the biggest style, and soared the most was on *Free Trade*. "Free Trade," said he, "Fellow Citizens, is the main log in our raft; we maintain that the Creator made us all *free* and equal, and gave us the air in the heavens to breathe freely, and the water of the earth for our free use, and the land and its products from one end of this vast world to the other, should be equally free to us. And it is contrary to divine law and judgment to put an embargo on everything we want to buy of our neighbors, whether they live on the farm that joins us, or over in England, France, Turkey, Russia or China, or any other part of the world; we have no right to say others shouldn't sell us their goods at any price they was a mind to, or give 'em to us if they wanted to. No, sirs, gentlemen, everything should be put on a free basis so far as business is concerned. We ought to get everything we want at the very lowest price that competing markets can offer, without being restricted by enormous tariffs that are gotten up in the interest of greedy capitalists and soulless millionaires, etc."

He would try to work upon people's prejudices and sympathy, and he would tell some stories to see how many laughed and how many didn't. While the laughing was going on he would calculate by the number that laughed and that didn't what course to take in the rest of his speech. He used his funny stories just the same as all of 'em do, as *feelers*. He would shape his remarks as he thought would please the majority. He spread himself in good shape, and in his flights of rhetoric and fancy, he imagined that he had converted every one to his ideas; and a seat of honor in the great fine capitol at Albany loomed up before him as the pearl of great price. He made a regular war on every successful manufacturer or railroad man. In fact, he give a blow to every one that was financially successful. He took the ground that free trade was the stepping stone to free money, and in his opinion free money was a big thing for the people to have. He was worked up to such an appreciation of himself and his abilities, that he dreamed in his sleep of the great Bigler that was to be. His joy, however, was like that of the child who sees the rainbow tints glistening on the surface of a soap bubble in the sunlight. The fourth of November burst the bubble, and there was nothing left.

He forgot to tell the people that the best citizens were those that were sober, honest and industrious; that they were the ones who spent the least time in talking politics, and made the least noise on election days. He forgot to mention in his speeches that the shiftless, lazy and profligate people were the ones that made the most noise about elections, and complained the most about monopolies and rich men. He forgot to hint in his speeches that nearly all the rich men of our country were born poor, and worked their way up in the world, that industry and frugality were the principal elements in their success. He forgot to say to the people that there was no country on the globe where honest labor received such high recognition, where the wage earner received so much for his labor, and where the way was open to a fortune for him, as this country. He forgot to mention a word about Professor Feeler's lecture or the examination he received at his hands. He forgot to give his real reasons for changing his politics.

As Tom Conners went through the county he so completely riddled Bigler's speeches, that there wasn't enough left to them to make a fly net to cover a kitten. He showed it up clear enough for the most stupid to understand that the first law of nature is self-protection, and what is true in regard to the individual in protecting himself and his interests, is equally true in regard to a community, a town, county, State and nation. All its interests should be carefully protected, and if the products of another country could be scattered throughout our country at such prices as to paralyze if not completely destroy our own industries, then they should be shut out by such a tariff as would place them in a fair competition with our products.

He didn't forget to call special attention to all those items that Bigler omitted. He didn't forget to show that the Democrats was alike interested with the Republicans in upholding and protecting the prosperity of our country, and all its industries, and in protecting every one in their right to vote, and in securing an honest count. Nor did he forget to refer to Professor Feeler's description of Bigler. The final result was decided last Tuesday. Tom Conners was elected by a majority of 4,387, which was just 392 short of all the votes cast in the county.

Since the election Bigler has been real sick; the strain upon his nervous system was more than he could stand. The exposition of his true inwardness hurt him as much as his defeat, for his ambition was not only knocked in the head, but his hypocrisy was unmasked, and dishonest Bigler could no longer fool the people of that locality with his numerous shams. He now declares he wont live in such a country; he is going to move to Chicago.

Clarissa says she guesses we will get along just as well without him, and perhaps better. That settles it in my opinion, for when Clarissa once makes a positive declaration of a principle or an idea, it is just as satisfactory as if I'd read it in the Bible.

Speaking of Clarissa thusly, makes me think how blessed and happifying it is to have such confidence in your wife, that when she tells you anything, you know it is positively true; and how much more happifying it must be to them that is of a opposite sex from what I belong to, by the nature of things, to have the same sweet confidence in what their husbands tell them. If such was the case generally, marriage bliss would go up in the market five hundred per cent., and the divorce business would be knocked higher than Bartholdi's torch of liberty lighting the world. I wish such was the case, but I'm forced to believe it aint. What might be if the sweet angel of confidence roosted on every front door, isn't, and I don't see any sign of a breeze that is likely to waft that condition of things to the human family in the very near future.

When I get to talking to Clarissa in a loving sort of a way, and tell her what perfect confidence I have in her, she generally, and at

BIGLER STARTS FOR CHICAGO.

sundry times, replies, "Well, Benjamin, I love you, 'tis true, but I can't exactly return the high compliment you give me." Really, I don't suppose she can, for ever since she found me acting sweet-like to the Widder Lewis, about two years after we was married, she has a vivid recollection of it, and how I mixed myself up in trying to explain.

The men think they are the sharp ones of the Creator's handiwork, but they are deceived; they haint one-half as sharp as the women, for just as sure as they get caught in doing something mean and wrong, they will commence lying out of it, and they'll mix themselves up so before they get through explaining, they'll have to confess they lied. But, if a woman gets into a difficulty, she will simply *lie* out of it, and stick to it until the climate changes temperature in the lower regions, before she'll confess.

Clarissa doesn't agree with me on that point, but the reason is plain enough. She has always been truthful and honest, and she thinks women in general are. Well, I think women, in general, are. I do not for a moment think the general run of women are liars, but when you do happen, by accident or otherwise, to find one that does prevaricate, the remarks I have made on that pretty correctly apply.

Domestic felicity depends largely upon domestic confidence. Chamfort says: "It is with happiness as with watches—the less complicated, the less easily deranged." I was trying, in my weak way, the other evening, to philosophize with Clarissa in an argument on this question of domestic peace and happiness, and gave her my ideas upon this confidence business, and told her what the world might be, if—and if; and she said: "Benjamin, those are my sentiments, but the '*ifs*' take all the starch out of sentiments. Balzac says: 'We are finite beings. There can be no infinite happiness for us. The soul that dreams it and pursues it, will embrace but a shadow.' I am willing to accept the situation, and embrace all the substance I can of everyday happiness, and not spend my time in running after shadows." Thus, my philosophizing, as usual when I get into an argument with her, ended. I think I can safely say, when I get into a discussion with Clarissa, nineteen times out of twenty I can appropriately write the word "Waterloo" at the end of my part of the discussion.

When I married Clarissa I thought just as a great many of them think, and as some of them act—that I was going to be boss, and have things about as I wanted them; but I soon found that Clarissa was my intellectual superior, and I concluded, for various reasons, that I had better adopt the advice of La Bruyere, who said: "It is often shorter and better to yield to others than to endeavor to compel others to adjust themselves to us." I have lived by his advice so long, that now it is a pleasure to yield to her.

I find I have been running off onto a different track from what I intended to, when I got through telling about the election and Bigler's defeat. The reason for it is plain. Clarissa made a remark, and I got to telling about her remark, and switched off. That woman switches me off my main track very frequently, if not oftener. I may have an idea in my head worth a whole column in a newspaper, but just as sure as she speaks to me it's gone, and I go off in admiration of her, and feel my own littleness so much that the idea is gone forever, and when I get back onto the main track again, I have to get a new lot of ideas before I can go ahead. I confess, it is a serious drawback, for ideas with me haint a quarter as abundant as they are with Clarissa and other smart men. Therefore I shall rely upon the patience and forgiving spirit of the readers to excuse the many sudden and unexpected breaks.

I was going to say that the political campaign this fall brought out some ideas more prominently than others; ideas that we all ought to think over.

First—If there is anything worth laboring for, it is worthy of protection.

Second—The source of supply to the laborer—viz.: capital—is as truly worthy of protection as the fountain that supplies us with water. The laborer cannot be protected when the source of his earnings is open to all kinds of attack and to destruction.

Third—The most important thing to all of us is a *pure* and *honest* government, where justice shall be accorded to all, regardless of any condition, and this can only be secured by the protection of every citizen in the country in his lawful right to vote as pleases him.

Bigler didn't adopt any progressive ideas, but resorted to all the little catches and points that in his opinion would make votes for himself. He failed to exhibit that high moral character or broad, comprehensive view of the country's needs that public opinion demanded of a man to represent them in the law-making body of the State. He played the part of a fox, and was treated according to his deserts.

Clarissa says that, while she doesn't pretend to be a politician, she reads a powerful sight, and thinks a little, and that, as near as she can remember, it has been the custom in this country for the opinion of the masses to be pretty near correct; that some years the

LETTER OF CONDOLENCE.

people kind o' go to sleep and forget that "eternal vigilance is the price of liberty," and in those spells of slumber the cunning political foxes and wolves go prowling around, and steal a victory at the polls; but it only serves to wake up the sleepers, and the next year public opinion is wide awake and hard at work, and it opens up graves and buries these animals out of sight and smell. Then the country moves along, prosperous, peaceful, and happy for a time. She says they woke up this year, and we won't hear anything more of Mr. Bigler in the political field for a good many years, if ever. I think just as she does on that point, of course.

Last night the ladies' sewing society had a meeting at Widow

Abby Standish's house, and they talked about the election more than anything else. And they concluded that, as Mr. Bigler was going to leave the neighborhood for good, they ought to do something kind of pretty for him. So they decided to have Mrs. Dave Kirk write him a letter of condolence, and a verse or two. Jane was never noted for being much of a writer. She said she couldn't write a letter fit for a cow to read, but as he was her cousin by marriage on Kirk's side of the house, she would do the best she could; so she wrote the following:

"CUZZIN B. B. BIGLER:—

" It is with mingled feelins uv sorrow and regret that I pen theze few short, breef sentences uv kondolence and konsolashun to you. I no it must be gallin to your dear good wife Mariah, to have your pollytickle kareer come to such a sudden and unplezant kloze. I no she iz naturally proud, and haz ben in the habit uv goin in respectable kumpany, and I uzed tu like to go to hur house a vizitin. I hope she will bare up under your disappointment, and not brake down in bodily helth. I regret you did not stick to your furst party and ben willin tu axcept some miner posishun on the ticket az you mite have pulled thru if you had.

" However, I spoze the Allmity noze better what we are all made uv better than we do ourselves, and probably it iz best you dun as you did, for we cant help believin that what iz your loss iz our gain.

" Du not be discouraged and give up, but go out West and go into the kattle bizness. David sez thare iz lots uv muuny in it, and if you cant make your mark in the world az a pollytickan, you can git to be a kattle king, and if thare iznt quite as much honor in being king uv the long and short horned brutes az a ruler amung the human kind, thare iz lots more munny in it, and a shinin silver dollar will kuver a good sized soar. With these tuchin and feelin remarks, and this little poem on behalf uv the Morganville soin society (in whoze interest I address theze lines) I bid you a disconsolate farewell. Your cuzzin, HELEN KIRK."

" Bizzy Bascum Bigler,
'Tho a wiley wigler,
With his pollytickle rake
Failed in taking the cake;
Partly becauze the young peeler
Was shown up by Mister Feeler,
But more becauze we saw
He didn't respect the law.
The greatest mistake he made
Wuz advocatin Free Trade,
And in not showin the truth
By good and suffishent proof.
The high and noble honors
Wuz given tu Tom Conners,
Who saw the way tu eleckshun
Wuz in the coze uv Proteckshun."

CHAPTER XII.

WITH a favorable breeze and an even sea, most any vessel with a reasonably tight bottom may venture on a short journey, but if a long voyage is to be made, I would advise the captain to see that his vessel not only has a tight bottom, but that it is thoroughly sound; that every beam and brace is sound, and properly secured; that in every way his craft is seaworthy.

Too many shipwrecks are caused by unsound vessels, commanded by incompetent masters. When a storm is encountered by such a vessel, the master is baffled, and loses control of it, and the rotten timbers give way, and total destruction follows.

They have had a big shipwreck, so to speak, in this community. George Waddles started on the voyage of speculation; he embarked in a vessel of his own construction; all the main beams and stays were composed of his professions of Christianity, and the thin covering of its hulk was his membership in the Methodist Church. When he first started out, everything went smooth and fine. He bought all the hogs and cattle in the country he could get hold of. He went to prayer-meetings and church service as regular as the pilot on shipboard consults his compass and chart.

When Jim Teeters moved to the village he went into partnership with Waddles in the stock-buying and shipping business, although, by a mutual agreement, it wasn't known that they was interested together in business, for by its not being known, they could work their schemes to better advantage.

Waddles had a set of large hay-scales down to the village, on which he weighed all the stock he bought. For a long time the farmers had sold their stock to Waddles, and drove it to the village, and had 'em weighed on Waddles' scales, and took his weight as correct. Waddles was always very polite to them, and would generally ask all about their health and their families, and was as honest in appearance to 'em as a man could be.

One day last week he bought sixty head of steers and 110 hogs of Clark Benjamin, a farmer in the town of Henderson. Benjamin is a very careful and prudent farmer, and an honest man, and has got to be a rich man.

Last fall he put into his barn-yard a set of Fairbanks' hay-scales, and when he sells any stock or grain or hay, he weighs it on his scales before he delivers it.

He weighed his steers and hogs before he drove them down to the village, but didn't tell Waddles anything about it, and when he got to the village with his stock, Waddles weighed them all and footed up the amount, and it was 2,000 pounds less on the steers than they weighed on Benjamin's scales, and 1,000 pounds less on the hogs.

Mr. Benjamin then informed Waddles that he couldn't have the stock at that weight.

"Why, what's the matter?" says Waddles, in great surprise; "don't you think that is correct? You saw the scales balance every time, didn't you?"

"Yes," said Benjamin, "I saw the scales balance every time, and noticed you took down the exact figures also; but I don't think it is correct—and in fact, I know it is not correct."

Waddles looked red in the face, and acted terribly hurt at Benjamin's remark, and told Benjamin to weigh them over himself, if he doubted it.

"Very well," said Benjamin, "I will; but first I'll just look them scales over a little."

He done so, and after a careful examination, he found that Waddles had fixed the scales so they would make just 100 pounds *less* than the actual weight at every draft.

There was a number of farmers and business men standing round the scales during this time, and when Mr. Benjamin showed up Mr. Waddles' trick to 'em, and convinced them all of the fact, by a comparison with the weights on his own scales, and also by the way the scales was fixed, Waddles fainted away, but by dousing him with cold water he came to pretty soon. He looked awful, but he couldn't say nothing. Mr. Benjamin demanded full pay for his stock, according to the weight on his own scales.

Waddles was so dazed he didn't say anything for some time. When he had recovered from the shock, he told Mr. Benjamin to go to the bank with him and he would give him the money, and take the stock at his weight.

The news of his fraud went all over the village like lightning. In a hour and a half three farmers that had delivered stock to him that same day had him arrested for swindling, and he was tried before 'Squire Dale. The proof was so positive that Waddles couldn't overcome it, but said he never done it; that Jim Teeters used the scales to weigh large amounts of butter and cheese, that he bought to ship to New York, and also hogs.

'Squire Dale bound him over to court. The whole thing came out on him so sudden that the people all over the village appeared thunderstruck, and when the 'squire turned him over to the sheriff, he tried to get bail, but he couldn't get any one in town to go on his bail for $1,000, and so he had to sleep in jail that night. The next day the bankers, after getting security on $2,000 worth of cattle, went on his bail for $1,000, and Mr. Waddles was let out.

This was only the beginning of a general tear-up. The next day Teeters was arrested for swindling. He was tried before 'Squire Dale also. There was plenty of proof to convict him, and the 'squire bound him over to court in $1,000 bonds. When the sheriff took charge of him he got the sheriff to bring him out to

WADDLES FAINTED; THEY DOUSED HIM WITH COLD WATER.

see me, and tried to get me to go on his bond. I said to him, " Mr. Teeters, I would willingly go on the bond of an honest man to help him out of a difficulty, but I have too clear a recollection of your dealings with me last summer, in the hog business, to sign my name to your bond, and you must excuse me if I say, once for all, *No*."

He looked as if he would sink, but I didn't have a mite of pity for him. The sheriff took him back to the village, and poor Teeters had to sleep in the jail that night. Somehow or other the Methodist folks didn't help either Waddles or Teeters out of their difficulty. Teeters had to give the bank a chattel mortgage on his store

REFUSING TO GO ON TEETERS' BAIL.

before they would bail him out; this was done the next day after he was arrested. Now there was a pair of our prominent men booked for trial at the next term of court, and everybody was talking about it, and most folks was surprised, especially in regard to Waddles, as he had lived there for a long time, and had been a leader in the Methodist Church, but I wasn't surprised at all about either one of 'em; I knew by experience that Teeters was a rascal, and I have been well satisfied for a good many years that Waddles was masquerading as one thing while in his heart he was another. I don't pretend to be very sharp, but I know a humbug when I see it, if I can't tell others how to detect it.

Things run along about ten days in the usual way, when on a Sunday morning, after Rev. Danberry had finished his sermon, and just before he pronounced the benediction, he requested all the members of the church to meet in the basement immediately after the close of the morning service.

They met in the basement, and the minister told them the object of the meeting was to consider the matter of retaining brother Geo. Waddles and brother Teeters in the church, after the damaging evidence that had been brought out against their characters. He wished to have an expression of the members in regard to it. There was a good many remarks made by different members. Some advanced the idea that they should be labored with, while others insisted that if they had deliberately gone to work to steal the livery of heaven to serve the devil in, if they had used the church for no other purpose than to assist them in swindling the people, it would be an insult to the church to even offer to labor with them. They took a vote on it, and by a very large majority they decided that the names of these two swindlers should be dropped from the church roll. When this was made known to Waddles and Teeters, they resolved to have revenge on some of these brethren that was so active in getting their names dropped from the church roll, so they circulated several stories damaging to their characters. Stories once started never grow less, but rapidly increase, both in numbers and magnitude. The surest way to make a lie the most effectual is to mix enough of truth with it to give it the semblance of truth, and then it goes well, and hits its intended victim every time. These gentlemen understood that scheme perfectly, and started their stories with a determination—that as they fell, others would have to go with 'em. The result has been terrible. The church has been nearly broken up. Nearly one-third of its members have been dropped from the roll, or labored with. Scandal seems to have been the order of the day, and each succeeding day developed new sensations. It was hinted around that Rev. Danberry was not above suspicion, that he had called upon certain sisters very frequently, and especially the Widow Crookshank, who runs a milliner store in the village. Things had come to such a pass that one was really afraid to meet his neighbor for fear he would hear some horrible news.

Clarissa said she was perfectly sick, hearing of so much wickedness, but she says, "It's not surprising that we hear so much all of a sudden, for when all kinds of meanness and wickedness hides itself behind a mask of piety and religion, it's like a stream that has been dammed up by floodwood and rubbish. After a while one or two of the larger pieces give way, and then the whole mass of rubbish goes out with a rush, filling the stream below with its mire and filth, but the fountain above is still pure, and as its purifying waters course along it cleanses away the filth, and in time purifies the whole stream. The church is no more to blame because bad men and women drop into its folds, than the fountain is for the driftwood falling into the stream. The Methodist Church is designed as an institution for the dissemination of high and holy principles; is an institution of honesty and purity, but some bad persons had got into it and drifted along. Corruption and wickedness hid itself behind great and loud professions.

"When Waddles and Teeters gave way, all the hypocrisy and wickedness that accumulated, rushed out upon the world. But it will all be over soon, and the church will be all the better by being rid of the shams and hypocrites that have found their way into it.

"The church never hurt a person in the world, and I want infidels to understand that. No person was ever made worse by any church, but vile hypocrites that mask as church members do an immense amount of harm, not only to individuals outside of the church, but to those who become its members from the highest and purest motives. Now a great deal of this slander we hear has been started by Waddles and Teeters in order to turn public talk away from themselves, and see if that can't better their case a little when it comes up for trial, and has no real truth in it. Time will set it all right, and justice will light in the right place, though it may seem to be a long time lighting." I believe Clarissa is correct in her opinion about this matter, and I will leave Waddles, Teeters and the Methodist Church in the hands of Father Time, while I straighten up matters around home and get ready to take Clarissa on a tour abroad.

CHAPTER XIII.

MRS. Jonas Buzzbee—Clarissa's second cousin on her great uncle's side, that lives in Syracuse, and whose husband is in the hardware business there, sent us a paper week before last, and marked an advertisement in it with red ink. Here is the advertisement she marked:

"GRAND EXCURSION."

"A GOLDEN OPPORTUNITY that may never occur again. Everybody should take advantage of it. A train composed of forty-eight magnificent sleeping cars, five dining cars, forty baggage cars,

EXCURSION TRAIN.

two refrigerator cars and one car for servants and dogs, will leave the Grand Central Depot in New York City November 15, for San Francisco, Cal., via N. Y. C., L. S. & M. S., C. & N. W., U. P. and C. P. Railroads.

"Tickets good for four months, including berths and meals, and privilege of carrying 2,000 pounds of baggage, and return via any route passengers desire, either via rail or steamship or both, only $45.00.

"Every ticket-holder is entitled to free transportation for one servant and two dogs. Stop-over checks will be given to passengers, at any point desired, west of Chicago. The many points of interest can be visited along the route with very little expense. Among these may be mentioned, Omaha, Denver, Colorado Springs, the Garden of the Gods, Pike's Peak, Monument Park, the celebrated bathhouses of Idaho Springs, Cheyenne, Black Hills, Ogden, Salt Lake City and its wonderful institutions, Helena, Boise City, Sacramento, the Yosemite Valley, the Geysers, Portland, Seattle and Sitka, Los Angeles, San Diego, the principal cities of Mexico and Central America, New Orleans, Mobile, the orange groves of Florida, and a few cities on the Atlantic coast on their way home.

"No one should miss this wonderful opportunity. Tickets from Albany, $44.00; from Utica, $43.00; Syracuse, $42.00; Rochester, $41.00; Buffalo, $40.00; Cleveland, $36.00; Toledo, $35.00; Chicago, $30.00. For further information and particulars, address Messrs. Holdem, Ketchem & Skinem, No. 211 Chatham Street, New York, or Jerusalem, Scalper & Co., 148 Clark Street, Chicago, inclosing a two cent stamp to insure a reply."

Clarissa and I have been saving what money we could for some years, intending to take a trip some time and travel, and we had got considerable on hand. I had made up my mind to see something of the world beside Morganville and the village before I died, and Clarissa was anxious to visit many places, and meet many distinguished people she has read about, and when we read this advertisement, it seemed like a big bonanza to us, and we wondered if there wasn't a kind of a Providence in having this excursion come at a time we was calculating to travel.

Clarissa wrote to her cousin Buzzbee, thanking her for the pa-

EXPERIENCE WITH HYPOCRITES. 147

per, and especially for the advertisement, and told her we would make her a visit a couple of days before the train left S. I arranged things around home so as to leave Abe and Mary and the hired man comfortable and all right, and went to the village and got me a new suit of store clothes, and rigged Clarissa out, or rather, she done it, and on the 13th of November we took the railroad for Syracuse, or rather the railroad took us to that place. We got there at 5:45 P. M., and Mrs. Buzzbee and her husband met us at the depot with a sleigh.

I never heard such a noise in my life as there was as we was going out of the depot yard. A dozen or more of the sassiest

ARRIVAL AT DEPOT IN SYRACUSE.

loafers I ever saw, was standing in a row, trying to get us to go to some hotel. One of the sassy scamps grabbed hold of my valise.

I hauled off and was going to plant a bean over his eyes, when Mr. Buzzbee said, "Come on, Uncle Benjamin, and don't pay any attention to them hotel hoodlums." That dumb scamp dropped it mighty sudden, and looked cheap enough. We got into the sleigh and had a fine drive up to a great, fine brick house where they lived. They seemed glad to see us, and although I never met Mr. B. before, he acted as if he always knew me. They have an elegant home, and everything wonderful fine in the house.

The next day he took us all over the city in his sleigh. I went down to his store with him, and I was surprised. He had more goods in his store than the whole caboodle down to the village have, all put together. He is a wholesaler, and does a big business. After we had gone over the city, and seen a good many things, we took the women home and had supper, and then Mr. B. drove down town again, and took me into what he called a private club-room, and introduced me to a number of gentlemen, all of whom he told me (afterward) was prominent citizens of Syracuse. Some of 'em was merchants; some was doctors and lawyers, and some was prominent politicians. One of 'em was the mayor of the city; he was very polite, and in a few minutes after I was introduced to him he asked us all up to the bar to have a drink. All but me took something. Some said, "I'll take a *sour*," while others called for a "straight," a "mash," a "cocktail," a "mint-julep," etc. Mr. Buzzbee said he wanted a "Thomas-and-Jeremiah." All these things was strange to me, and I couldn't understand what they meant. The mayor says to me, "Come, Uncle Ben, what will you have?" I said, "Nothing, if you please." They all looked at me, surprised, and says, "What! don't you drink?" Says I, "Gentlemen, I drink good, fresh water, when I'm to home, and sometimes milk, but that's all." The mayor said, "Well, you know you aint to home now, and when you are in Rome, you must do as Romans do. We don't drink at home, do we, gentlemen?" and all responded, "No, of course not," and "Here is some kernels of roasted coffee you can eat, and when you go home your wife can't detect you by your breath." I replied, "Gentlemen, you will please excuse me; I don't believe in *shams*. I don't believe in pretending to the world to be sober and temperate, and then get into some back room, as you are here, and give a lie to all my pretensions; and, more than that, I don't believe in shamming to my wife who, of all others, should know the truth in regard to my conduct. I can't see the difference between this place, fitted up in such a grand style, with marble counters and great big looking-glasses, and fine pictures and pretty carpets, and patronized by the prominent citizens, including the mayor, and a common country tavern bar-room, with its dirty, low walls, muddy floor, and few broken wooden chairs and benches, filled with blear-eyed, besotted, ragged wretches; its air laden with the sickening smell of cheap rum and whisky, and its principal sound the discordant combination of oaths and curses and foul vulgarity, except *pride*, pride in appearance, pride in association, pride in not being seen by the outside world, pride in everything except *principle*, and the material you obtain here is the surest destroyer of *pride* and *principle* that I know of. Give it time, and it is sure to kill both. I beg your pardon, gentlemen, if I have said anything to hurt your feelings; I don't mean to do that, but I am a plain farmer, never was away from home before, never saw a city until now, and never met prominent citizens, especially in such a place as this; but Benjamin Morgan is opposed to shams, and opposed to men losin' their heads to satisfy their greedy stomachs. If it is all right to drink this stuff, and sell it, then have places along the sidewalks, or like other places for refreshments, where it can be sold, and where a man can stop with his wife and daughters, and sons, to drink, and not have burnt coffee to eat after drinking; and let the mayor, and prominent merchants, doctors, lawyers and politicians see that licenses are issued to every one that wants to sell it. I am opposed to playing the double game of good Lord and good Devil. Hypocrisy don't pay. When you have to settle accounts at the closing up of business, you'll have to tell so many lies in explaining things that the lies will down you."

Then I turned to Mr. Buzzbee and said, "Let's go home; it's pretty late, and Clarissa will be worrying about me." I saw Mr. B.

was terribly red in the face, and so was the mayor; and I could hear some of the others laughing and say something about *"country crank."* I didn't know what they meant, unless it was a machine for winding up the country with.

Mr. Buzzbee and I went home. On our way home Mr. B. said he was sorry I spoke so plain—not so much on his own account as on account of all those gentlemen, for they were all his friends. I told him I was sorry on that account that I had said anything, but I told him he could explain to 'em the next time he met 'em, that I was an ignorant old fool, from up in the country, and didn't know any better than to beller out what I honestly thought. He said that would be entirely unnecessary, as they all understood that now.

I haint used to very refined society, I know; but I know enough to feel a stab like that Mr. Buzzbee gave me, and appreciated it just as perfectly as if a mule had kicked me for fooling with his heels.

After we went to bed, I told Clarissa all about our trip down town and back, and what was said, and how Buzzbee gave me a stab. She said, "Well, Benjamin, we haint to home, and you had better keep your mouth closed and your eyes open, and you will learn just as much, if you don't do so much good," and then she said there was going to be a big temperance meeting at the M. E. Church, to-morrow night, and Mrs. Buzzbee wanted us to go, and as our train did not leave until midnight, we would have plenty of time to go, and visit afterward. I told her I would like to go first-rate.

CHAPTER XIV.

THE next day Mr. B. and I went down to the railroad depot to get our tickets. We told the ticket agent we wanted two excursion tickets for San Francisco and return. The agent proceeded to fill out the tickets, and asked how many servants and dogs we had. I told him I had a hired hand I had left to home to help Abe take care of the farm, and I had never raised any dogs, as Clarissa wouldn't have the dirty things around the house. He laughed and

BUYING TICKET IN SYRACUSE.

said he merely wanted to know how many we wanted to take with us, so he could include them in the ticket. When he got the tickets ready I counted out $84 for the two tickets, and he said it would be $200 more. I was thunderstruck, and pulled out of my pocket the advertisement Clarissa cut out of the paper, and asked him what they meant by that? "Oh!" said he, "that's all right; you have to pay us $142 for the ticket, and when you get to San Francisco you take what you have left of your ticket into the company's office there and they will give you a rebate of $100 on each ticket; that is, they will pay you back $100. Don't you see, Sir, that the company is protecting its passengers in doing thus? for they might have their money stolen from them before they arrived in California, and in doing this each passenger is sure to have at least $106 when they get there, and their return tickets." I had never thought of that, and at once I concluded that the managers of this excursion was Christians, and was looking out for the safety and welfare of their passengers; so I very readily paid him the other $200 and took my tickets and also a card of the company's agents in San Francisco, which read, "Dodgem, Skipem & Oppenheimer, brokers and dealers in Second hand Tickets, 1496 Oakland Street, San Francisco, Cal."

After going down to Mr. Buzzbee's store and gaping around town about an hour, we went home to Buzzbee's, and I explained to Clarissa all about the ticket business. She didn't exactly see the Christian part in the ticket performance, unless it was to create *faith* in the honesty of a lot of men the public didn't know, and as faith was one of the principal elements of professional Christianity it might possibly have a distant connecting link between this company and Christianity, and it might not have. But inasmuch as we had bought the tickets we would go and not worry about it.

After supper, we all went to the M. E. Church. I set next to Buzzbee. The church was filled in a short time, and a young man addressed the audience in regard to the object of the meeting. He was very enthusiastic on the subject of temperance, and said they wished to organize a new temperance society, and push the cause of temperance in every part of the city, and State and nation. He said the Rev. W. P. Waterhouse would offer prayer, after which we would listen to an address from one of Syracuse's brightest lights and noblest workers, the Mayor.

The minister offered his prayer, but I didn't hear a word of it, for I couldn't help thinking about the mayor that was to speak, and wondered if it was the same mayor I met the night before. After prayer was over the mayor was introduced; it was the same man, and he talked for about an hour on the evils of drinking, and even made reference to my country tavern bar-room, to show the degradation that strong drink was liable to bring a man down to, but never hinted a word about the fine genteel club-room. I was so

HE BROUGHT HIS FOOT DOWN ON BUZZBEE'S CORNFIELD.

confounded indignant at his mean hypocrisy that I brought my foot down with a heavy thug, right on Buzzbee's corn-field, and he almost fainted. I didn't much care, for his particular friend, the mayor, by every word that he was electrifying the audience with, to me was establishing him as a grand rascal and unmitigated liar, and Buzzbee and the "leading merchants, doctors, lawyers and politicians" knew it.

When we went home to Buzzbee's, I was so mad I couldn't act decent. Buzzbee said, "Uncle Benjamin, you haint used to it. After you have lived in a city a few years you won't notice anything of that kind. You'll find that the lawyer pleads cases at the bar, not for the sake of the client, but for pay; it is his profession. The doctor visits his patient, not because he considers it his Christian duty to cure the invalid, but for pay; it is his profession. The minister that preaches two long sermons every Sunday, and visits and smiles and shakes hands six days in the week, doesn't do it because he thinks the Almighty will destroy him if he doesn't, but for the *pay*. The larger the pay the louder the call to 'go preach;' it is his profession, and the man that delivers temperance lectures doesn't do so because he thinks 'his Satanic majesty will call him on a blind' if he takes a drink, but for the *pay;* it is his profession. And when a city mayor makes a temperance speech one night and treats the leading citizens in the club room the next night, you can calculate he is acting strictly professional.

"Uncle Ben, come and see us when you get back from California and let us know if you find any one else that you think is as badly off as our mayor."

I kinder got over my huff, talked more pleasant-like until time to go for the train. They took us to the depot, we bid 'em good-by and we got aboard the train, which pulled into the depot about the time we drove up.

CHAPTER XV.

WE entered a sleeping car for the first time in our lives. As we entered at the wash-room end of the car, a nigger met us and asked us for the number of our berth. I told him that was a delicate question for a nigger to put to a stranger, and as Clarissa was my second wife I didn't care to tell when either one of us was born, and furthermore, I didn't know that it was any of his business when we was born.

"No, no," said he, "you don't understand. I am the porter in this car; I take care of the car, make up the beds and assign the beds to the passengers according to the number on their berth ticket or bed ticket."

"Oh," said I; "well, why didn't you say so in the first place?" And I pulled out my $284 lot of tickets.

He looked them over and said, "Your berth tickets are not with these."

Said I, "That's all the agent give me."

Said he, "He should have given you berth tickets."

By this time the train was moving out of the depot, and it was too late for me to get it fixed there. I asked him what we should do. He said he had one upper and lower together left he could let us have.

"Well," said I, "let's have them, for I'm mighty tired." "Said he, "They will cost you $3 a day as long as you occupy them."

Said I, "What kind of a swindle is this, I'd like to know?" and pulled out the advertisement and showed it to him. He said it was no swindle. "The agent at Syracuse was at fault for not giving you the sleeping-car tickets. You will have to pay me three dollars a day for the time you occupy them, and the last day I give you a draw-back check, which you will present to the company's agent in San Francisco, and they will pay you back the money you pay me." "Yes," said I, "that is another one of the company's Christian acts." The nigger laughed, and said "'twas his orders, and he had got to obey orders." Well, it was no use in quarreling with the nigger, and we was disturbing the passengers that had gone to bed, so I paid him three dollars, and went to find our beds. He took us to the other end of the car, and gave us what he called section one. Clarissa said she preferred to sleep down stairs, so I had to go up chamber to get to my bed. Things was terrible awkward to me. I couldn't find a boot-jack, and I had to work a good while to get my new boots off, they was so darned stiff around the instep. When I got them off I threw them under Clarissa's bed, then I climbed up a short ladder, and got hold of a rod and sprained my back considerable, and then I had the darndest time getting my breeches off I ever had, and when I got them off I didn't know where to put 'em; finally I put them into bed with me, and held them in my arms so no one would get my pocketbook without waking me up. I got to bed after awhile, and was just getting into a drowse, when the feller that slept in the next room to me broke out in the most horrible fit of snoring I ever heard in my life, and kept it up for more than two hours; then I got to sleep. I woke up in the morning, and the nigger (I suppose it will sound better to say porter) called out "Buffalo." I got up, and had a worse time in getting my breeches on than I had in getting them off, and then I called for the ladder, but I couldn't get neither the nigger nor ladder, so I had to hang myself to the curtain-rod and fall down. Clarissa had got up and dressed before I came down stairs, and was in t'other end of the car, washing and combing. I hunted for my boots, found them all polished up so you could see your face in them ; I wondered who done it.

UNCLE BEN GOES UP CHAMBER TO BED.

Just then the porter came along and wanted to brush me off. When he got through, he said, "A quarter, if you please."

"What for?" said I.

"For shining them brogans," said he.

"Oh, yes, certainly; I forgot that," said I. "I haint got used to the city nor the customs of a sleeping-car yet," and handed him a quarter, with the remark, "I suppose I'll get this back from the

"MISTER, WONT YOU BUY A MORNING PAPER?"

company's agent at San Francisco?" "Certainly," said he. I then asked the porter (whom I began to reverence by this time as a partner of the president of the road) how much it would cost me to wash and wipe in that wash-room and look in that fine glass. "Oh," said he, "nothing; that is free." I breathed a sigh of relief, and said, "Young man of auburn complexion, that is one thing that the company's agents at San Francisco don't pay back, does it?" "What?"

said he. "Why," said I, "the amount required for washing and wiping and looking in the glass, nothing."

We had got into the depot at Buffalo, and came to a full stop. I had washed and wiped, and was ready for breakfast, and Clarissa had done the same. We felt as though we'd like to step out and look around Buffalo a little. I asked the porter how long we staid there, and he said twenty minutes. I asked him where we could get breakfast. He said we would have breakfast in the dining-car about half an hour after we left Buffalo; but if I was hungry, I could get a very nice lunch in the eating-house, on the right-hand side of the depot, and pointed it out to us. Clarissa said we had better eat our meals on the cars, as they was to be included in our tickets, and she kind of wanted to see how they managed to set a table on the cars, and cook and wash dishes, so I concluded not to go into the eating-house, as Clarissa had settled it.

It wasn't much satisfaction in trying to see Buffalo in twenty minutes; we only got a chance to go on one side of the depot and look out of the door a minute, when we would hear an engine-bell ring, and thinking it was our train starting, we would rush back to the train, only to find that it was some other engine going through the depot. Then we went on t'other side and looked out of the door a minute, and heard another bell ringing, and back we rushed to the train, only to find we was fooled again. We concluded we would walk up and down the platform, close to the train, so we wouldn't get left. A few minutes passed, when the conductor yelled out, "All aboard!" and we made a rush for the car, and obeyed the conductor's orders. I don't suppose I have got a very correct idea of Buffalo, although I can say, if any one asks me if I have been there, that I have.

While I was walking on the sidewalk outside the depot, a little boy with a pair of bright eyes and a dirty face, clothed in rags, came along with a lot of papers under his arm, and said, "Mister, won't you buy a morning paper?"

"How much be they." said l.

"Five cents," he replied.

I didn't care for the paper, altnough Clarissa said she would like one, but I thought that there was a bright, honest little boy, no doubt earning what he could to take care of a poor, sick mother or crippled father, or perhaps both, and it was a Christian and neighborly act to help him, so I said, "Yes, I'll take one, and pulled out a two-dollar bill and gave him, and he counted back the change to me, one dollar and ninety-five cents. I gave him an extra five cents, and told him he was a nice little bub, and put the change in my vest pocket.

He seemed to be wonderfully pleased, while I thought to myself, "How much more blessed it is to give than to receive." The great mass of people don't exactly understand this giving business. If they are asked to give something to a charitable cause they are a long time pulling out their pocketbook, and when they get it out they make a horrible face, and feel as though they was about to have an arm amputated. Now, in such cases, what they give does 'em no good—in fact, it does them a positive injury, because they have violated the true principle of giving—they have, in fact, given nothing, but simply undergone the operation of squeezing. A gift should come from the heart, and when it does the reaction on the feelings of the giver is worth more than the amount of money handed to the applicant. He has a calm and peaceful mood onto him that seems to pat him on the back and say, "Good feller; you'll pass in."

I had this kind of feeling come all over me, first commencing at my toes and gradually creeping up over my visible person, ending on the topmost spire that towers aloft from the summit of veneration bump that surmounts my upper deck, when I gave that extra nickel to that honest little newsboy. And I thought to myself "Why can't folks, when they contribute anything, instead of acting so all-fired stingy about it, thereby shutting out the *Comforting angel of satisfaction*, give the amount of their donation with a free and pleasant spirit, and have that same happyfying feeling I have referred to, roost upon their crowning spires?"

The widow's mite was a blessing to her, not on account of the

"BREAKFAST IS NOW READY IN THE DINING CAR FORWARD."

large amount of property it represented, but the true spirit that prompted the gift.

We had been gone about twenty miles from Buffalo, when a big, fat nigger, with a white roundabout and apron, hollowing like a boss at a barn-raising, "Breakfast is now ready in the dining-car, forward!"

CHAPTER XVI.

WE followed the other passengers (who seemed to be better posted than we was) into the dining-car. They give us a seat, and handed me a tract to read. I handed it to Clarissa, and told her I was too hungry to read tracts—I'd read it after breakfast. The waiter said it wasn't a tract, but a bill of fare for me to order my breakfast from.

"Oh!" said I, " I didn't know that. Well, never mind that now; Clarissa can get her breakfast out of it if she wants to, but you can just bring me a good, square breakfast. Any good, common victuals, such as you use every day, will do me. I don't want you to put yourselves out on my account; only bring me enough of it, for I am pretty hungry." Clarissa read every word of her bill of fare, and then said she didn't exactly understand all of it, but she would take "beefsteak with toadstools, and some chicken *a la* fricka with cranberry sass, and some—some—some pancakes *a la*—say! waiter, what is that other word?" "Francaise; it means French style." "Oh, yes," said Clarissa, "I know what it means, but my eyesight is a little poor, and I couldn't quite make out the word; well, I'll take some of them, and some of that stuff there (pointing the waiter to another word that her eyesight was too poor to make out), and some coffee, and I guess that's all," and the waiter started for the other end of the car, where they do the cooking.

After he had gone, I said to Clarissa, "What did you pretend to that nigger you understood that stuff you read, when you didn't know what it meant any more than I know Greek?"

"Well, Benjamin," said she, "what is the use of my confessing I was ignorant to that waiter, when I could just as well lay it onto my eyes as not?"

"Well, in the first place, that is *shamming* in a small way, and you despise that kind of business as much as I do, and then you don't fool the nigger a mite, for he knows you don't know anything about French, and it brings you down even in the estimation of the nigger, for he'll know you are pretending to know something you don't know."

The car was beautiful inside; looking-glasses all around, everything nice. While they was getting our breakfast ready, the landlord of the car handed us a plate of grapes and oranges, and they was first-rate. Pretty soon the waiter came with our breakfast. Clarissa got her bill of fare breakfast, and I got a good, square breakfast. Mine was better than her'n, for there was more of it. I got some good pancakes, and I'll be blamed if I could see any difference between them and her *pancakes a la Francaise*.

We had a mighty good breakfast, and told the landlord he set a good table, and started to go back to our car, when he said I hadn't paid for my breakfast. I told him I guessed I had; I pulled out my tickets and showed them to him, and then I pulled out the advertisement of the company, and showed it to him.

He smiled, and said that the company would no doubt do as they agreed to, but that the dining-car was run by an independent company, and not by the excursion company; that I had no ticket among those I bought in Syracuse that entitled us to meals; that I would have to pay him for what meals I got, and he would give me draw-back checks for each meal paid for, and when I got to San Francisco I could present them at the company's office there and have the money all refunded.

"Yes, just so," said I; "this is another Christian act. Well, here is your money," at the same time getting the change out of my vest pocket that the poor little newsboy gave me in Buffalo. "How much is it?" said I.

He said it was seventy-five cents apiece.

"Whew!" said I, "it's a good breakfast, but it's a dumb big price for it." I handed him the change—a one-dollar piece and a fifty-cent piece. He examined them closely, and then threw them on the table, and handed them back to me, saying,

"Those are both counterfeit, sir—good for nothing."

I was perfectly dumbfounded, and explained to the landlord how I got them. He said he had no doubt of the truth of my statement; that it was an everyday occurrence at that depot. I asked him if they didn't have policemen at the depot in Buffalo.

"Oh yes," he said.

"Well, then," said I, "why don't they arrest them little villains?"

"Because," said he, "they get part of the swag."

I paid him good money for our breakfast, and went to our car. When I get back to Buffalo I am going to have that little scamp arrested, if it takes me a week. I wouldn't be a bit surprised if he wasn't some relative of Jim Teeters'.

When we got back to our car they had got the beds all put out of sight somewhere, but I couldn't see where they went to, and the car looked fine. We got nicely seated and Clarissa had adjusted her gold-bowed specs, preparatory to reading that one-month-old paper I bought of that little villain, when an old gentleman sitting in the seat right in front of us turned round, and with a voice that sounded like wind blowing through an ivory fine-comb put up against a hole in a window-glass, said,—

"Good-morning; it's a fine day. Are you going very far out this way?"

I replied that we intended to go as far as the lay of the land and the contingent fund would allow us. In other words, the Pacific Ocean was our present boundary, geographically speaking, and a reasonable purse our financial limit; and unless the Ketchum, Holdem & Skinem Company didn't rob us of every dollar I had, that me and wife Clarissa (pointing to her at the same time), intend to pillow our heads on the sunny coast of the great Pacific, and see if our dreams will be like the old forty-niners; that we are engaged in the occupation of picking gold dollars off the bushes, and loading them into ships to be transported back to the land of their nativity.

"Well, I am glad you are going out there, for that's just where I am going, too," said he.

"I supposed so," I replied, "and I suppose all the passengers on this train are bound for the same place—California."

The old gentleman had a long, narrow, rounding face, large, gray eyes, a large, crooked nose, the end of which swelled out like

THE OLD INQUISITOR.

a feeding-bottle, and was ornamented on the left side with a huge seed-wart. His complexion was between a carroty and a strawberry color, and his face was surrounded by a deep fringe of white whiskers, Horace Greeley style. He skewed himself around in the seat, so he could get a good look at us, and opened out the following conversation:

"I've got a son and two sons-in-law living out in that country, and I haint seen 'em for a long time, and when I found out this excursion was going to take folks through to California so cheap, I thought I'd better go out and see the chidren once more before I died. You see, I'm getting pretty well along in years; I'll be seventy-seven years old if I live to see a year from the 31st of next May. I live in Vermont, up in Windham County, and I was down to Albany visiting my wife's brother, when I heard of this excursion, and concluded I'd go, so I wrote up home to my son Thomas, who is running my farm, to sell off half a dozen cows and an old kicking mare I have been wanting to sell for a good while, and send me the money, as I was going to California.

"I got the money last Saturday, and now I'm on the way there, but I'll be goll-darned if I can see through this scheme of charging us a hundred dollars extra for our tickets, and then give us a drawback check, can you?"

I said I didn't at first, but the agent at Syracuse explained it to me, and under his explanation (which I gave to the old gentleman) I thought it was a Christian act; however, since we got aboard of this train I have seriously doubted the Christian motive, and I am inclined to think it is a sort of "an s. s. arrangement."

"'An s. s. arrangement?'" said he. "What is that?"

I told him it was a "soft snap" for the K., H. & S. Company; however, we could tell better when we got through.

I found we had got a very inquisitive neighbor. In two straight hours he had told us his entire family history and given us the line of his pedigree as far back as he could get, and then he began a series of questions with a view to investigating my record and etcetera, but I declined to be put into the witness box. Clarissa got him engaged in a argument on the temperance question. Somehow or other she thought she could see behind that red face and bottle nose a whole distillery, and she just fired shot after shot of good sound temperance logic at him, and got the best of him every time, and completely downed him. He took his little satchel and went into the men's wash-room end of the car, and in a few minutes returned, and his breath smelled as though he had opened a door to a country tavern. Across the aisle, at the other end of the car, four gentlemen had got a table put up between them and was playing cards. They seemed to enjoy themselves very much, and seemed to be pretty smart men. I always supposed that no one but gamblers played cards, but I have learned in the few days I have been away from home that real good ladies and gentlemen play cards for amusement. Clarissa's cousins, the Buzzbees, at Syracuse played cards, and they belong to the Methodist Church. I told Clarissa I was going to learn to play, and then I would learn her how to play, and we could have considerable sport evenings and other times when we hadn't got anything else to do. Clarissa said she hadn't a mite of objection to my learning to play cards if I wanted to, but as for her, she hadn't got any time to fool with cards, for she had more reading on hand than she could manage to attend to.

I went over where they was playing and said "Gentlemen, I don't want to be impolite, but I would kinder like to watch you play, if you have no objection."

"Certainly not," they responded; and one of them very politely offered me his hand and place in the game.

I thanked him, and told him that I didn't know one card from another, and never tried to play any game with them. That my name was Benjamin Morgan, from Morganville, Blank County, State of New York; that I never traveled any; never was forty miles away from home before this trip in all my life; that me and my wife had been tolerable saving in our lives, and had got quite a little ahead and thought we would take a trip to California and around the country some.

I had made up my mind to learn what I could, and I was going to learn how to play cards so we could have a little amusement to home with the children and neighbors.

One of the gentlemen, a very nice-looking fellow, and dressed real nice and who I judged must be pretty well off, as he had an elegant gold watch and chain, says:

"Here Uncle Benjamin."

"That's right! that's right!" said I. "Where did you ever see me before? I don't remember of ever meeting you before."

He replied that he had never met me before, and wanted to know why I thought he had.

"'Cause," said I, "every one calls me *Uncle Ben* at home, and I didn't know how you knew my name was Uncle."

"Oh," says he, "that's nothing. Whenever I meet a man that I can see at the first glance is an *honest* man, *plain*, *frank* and *generous*, *unsuspecting*, *unassuming*, and that can't play the part of a hypocrite because he is so honest by nature that he thoroughly despises hypocrisy, I always call him *Uncle*. I do so as a compliment, and that brings him into the closest relationship to me that it is possible, without including him in the direct family line. And as I saw by the first glance that you were such a noble, true man, I could not resist the desire to call you *Uncle*. I hope you are not offended?"

"No sir," I replied, "not at all. I thank you for the compliment."

"Well, then, Uncle Benjamin, I have no doubt you are on your way, like all the rest of us, to California?"

I informed him that that was my destiny.

"Well, it's a long trip, and we might as well all get acquainted and enjoy ourselves."

I told him I fully acquarificated in his views of the situation.

"Now," says he, "you just sit down here in my place and I'll learn you how to play." So I sat down in his seat. "Mr. Morgan," said he, "my name is Richard Smooth; I am from Providence." "Is that so?" said I, and I jumped up and clasped his hand in a most cordial manner, and then I examined his hand very closely. Said he, "Uncle Benjamin, what do you find so peculiar about my hand?" "Nothin' in particular, only I've heard George Waddles and the other Methodists down in our village say so much about the hand of Providence. If anybody dies around there, the '*hand* of Providence' has something to do with it. If anybody prospers, the '*hand of Providence*' has blessed the prosperous party, and I have always had a strong desire to see the '*hand of Providence*,' but of all places I should look for it, the last place would be on an excursion train, managed and operated by the Holdem, Ketchem and Skinem Company, but here I've found it, and now I hold in my hand the '*hand of*

THE "HAND OF PROVIDENCE."

Providence.' It looks just like anybody's hand, but it's awful *smooth* and soft."

"Uncle Benjamin," he said, "don't get the wrong impression. The *hand of Providence* the Methodists down in your village refer to belongs to another party entirely; he is from another Providence. I'm from Providence, Rhode Island. The party your Methodist friends refer to, has never even visited the city I am from."

You can imagine my great disappointment in having all those

bright fancies and delights that was for the moment dancing in my heart, and holding high carnival within its realm, suddenly dashed to pieces by the real owner of that section of human anatomy I was at that moment clinging to. I felt myself relax into a withering and lifeless piece of clay. However, I regained my usual calm habit in a few minutes, when I asked his pardon for my ignorance, and assured him I meant all right. He then introduced me to the other gentlemen, as Dr. Montee, of New York City, Thomas Three, of Lowell, Massachusetts, nephew of B. B., and Jackson Kard, of Montreal, Canada, a very successful speculator. Who would ever have dreamed that the plain, homespun Benjamin Morgan, of Morganville, Blank County, New York, who less than a week ago was stripping ten cows and a heifer every night and morning, was now sitting in a elegant palace car in company with four highly educated and polished gentlemen from different States and nations, Messrs. Smooth, Three, Kard and Montee, and the gentleman from Providence trying to learn me the mysterious and highly interesting art of playing cards. He proceeded to inform me that the game they was playing at that time, was *Seven-up*, or what used to be called Old Sledge. "Now, uncle Benjamin, they will deal off six cards apiece and as you are the first player at the left hand of the dealer, you have the privilege of begging, if the trump don't suit you, or standing your hand if it does suit you. Well, there! don't you see he has turned a spade; now spades are trumps, and you have got a good hand; there is the ace, the king, the jack and deuce; you want to stand your hand; you will make four times on that hand;" and so he went on, trying to learn me the game, but I couldn't get a mite of head or tail to it. "I am too stupid to ever learn this game," said I, "and I am just spoiling the game for the rest of you, and I'll get up." "No, no! Uncle Benjamin, you are doing splendid. I never saw a beginner do so well; did you, boys?" said Mr. Smooth, and all joined in the chorus, "No, never. He has beaten us this game, already." And I was just big enough fool to keep on trying to learn. But the more I tried, the more I became disgusted with it, and Dr. Montee said, if Mr. Morgan didn't care to play any longer they ought not to insist. "Oh! certainly not," they all responded, and we quit just as the same nigger come through the car, hollering, "Dinner is now ready in the dining car, forward," I took Clarissa to dinner and I told her all about these nice gentlemen, and she shook her head and said, " Benjamin, you had better let them men alone; there is something, I don't know what it is, but something or other tells me that they don't mean you any good, and I'd advise you to have nothing to do with them."

CHAPTER XVII.

WE had a fine dinner, and as I had to pay seventy-five cents, I concluded I'd eat all I could at dinner, then I wouldn't get any supper, and in that way I would save seventy-five cents. Things went on the usual way; we had a splendid dinner. I tried the bill of fare arrangements, but I confess I don't like that way of getting my victuals. I'd rather have 'em bring me the best they have got in the house, without a bill of fare, than to spend twenty minutes or half an hour in trying to find the best they've got, and then run a risk of getting fooled on a good share of it that I can't fully understand. I may get used to it before we get home.

While we was eating dinner, Clarissa and I talked together considerable, and she kept an eye on those four new acquaintances of mine. When we went back to our car, she said she believed them fellows was sharpers.

"Oh! no," says I, "they are all fine gentlemen. That fellow there, sitting next to the window, with that large red moustache, is Dr. Montee of New York City, and that gentleman with a gray moustache and keen, black eye, sitting in the same seat with the Doctor, is Judge Three, of Lowell, Massachusetts, and that fellow with his back to us, is Jackson Kard, from Montreal, Canada."

Just at this moment Mr. Smooth approached me, saying,—

"Uncle Benjamin, wouldn't you like to join us in a social game of cards? I'll learn you a new game."

Says I, "Mr. Smooth, let me make you acquainted with my wife, Clarissa."

Mr. Smooth was very polite, and done his level best to make himself agreeable to Clarissa, but she acted very cold, almost frigid. I was ashamed of her, but Mr. Smooth didn't seem to mind it a particle. He settled down into the seat in front of us, and began talking to that wife of mine just as if he had known her forever, and finally he got her interested in talking history. He seemed to know something of everything; he was a regular walking, talking and acting encyclopedia.

While Mr. Smooth was entertaining Clarissa, Dr. Montee mo-

"SHE ACTED VERY COLD, ALMOST FRIGID."

tioned with his hand for me to come over to his seat. I done so, and the Doctor become very interesting to me. He was telling about his travels in this, that and the other country. Presently Mr. Smooth returned to his friends and said,—

"Mr. Morgan, wouldn't you like to learn another game of cards? We can learn you a very simple game, the easiest learned of any game with cards. It is called 'Poker,'" and he went on to explain it all to me. He showed me how four aces could beat anything, and how four kings could beat four queens, and four queens could beat four jacks and so on, and that three of a kind could beat two pair, and a flush could beat threes, and a full hand could beat a flush, etc., etc. I thought I could see into that right away. After I thought I could understand it pretty well, Jackson Kard proposed that we try our luck on a few games.

"Well," said I, "if Mr. Smooth will stand by and assist me, I don't mind if I try a few games."

It was my turn to deal. I dealt 'em all round. Judge Three, my left hand neighbor, said:

"I'll anty one dollar, call two dollars."

Said I, "What do you mean about bringing your aunt into this game for one, two or any number of dollars? What has she got to do with this game any way?" I begun to feel a little indignant, but Mr. Smooth explained it all to me so I understood it all right.

After they all got around and called for what new cards they wanted to fill their hands with, I didn't bet anything, for I didn't have a very good hand, but when the other fellows dealt I got first rate good hands, and I won several small bets of five or ten or fifteen dollars, and once or twice I lost a little. Pretty soon, when Dr. Montee was dealing, he dealt me four aces and a queen. When Mr. Smooth saw my hand, he whispered to me that I had the best hand it was possible to get, and to just make a heavy bet, for I would surely win. So I said, "I'd bet $100." Dr. Montee said, "I'll see you and raise you fifty." Smooth whispered to me to see him and raise him fifty more, that would be $200. I done as Smooth thought best, as he was my assistant. I thought if I could win a couple of hundred dollars from some fellows that was determined to lose it any way, it would kinder make me even in case the H., K. & S. Company's agent in San Francisco should try to beat me, so I said, "I would raise the Doctor fifty more." The Doctor regretted he could not see me at $200, as $150 was all the change he had. Most of his money was in drafts on the Chemical Bank of New York. He always considers it safer to carry his money when taking long trips like this, in drafts, which he could get cashed at any time at any of the banks.

He produced one of his drafts; it was for five hundred dollars. He said, "Mr. Morgan, if you have got that amount of currency about you, and will cash it for me, I'll meet you in your bet on $200." I thought it over, I thought it was just the same as money, and I was sure to win his $200. So I said, "Gentlemen, I don't know any-

"BENJAMIN MORGAN, WHAT ARE YOU DOING HERE?"

thing about it, whether the bank is good or not." "Oh, yes," they all responded, "that is the best bank in New York City. If you wish to accommodate the Doctor, we will indorse the draft with him." So I said, "Well, gentlemen, you indorse the draft and I'll give you the money for it."

Just at that moment Clarissa (who had been watching us) came up where we was, and in a searching manner and a Major-General tone of voice, said: "Benjamin Morgan, what are you doing here? What are you pulling your money out here in this manner for?"

I explained to her what had been done, and what was about to be did. She said:

"Well, you put your money in your pocket, and let that piece of paper alone, and let these men alone, and come along with me to our seat."

I said, "Gentlemen, I am sorry to disappoint you, and sorry I couldn't play this hand out, for you can all see I would have won it (at the same time showing my hand by throwing it on the table), but when my wife Clarissa speaks in that manner, it settles it beyond any question, and all further debate is unnecessary."

I left 'em and went to my seat with my garden angel, as she proved to be on this as on former occasions. She told me after we was seated in our own bedroom end of the car, that them fellows was all regular gamblers and blacklegs, and that Smooth was the leader of the gang, that the draft I was about to give them five hundred dollars for was worthless, altogether likely a forgery, and by my getting my money out before them exposed what I had, and if they had got the $500 they would get the rest before they left me. "Now, you mark my word they'll get that money from you yet, unless you keep away from 'em."

I told her I wouldn't play cards with 'em any more, and I'd be dumbed if I'd play another card if that was the kind of company it got me into, but I couldn't believe them fellows was rascals.

I had, in a long pocketbook that I carried in the inside pocket of my coat, $1,150. I knew just the amount, as I counted it all over at Buzzbee's house in Syracuse, when I was putting on my breeches. I got one gallus on, and just happened to think that I'd better fix my money and know just how much I had; and I didn't wait to hitch up 'tother gallus, but counted over and put $1,150 in this book. It was a new one that I bought the day before in a store on Salina street. My old one was about wore out and not much account, and I kept $300 in my old book that I carried in my breeches pocket.

While Clarissa was talking to me she noticed that there was a button coming off my new coat and a place under the sleeve where it was ripped about three inches. So she says:

"Benjamin, if you'll take off your coat I'll mend that before it gets so dark I can't see." She got a spool of thread and a thimble out of her pocket while I pulled off my coat.

"Oh say, Benjamin," said she, "did you buy that paper of

"I DIDN'T WAIT TO HITCH UP T'OTHER GALLUS."

needles for me that I asked you to in Syracuse? I forgot to ask you for 'em before."

"Yes," said I, "here they be, I think," and I pulled out my old pocketbook and handed it to her, and said I put them there. I thought I'd go and wash while she was fixing my coat, as it was pretty nigh supper time.

When I had finished my toilet operations and returned to my seat, Clarissa had the coat all mended and held it up for me to put on, and gave me the pocketbook, which I shoved down my right hand breeches pocket, where I always carry it.

We was now approaching Cleveland. Mr. Smooth came to me and in a very polite way asked me if I wouldn't like to take a walk around the depot a few minutes, as the train would remain there twenty or thirty minutes. I felt kind o' tired of being boxed up in that car all day, and just wanted a chance to get out a little while, and said, "If Clarissa is willing, I'll go along with you." Clarissa said she didn't care, but she wanted me to remember what she told me. "All right," I told her.

We had at this time arrived in the depot, and I joined company with the four fine gentlemen for a walk around the building. Pretty soon we saw a big crowd around the ticket window, and some one was talking terrible loud, and it looked as if there was going to be a big fight. All the gentlemen said, "Let's hurry up and see the fun." So I rushed up with the rest of them, and in less than two minutes I was jammed right into the middle of the crowd. I couldn't get out, for the crowd kept getting bigger and bigger every minute. My friends and I got scattered, and when I got out of that crowd our conductor was hollering, "*All Aboard!*" I made quick time for the train and got on the steps just as the train was moving. There stood Clarissa on the platform, looking pale and trembling. I asked her what was the matter.

She said, "Oh, Benjamin, I have been so anxious for your safety that I'm all unstrung. I watched you from the moment you left the car until I lost sight of you in that horrible crowd. I was so afraid something would happen to you, or you'd get left!"

"Well, I'll be dumbed if I wasn't afraid I'd get left. I never was caught in such a jam as that before, and I never intend to be again."

Says she, "Where are your friends?"

"Goll dumb it," said I, "I'll bet a cent they are right in that crowd now and can't get out. Now that's too darned bad." I hollered to the conductor and asked him if he wouldn't stop the train and back up to the depot—that those four gentlemen was left.

Said he, "Do you mean those four fellows you was playin' cards with?"

"Yes," said I.

"Oh, well, don't worry about them; they didn't intend to go any further. Their tickets was for Cleveland."

"Well, but they told me they was on their way to California, and was glad I was going along so they could have my company."

"ALL ABOARD!"

"Well, sir, that gang have been on their way to California for the last half dozen years, but they never get any nearer California than Chicago, nor much further from that golden State than Buffalo. I have no doubt they was glad of your company; they are quite a lonesome class of fellows—always trying to make new acquaintances. Generally they pick farmers. The more honest the farmers seem to be, the more readily do they select them for acquaintance."

"Well, I'd like to know how they can tell farmers from anybody else on the train?"

The conductor smiled and said: "That is a puzzler. I can't exactly explain the art, but somehow or other anybody that has traveled much can pick a farmer out on a train of cars every time. I don't know how it's done, unless it's because they pick the honest looking ones. But my friend, I haven't time to talk with you any longer, as I have a heavy train to look after. You may discover why those fine gentlemen didn't get on again."

Supper was called for the dining car, and although I thought I would make a big dinner do for supper also, I was just as hungry as if I hadn't had dinner. So we went to supper. We gave our orders for supper, and while the waiter was gone Clarissa and I talked about what had happened, and I asked her if she could understand it, She replied with an expression of pity behind a veil of sarcasm :

"Benjamin, I admire your honesty, but I am getting pretty tired of your simplicity. I knew you was a honest and well-meaning man when I married you, and I thought in time you might learn something, and that after a while I might be proud of you. Sometimes I think I am, and sometimes I *know* I aint. Ever since we left Syracuse you have acted foolisher and foolisher. I thought I'd let you go and have your own way, and would have done so had I not seen you in the act of giving away our money, and also doing still worse, trying to get their money from them just because they calculated wrong on some cards. Then I thought it was the duty a wife owed to her weaker half to save him from loss of money, and from the temptation the Devil always holds out, Money! Money! to take you away from them.

"I don't think it would take much to pick you out, the way you have been acting to-day. Now, I want you to steady down and act like a man becoming one of your years." The waiter had already spread a delicious supper before us; we had supplied the cravings of our appetite and arose from the table. I put my hand into my right hand breeches pocket, to get my money to pay for our supper, and my pocketbook was gone. I felt in t'other breeches pocket but it wasn't there, then I felt for my long pocketbook in my coat pocket and it was gone. I felt in every pocket I had, but not a sign of either pocketbook.

"Clarissa," said I, in great excitement, "I've been robbed! I've been stolen! I've been waylaid! I've been murdered! No, no, not murdered, but everything else; what shall I do? I haven't got a dollar, nor a ticket of any kind, nor a drawback check of any kind; they were all in them two pocketbooks," and trembling like a poplar leaf in a September gale I sank into a seat and was about to faint away, when the conductor came along and inquired what was the matter. They told him, and he said he thought I'd find out why the four fine gentlemen didn't get on again at Cleveland. That made me a little mad, and I spunked up some. Clarissa paid for the supper out of some of her private money. I told the conductor I didn't know what to do, for my tickets was gone, and I hadn't got a dollar to get back with. The conductor said he would carry us through to Chicago any way, and then I could telegraph home for money.

We went back to our car; Clarissa didn't seem to worry a mite, but seemed to enjoy my discomfort. I said to her that we would have to get back home, some way, from Chicago. She plainly said in a cold and unsympathizing voice, that if I wanted to go back to Morganville and be the laughing stock of that whole country I could go, but she wouldn't go one step back until she had pillowed her head in California and dreamt her dream. I asked her if she meant what she said. She informed me in a very decided manner that she did; when I saw there was no room for doubt, I asked her how she expected to get through? She said she knew several rich folks in Chicago, and she intended to stop there two or three weeks and visit, and she would borrow enough from them to take her through

"NOT A SIGN OF EITHER POCKET BOOK."

if necessary. I asked her if she thought she could borrow enough to get me through too. She said she didn't suppose she could. I was now on the saw-tooth edge of despair, and felt as if some one was liable any minute to move the edge and cut me into fragments. I told Clarissa I didn't know where to sleep to-night as I hadn't got enough to pay for my lodging nor hers. She said it was good enough for me, it might learn me the lesson she give me in Syracuse, viz., "to keep my mouth shut and eyes wide open, and know where my pocketbook was. Them fellows played you for a S. S. and took you in." She kept on torturing my half-crazed brain with such cold remarks, and even went so far as to ask me if I didn't want to exchange photographs with my highly educated friends, Smooth, Three, Kard and Montee, and take their address. I told her that I should be highly pleased just at the present time to have their photographs and address; I thought I could make good use of them.

She said she had got money enough to pay for our beds, and we would be in Chicago in the morning, and for me to go up stairs to bed and go to sleep, and perhaps in the morning I'd know something. I always knew her superiority over me in point of intellect and perception, but never before did I have that complete feeling that she was the *master* and I the *under dog*. I went to bed according to her orders, but I didn't go to sleep according to her orders. I never slept a wink all night. The whole experience of the day and evening passed before me like a great panorama; there it was all painted out; the car, the old inquisitor, the four gentlemen, the slick Mr. Smooth and the mistaken "hand of Providence," the game of seven up, the simple but very interesting game of poker, the bets, the hand of four aces and a queen, the bet of $100, the raise of fifty, my raise back, the draft for five hundred dollars, Clarissa's timely interference, the exposure of my money, the invitation to walk in the Cleveland depot, the walk, the crowd, the horrible jam I was in, the close connection made with the moving train, the interview with the conductor, the episode at the supper table, Clarissa as my master and I obeying her orders, and now tumbling and rolling on an attic bed trying to do what it was impossible for me to do, sleep. All this moved by me under the glare of a strong electric light, in less time than it takes to tell it, and then passed backward under a red light, then back again under a green light, and again it rolled by under a blue light, when I spoke out so loud as to wake Clarissa up and said, "Damn that panorama."

Clarissa spoke up and said, "Benjamin, you let the panorama alone and go to sleep; it ain't a panorama, any way; it's my curtain you are shoving one way and another."

After what seemed to me a month's time had elapsed, daylight broke the horrid, dismal night, and I climbed down and washed up. As I finished, we was pulling into Chicago. It seemed to me we was over an hour from the time we got to where the houses was thick till we got into the depot. In the frenzied condition of my mind, I wrote the following ode to myself. I wrote it on the starched part of my shirt bosom:

> "Benjamin Morgan is a big fool,
> To allow himself to be a tool
> For gamblers and thieves, himself to plunder;
> Better always to have staid at hum,
> Than to go away on such a bum.'

CHAPTER XVIII.

WE had left the train and was standing in the great depot of the great Lake Shore & Rock Island Railroad, in the very heart of the great city of Chicago. Like the babes in the woods, we didn't exactly know which way to go, and I didn't care much which way I went. All I wanted just then, was to go home and stay there, and let them travel and see the world that wanted to. For my part, I had had enough of it.

Of course we couldn't stay there. So Clarissa said we'd go to the Palmer House. She had read a great deal about it, and she always wanted to see it, and we would stay there one day, and she would inquire of Mr. Palmer where her friends lived, and then we'd hunt them up. So we followed the crowd along to the door on the right hand side, where we saw a policeman, or we supposed he was, as he was dressed in uniformity. We asked him if he could show us where the Palmer House was. He told us to take the second bus (pointing to it), and it would take us there. We got into the bus, but before they would take us a foot, we had to pay the fellow fifty cents apiece. Then the fellow started up and drove like fury up one street and down another, and around several more, and finally pulled up in front of a monstrous great big building, and said it was the Palmer House. I never saw such a big building before in my life.

There was a nigger standing at the door of the bus to take our things; he had got Clarissa's umbrella and reticule and was just taking my valise, when I happened to think it wasn't locked, so I said, "Look here, Mr. African, please wait a minute, I guess I'll take care of that valise myself. He politely handed it to me and trotted along ahead of us.

I was looking up at the top of the portico where we was, seeing how awful pretty it was, and didn't notice the steps until I tumbled over the bottom one and fell my whole length on the entry floor.

I got up spry and felt ashamed enough. Clarissa said, "Ben-

"BENJAMIN, WHAT IS THE MATTER WITH YOU?"

jamin, what is the matter with you? Why don't you look where you are stepping?"

We went along into the end of the hall where the nigger give Clarissa a seat, and told me to go out into the office with him. She set down there while I went out around a big stairway into a monstrous great big room, and up to a marble counter, behind which stood a smart looking young man with a pen in his hand, which he handed me, and shoved a book in front of me.

I said, " Good-morning, Mr. Palmer. I don't want your pen; I merely come in to ask you if it would be convenient for you to keep me and my wife a day or two, or until she found some of her friends here." " Oh, certainly," he replied, " but you take this pen and register your names, so that we can assign you rooms."

I shook my head noways, and said I'd go and see my wife first before I put my name on the book. I went back where she was and told her how that it would be convenient for them to keep us, but that they wanted me to sign a big book, and I thought best to ask her opinion before signing.

She said she would go with me and see what it was. So she went with me back to the counter in the office, and looked at the book. Then the smart looking young man, with a warm hearted smile, explained to Clarissa the object of our signing the book, and she said she guessed 'twas all right. So I wrote our names down, " Benjamin Morgan and Clarissa, Morganville, N. Y." The young man read the names over and said, " Mr. Morgan, this is your wife, I suppose?" " You supposed right, the first time," said I, " I don't intend to go around the country with anybody else's wife, so long as I've got a good one of my own." He smiled and put down some figures behind my name, rung a bell on the counter, got a key out of a lot of boxes and handed it to a boy and said, "Show Mr. and Mrs. Morgan up to room 984."

The boy started, saying, " Right this way, please," and took us right back to where Clarissa was sitting, and presently a little house came sliding down a big hole in the wall, a door slid open, and a lot of folks walked out, then a lot walked in, and the boy told us to walk in, which we did. Then the little door was slid shut, and our room begun to go up. We passed story after story, and I was a little uneasy, and I said to the nigger that had his hand on a rope, " When did you advertise this balloon ascension? I hadn't heard a word of it before. We was lucky to be here in time to go up in it. Where do you suppose the dumb thing will land? I don't care much where, only I aint been to breakfast, and I don't want to have to walk too far before I get something to eat."

By this time it had reached the ninth floor, and the nigger laughed, and said the balloon had landed, and we could get off. The door slid open, and the little boy with our things in his hand led us down a long hall and turned to the left, and went down another long hall an awful ways, then turned to the left again, and went halfway down that hall and took us into a large room on the right-hand side.

Said I, "Young boy, are we still in Chicago, or have we left the city?"

"Yes, sir," said he, "you are still in Chicago, and still in the Palmer House; you have not left the Palmer House since you first entered it."

"Said I, "Young boy, I don't want to be imposed upon; I don't want you to lie to me; I can't believe that we are in the same tavern we first came into."

The boy pointed to a card that was tacked on the door, and said, "Read that, if you think I am lying."

We read it. It said, "Rules and Regulations of the Palmer House." I was satisfied the boy was truthful, and he was about to leave, when I asked him how we could find our way out to the office, and where the dining-room was, and when breakfast would be ready?

He told us breakfast was on now, and we could eat any time we wanted to. He showed us a little white button in the wall near the door, and told us when we was ready for breakfast to press on that little button, and a waiter would come to show us wherever we wanted to go, and we shut the door and looked around the room. It was awful nice, but when we looked out of the window all we could see was the roofs of houses, and high, smoking chimneys; as far as we could see, it was chimneys, roofs, and steeples.

I set down while Clarissa done up her hair and changed her

dress. I was blue as indigo. Clarissa could see by my dejected looks that I was feeling dreadful, and that unless I had a change in spirits my two feet would soon be meandering toward the graveyard. I have no doubt that my melancholical countenance aroused her pity, for she came and threw both her white arms around my neck, pushed my face up with her hands, and planted two lovely kisses right on my dry and withering lips, and she spoke in a most cunning and loving manner, and said, "Benjamin, don't feel so bad any longer; we'll go right on and finish our trip according to our original calculations, and will have a good time."

"Yes," said I, "that's well enough to talk, but where is the money coming from to do it?"

Says she, "I've got $1,150 right there in that book (handing to me my new long pocketbook, with the contents in it just as I had fixed it at Buzzbee's house), and here, rolled up in this paper, is 229 dollars and seventy-eight cents, and our tickets and drawback checks, the paper of needles, and all the other papers you had in your old pocketbook—every penny is saved."

I was completely dumbfounded. I jumped up and hugged her and kissed her forty times or less, then I wanted to know how it was.

"Well," says she, "I was well satisfied that them fellows was scoundrels and was bent on getting your money away from you. I wanted you to learn a lesson, and was satisfied you had as good an opportunity to learn it then as you would ever have. I watched every move they and you made, and when you drew out your new long pocketbook I knew it had gone far enough. I then interfered and got you away from them. I got your coat to mend so I could slip out the new long pocketbook and take care of it. I got your other pocketbook to get the needles, and while you was in the wash room I took all the contents out of it, rolled them up in this paper, took some old newspaper and stuffed the pocketbook as full as usual and when you come in from the wash room I handed you the pocketbook, which you put into your pocket, and of which you was robbed last night by those rascals. I hope the lesson is one you wont forget, and you will be more careful in the future who you get acquainted with, and who you trust."

I hugged and kissed her again, and said: "Clarissa, you dear old soul, you have always proved yourself to be my garden angel, and this is the strongest proof I have ever had of it. I know you are garden and garden and garden me continually, and no one on earth or in heaven ever had a more gardener angel than you have

PALMER HOUSE.

proved to be. And now, Clarissa, I have to confess my complete inability to take care of money. I confessed it to you after I got swindled in the hog business, and now I confess it again, and ask as a favor that you please take all the money and take care of it. Just give me each morning what amount you think I ought to have, and keep me from being swindled and robbed."

She said she would, and she counted out $8 and said I had better take that much as I would probably need considerable in going round the city.

My countenance underwent a change from indigo blue to the hottest kind of red in less than five minutes. I could have danced a hornpipe if I'd a knowed how, and had Lank Stevens to fiddle and call off for me. Our joy having become permanently established over our sorrow, and our toilet being completed, I pushed the button, and presently a waiter boy come and I asked him to show us to our breakfast room. He done so, bidding us to lock our room and take the key to the office if we went out, so it wouldn't get lost.

We went back the same way we come until we got to what I thought was a balloon, but which they told me was an elevator. We stepped inside the *ele* and slid down just as nice as butter in August till we got to the parlor floor, when the waiter led the way and we followed around through a magnificent hall, the floors of which was covered with thick velvet, the walls most beautifully painted in artistic designs, solid marble panel work on the sides, elegant massive fireplaces, and the largest looking glasses I ever saw, and on the side of the hall opened a number of elegant parlors, of which we only caught glimpses while on our way to the dining hall. We were now ushered into the dining hall by a portly and fine specimen of the African race. He was dressed in the very height of fashion; white vest and claw-hammer broadcloth coat, white gloves. He was very polite, and gave us choice seats at the head of a great square table. Presently another gentleman from Africa, with Methodist minister's clothes on, handed us a bill of fare. I was so busy looking at that room, the wonderful paintings overhead, and the great marble floor, and tremendous big looking glasses, that I didn't pay any attention to the bill of fare until the waiter whispered in my ear:

"Say, Clover, what are hogs worth?"

Says I, "I sold mine to Jim Teeters for 3¼ cents, but the

dumb scamp cheated me, for they are worth 4 cents. But my name aint Clover. You're wrong. My name is Benjamin Morgan, from Morganville, Blank County, New York. How the deuce did you know I was a farmer?"

The nigger laughed, and said, "By your honest countenance. But hadn't you better order your breakfast?"

"Excuse me," said I. "Yes, just bring me a good hot breakfast—anything you have a mind to, only have enough of it."

He left and I showed Clarissa all the pretty pictures and things I saw, pointing out with my fork the most interesting points I discovered. The waiter returned in about half an hour with our breakfast, and my, it was good enough for a Vanderbilt or the Queen of England to set down to. Such a beefsteak I never tasted before.

I asked him if Mrs. Palmer done the cooking in that house? He said, "No." "Well," said I, "I didn't ask to be impudent, but whoever cooked this breakfast is a dumb fine cook, and could get two dollars a week any minute in our parts. I'd give her that myself and send Mary off to school."

The nigger grinned all over, and said he'd tell the cook, and perhaps he'd like to get a place with me, and went out a laughing.

After breakfast we looked through the house some and went down to the office and inquired of the young man behind the counter where Clarissa's friends lived. She gave him the following names: "Carter Harrison, I used to go to school with him, and we used to have pretty good times, but he used to be dreadful big feeling; and Mr. Van Pelt, Mr. N. G. Rosster, Mr. A. W. Kinney, Dr. Butler, Mr. G. H. Olliver, Mr. Mucklevain, Miss Eudora Slick and Mr. Will Worthington."

"I can tell you where some of these live, and some I can't," said the smiling young man. "Mr. Carter Harrison has an office in the Court House, or rather the City Hall, but you'll be more apt to find him around on Clark Street. You step into Mike McDonald's and he can tell you where you can find him in case you don't see him in the City Hall. He and Mike and the Hankin Bros. are real good friends, and they generally know where each other are most of the time. Mr. Van Pelt, (let's see—George, do you know who Mr. Van Pelt is?" said he, addressing another clerk.

"Yes, he is one of the County Commissioners," was the reply.

"Oh, yes, I know now, he is the fellow that has been connected with a good many fat jobs, and things in connection with county and city affairs. Well, Mrs. Morgan, it will be very difficult to find him, as the papers say he moves about considerable, and manages during the year to live in every ward in the city. I don't know whether this is true or not, as the papers tell a good many funny things about him and Carter, and Mike McD., and Joe Mackin, and Gallagher and all those old chums. I don't pretend to believe one-quarter I read in the daily papers. They print a lot of stuff one day so as to have material to correct in the next issue, and that enables them to fill up their columns at half expense. Mr. N. G. Rosster is one of Chicago's most successful Board of Trade operators, and one of the wealthiest men in this city. He used to be a cattle dealer in a little town out West, but he made a very rapid march on to fortune. He has just completed one of the finest residences in this city. I think it is down on Indiana Avenue. Mr. A. W. Kinney; oh, yes, I know him well. He is one of the best artists in Chicago, and a royal good fellow; he has a nice studio in the Lakeside building, right over here on Clark Street. Dr. Butler is operating the Chicago Sanitarium, a private hospital. Mr. G. H. Olliver? Yes, I know him. He is a fine fellow; he is an old time missionary. I think he used to travel among the heathen in the far West. He is now in the wholesale wall paper business down on Wabash Avenue. He is very agreeable and wide awake, a regular Chicago man. He lives somewhere on the North Side, I don't just remember where, but you take this City Directory and you will find just where any and everybody lives in the city, and where they can be found."

Clarissa took a card and she put down the names of all those she wanted to see, and then we found what street and number they lived in. Then we thought we'd take a walk a little while, and started out; we went out the front door of the hotel and we was on State Street. My, my, what a sight! I never saw such buildings in my life before, and such a wide street, and sidewalks that was dumb nigh as wide as a whole street in Syracuse. "Why," says I, "Clarissa, Syracuse haint no more to be compared with this city than our village is with Syracuse."

I got out on the corner of State and Monroe streets and thought I'd look up to the top of Mr. Palmer's tavern, and while I was trying to count the windows up next to the roof, some dumb scamp run right into me and knocked me clean off my pins; and when I was down and looking to see how I came there, a ragged little villain with papers hollered, "Clover, ah there, stay there!" but I didn't stay there worth a cent; I was on my feet in less'n a minute, and making for that little villain my best licks.

Says I, "You little rascal, you are the same fellow that give me that counterfeit money in Buffalo. How in thunder did you get here so quick?"

He hollered at me, "Say, Old Clover, come off from the load," and I turned round and I'll be darned if there wasn't fifteen or twenty more just such looking little villains, all staring at me, some hollering, "Mister, have a shine? Shine for a nickel, Mister." "Morning *Tribune, Times* and *Herald!* Have a paper, Sir?" I was perfectly bewildered. They all pitched right at me, and there was hundreds of other folks on the street, and they didn't bother them.

I got back to the corner where I had left Clarissa, and took her arm and said, "Let's go down this way," pointing north, though I didn't know it was north at that time. We walked, but didn't go very fast, for when we wasn't stopping to look into store windows, there was such a crowd on the streets they kept knocking us one way and another. We walked about two blocks when we saw some cars moving right down the middle of the streets, and not a thing to make 'em move—no horses, no engine—and nobody pushing 'em. That beat anything I ever saw.

I saw one of them things dressed in uniformity. I went up to him and says, "Can you tell me what makes them cars go?" He looked at me a minute as though he thought I was a fool, and said, "A cable, they are called cable cars; there is a wire rope running under ground that is constantly in motion, and these cars attach

"I SAW ONE OF THEM THINGS DRESSED IN UNIFORMITY."

themselves to that cable by means of a grip, that is operated by that man in the front; that is called the grip car."

Says I, "How far does them cars go?" He said, "About six miles." I asked how much it cost to ride? He said, "Five cents each way." Says I, "Clarissa, let's take a ride on 'em, we can get a dumb big ride and see lots of the city for five cents apiece." She thought as I did, so we got onto the grip car and took a front seat, so we could have a clean look at everything. We went as far as the cars went and come back with 'em. Well, it was the most interesting ride I ever had; it was city, city, city on both sides of us, in front and behind us, and as far as we could see it was city except when we got down where the great Stephen Douglas lay pinned into the ground with a tremendous shaft of marble surmounted by a bronze statue of himself. There we could see considerable of Lake Michigan.

We passed thousands of monstrous great stone houses, some with gray, some with brown, some with red stone fronts, and some brick. We passed a great fine stone building, with towers and turrets, standing in a yard by itself, up near the resting place of Douglas. They told us it was "The Chicago University." Farther down on Cottage Grove Avenue, we passed a peculiar building, and asked the conductor what it was. "Well, Sir," said he, "it isn't generally known what that is, but people who live down this way and who pass it every day of their lives say it is a manufacturing establishment where they make *little pill doctors*. They call it 'Hahnemann College.' They do quite an extensive business in the city, and I understand they have a number of orders from country towns for their doctors, and they manage to supply all their demands." I told him I never heard of it before. "Did you Clarissa?" I asked.

He said, "You don't keep posted, I'm afraid."

"Well, yes," Clarissa answered, "I heard a woman in Syracuse saying she had a son they had been trying to educate for business, so he could help his father in the store, but the boy was so frail and tender the teacher said there wasn't any use of trying him any longer. His health was too poor to put him at hard work, and being discouraged in trying to fit him for business they thought of one place he might be fitted for, and that was a *little pill doctor*. And so they sent him to this college. He is here now, and they say he is doing fine, and expects to graduate this coming winter." And Clarissa terminated her remarks by saying, "That everything is designed to fill a proper place, and I suppose this institution sends out the necessary things to fill long felt vacancies."

We had made a turn onto a business street they called Twenty-second, and in a short distance turned again to the right, onto what they called Wabash Avenue. "That large house is the Jewish Syn-

"WE TOOK A BIG RIDE FOR FIVE CENTS APIECE."

agogue;" a little further down we passed a large, square, lonesome looking building with a sign board circling over the front door, saying, "Home of the Friendless." I thought to myself that if ever there was a Christian act done by any one in this world, it was done by the persons who got up this institution, and who carry it on. Clarissa said she intended to visit that place before she left the city, as she had read a great deal about it. She said it was conducted and maintained entirely by free contributions.

Says she, "Just think of it, a place where a poor, moneyless, friendless woman or girl can go and be cared for, nursed and doctored in sickness and supported in health until such time as they can find self-support. I tell you, Benjamin, that if ever the hand of Providence was reached out to anybody, it certainly is reached out to poor friendless mortals in this city by the maintaining of that institution, and it's the duty of every one that can spare a little to send it to that institution; and I'm going to give 'em ten dollars before I leave."

"Well," said I, "you have struck my sentiments exactly, and to-morrow morning, when you count out what money you are going to allow me, just add ten dollars more to it, and I'll give 'em as much as you do, I'll be blamed if I don't."

For I believe that all we can do in this world that is really and truly Christ-like, is to heal the sick, raise the fallen, care for the wounded both in flesh and spirit, wipe away the orphan's tears, assuage the widow's grief, and in all the little things of everyday life do just as we would be done by. Some folks tell us that all this may be done, and still if we have not faith in certain creeds and dogmas, we are the children of the evil one and heirs to perdition. Well, all I have to say is, that if the fruit does not give evidence of a right spirit, then let the cant religionists apply their brand, and burn it in as deep as they please.

I find I am philosophizing, which aint my intention, so I'll resume about our car ride. We had now got down to the Panorama of the Battle of Gettysburg. Clarissa said, "Benjamin, I have read so much about that panorama, I do want to stop and see it." So we asked the conductor if he had any objections to our getting off there. He gave his consent, and we went into the Battle of Gettysburg. My! my! I'll never forget it as long as I live. How we got up on that hill, right in the thickest part of the fighting, I don't know, and I'll be dumbed if I can tell. We went up some dark, winding stairs, and all of a sudden we was right on

BATTLE OF GETTYSBURG.

top of a hill in bright daylight. The smoke of the battle seemed to curl up in our faces, and it seemed as though we could hear the moaning and groaning of the dying brave boys. And while General Hancock on his black horse seemed to be in a commanding position, I held my breath for five minutes in suspense, expecting just as much as could be that he would be the next to fall. Everything about it seemed so real, that we seemed to be fastened to the place. I never saw a battle, but I know that when we left that place I was as faint and nervous as if I had been fighting there. I don't want to ever be any nearer a battle than that. I tell you, I don't want to be shot all to pieces, and carried off behind an old straw stack or cow stable, and be sewed and glued together, even if every hair of my head, including my scatterin' whiskers, had a flag of glory flyin' from the tips of them. Glory is a fine thing, but it don't restore life nor make new legs, and arms and eyes, nor mend shattered constitutions, nor give that vigor that long service in the army has taken from you, nor bring back again all the well laid plans for a future that have been destroyed and forever banished from you. It is all well enough for ambitious or tricky politicians and avaricious, money-making schemers to get the country into trouble, and precipitate a war, using any cause but the right one as a pretext, and then call upon the men of strength and vigor, in the country, to come out and fight, and prate about the glory there is in store for the heroes that will venture their lives and health to restore order and peace again, but you can just please excuse uncle Ben Morgan from taking a piece of glory off of that plate. I tell you, that all the *flowers* strewn upon the graves of our fallen dead, all the songs of praise to their noble deeds, and all the pretty things said about them is no more of a recompense to them for what they have suffered, and for the thousands that have had home and competence swept from them by the loss of their dear ones, than a handsomely executed and finely engraved certificate of membership to a defunct insurance company is to the victim who has dropped his thousands into its lap. I don't mean to be unpatriotic, nor do I, in any sense, fail to appreciate the benefits I receive from our country, but I had rather have my whole body, and my family, than to have a whole world full of *glory*, and not the former.

Talk about recompense! If Uncle Sam would give to every single survivor of the late war, and to the families of every man that was killed, a home complete, worth not less than five thousand dollars, it wouldn't be any more than a just recompense. Clarissa asked me how Uncle Sam could do it. I told her that was easy enough. Just let these congressmen and senators that prate and blow so much about patriotism and glory, just before election, go down to Washington, and for ten straight years do their best to make good, wholesome laws, and economize in all the expenses, and just take one-half off from their salaries and put it into a fund for the purpose I have mentioned, and without another dollar, every Union soldier living, and every dead soldier's widow or family would have a home, paid for out of that fund, worth not less than $5,000, and our congressmen and senators would be covered all over with glory, and future history would hold 'em up as specimens of humanity that the world never knew before, and in all probability never would again.

If our Congress and Senate was to be governed by a law that compelled such a state of things, for the next ten years, I'll bet every dollar that my wife counts out for me to-morrow, that you couldn't possibly make up a Congress and Senate, and find a present member in the lot.

Here, I am wandering off on some philosophical speculation. Seeing that Battle of Gettysburg set me to thinking, and just like a good many others, I've been thinking out loud.

Well, after we came out of the battle, safe and sound and not a scratch on either one of us, we saw another train of cable cars coming along, and stopped them and got aboard, and away we went, spinning along down Wabash Avenue. It was a fine sight.

Away down, as far as you could see, was two rows of mammoth structures, seeming to come together in a great distance beyond us. vehicles of every description passing to and fro in constant motion, and crowds on the sidewalk moving, some slowly, but most of them at a break-neck speed, backward and forward. It was so different from what it was on the old farm or even down to the village, that I got all fuzzed up. I was just bewildered with excitement. Presently we took a turn up on to State Street, and I told the conductor I'd give him an extra nickel if he'd stop at the Palmer House and let us off. He said he would, and in a few minutes he stopped his train and called out " Palmer House !" Sure enough, we was there. I knew the place by two great big marble women (I supposed they was marble) sitting up over the big front door. We went into the office; it was one o'clock P. M. I asked the clerk if we was too late for dinner. He told me we was just in time ; that meals was served in that house nearly every hour from seven o'clock in the morning until twelve o'clock at night. So we went up to our room. We got so we could find the elevator, and after we was landed on our floor, we could find our room.

CHAPTER XIX.

WE had a splendid dinner. I used to think Clarissa could beat the world getting up fine dinners, but she can't hold a torchlight to such a dinner as we had. I was surprised; honestly, we was an hour and a quarter to dinner, and was busy. I thought I'd try the bill of fare, and I started in with the whole bill, but I don't think

"WHILE I WAS RESTING CLARISSA WAS READING TO ME."

I got more'n half there was on that bill before I was as full as I could get, and I hadn't got down to pie and icecream, figs, raisins, nuts, cake, etc. I told the waiter to put that part away for me, where t'other boarders couldn't get it, and I'd have it at supper time. He smiled and said, "Yes, Sah." I don't think I ever ate so much in my life at one time. The sight in that dining room, the host of people coming in and going out, the elegant tables, the army of African waiters that march in, in military style, the beauty of that room, and the grand dinner, was worth the whole expense of our trip so far.

I had to go and lay down an hour after dinner, and while I was resting Clarissa was reading to me. She was reading about the anarchists and their trial, and the sentence the judge give 'em, and I tell you I think the judge was level-headed. I know there are some weak-kneed, sentimental, gushing kind of folks in the world, that say that a man shouldn't be hung nor imprisoned for speaking and printing what he wants to, for this is a free country, where free speech and free press has the right of way. Well, I want to ask those people if a man should have a right to carry poison around and put it into the wells and cisterns of people, and thereby scatter death throughout the land, because this is a free country? Now, the anarchist doctrine that has been preached, and printed, and heralded all over this land from ocean to ocean, and from the lakes to the gulf, is as rank poison to our laws and good order, as strychnine is to water and food, and if the one is a crime the other is equally criminal. Strychnine produces death; and we follow out the *intent* of the criminal, who deliberately gives it to his fellow man for that purpose, and put a gallows with him swinging from it, at the end of it. We follow out the intent of these law and order poisoners, and we find murder of the foulest kind all along its line, premeditated murder, and we ought to have a gallows at the end of it. There is not one mite of sense in any way, shape or form, in all this sentimental sympathy for the condemned anarchists.

I said to Clarissa, "I'd like to see them criminals." She said she had no desire to see 'em, but she would like to see the judge and the men that composed the jury before whom they were tried. I shall always believe that Lawyer Grinnell and that judge and jury done the greatest deed for the benefit of Chicago, the State of Illinois and the whole United States, that has been done since the close of the war. "But," says I, "Clarissa, here we are up in this room talking about the anarchists, when we ought to be out around the city taking in the sights." She fully agreed that we ought to be going around town, and she put on her things and we went around to the ele—and took a ride away down to the bottom of Mr. Palmer's tavern, and then walked out onto Monroe Street. There was a brass band riding through the street on a big, high wagon, and they were playing wonderful pretty music, and there was a great big cloth sign pinned onto the wagon, saying: "Fat Stock Show, at the Exposition Building."

That struck me as just the place I'd like to go to, so I says to

"WE WILL JUST FOLLOW UP THIS BRASS BAND."

Clarissa, "Let's go to that fat stock show. I have read considerable about it, and I'd like to go and see it." "All right," says she, "I am in for seeing all we can while we are here, for we may never be in this city again."

She asked me where it was. I said it was at the Exposition Building, but I didn't know just where that was; but said I, "We will just follow up this brass band, and we will get there when they do." So we followed them. We was on one street, then another, and then another, and so on. We walked and we walked. I believe we walked for three hours and a half. Clarissa was just tuckered out. She wasn't used to walking on them hard stones, and I was just about petered, when I yelled out to the driver on the band wagon, just after the band got through playing a tune, and asked him how much further it was to that *fat cattle show*. He said, "Klopher." Says I, " That aint my name; my name is Benjamin Morgan, from Morganville, Blank County, New York." "Vell, den, Morgan, you vos more ash two miles und a quawarter from doze kattle." "Is that so?" said I, "what time do you expect to get there?" " Ve dond oxpect to vos got der enny leedle vile this veek," he said. "Ve vos hired to trive a leedle ofer all the city to advertise dose show," he replied.

I never was so golldarned mad in my life, to think that Clarissa with her big bunion, and I with two big corns just a-killing me, had been following up that confounded Dutch brass band to find the show, and here we was, way down on a street where we didn't know where we was. I saw a policeman and asked him where we was, and how far we was from Mr. Palmer's tavern. He told us we was away down on Biler Avenue, about two miles from the hotel. He very kindly showed us where we would find a street car that would take us right down near the hotel. I thanked him, and Clarissa and I got back to our room about six o'clock, completely prostrated with fatigue. I think that was one of the biggest shams I ever had paraded in front of my physiognomy. After we got rested and had a good supper, I went down to the office. I asked the clerk ('twas another fellow this time, more stiffy like than the one that was there in the morning. He had a great big glass pin on his shirt front, and a sort of air of Boss-of-the-United States, onto him) how far the Exposition building was from here. He said it was only two blocks, right down here at the foot of Monroe Street. I asked him what in the name of common sense they let them dumb brass bands go around the city deceiving folks for. He said he never knew they deceived anybody. "But," said I, "they have; they deceived me and my wife to-day." And I told him all about the tramp we had, following up that dumb Dutch brass band to find the show. I thought he would die a-laughing, and that drew a big crowd of fellows around us, and they wanted to know what the fun was, and the clerk up and told 'em my experience, and one tall, lean, cadaverous looking cuss, with a hook nose and a pair of snapping black eyes and one eyeglass, asked the clerk for an introduction to me. The clerk asked me the number of my room. I told him, and he stepped behind a desk and looked at something; then stepped right back and said, " Mr. Tellemall, this is Mr. Morgan."

"Yes, sir, Morgan is my name; they call me uncle Ben Morgan at home. I am a farmer, sir, from Morganville, Blank County, New York."

Said he, " Uncle Ben, I am very happy to know you, and while you remain in the city, shall be pleased to have you drop into my office and make yourself at home.''

" Thankee, sir; thankee," said I, " where abouts is it ?"

" It is the reporters' room in the *Tribune* building, corner of Madison and Dearborn streets. I belong to the reportorial staff."

" The whatatorial staff?" said I.

" The reportorial staff."

" Well, what kind of a staff is that?" He went on and explained what his duties was. "Oh, yes," said I, " your business is to stick your nose in everybody else's business, and run and tell the paper all about it before t'other fellow has even concluded on his business. In other words, you are a regular town tattler, are you?"

Well he said he guessed that come pretty close to it. " Well," said I, " have you got a brass band running through the streets, advertising where your office is? Because if you have, you needn't look for me to call, for I just tell you I've got through running after them dumb shams. Come to think of it, Mr. Tellemall, there are so many fellows in the same kind of business in a city, you don't have to advertise, do you?" He said, " No." " Well," said I, "don't you kind o' hate that business? I should think you would. Say—you'd better sell out and come down to York State, Blank County,

Morganville, and buy a farm, or go down to the village and buy out Jim Teeters' grocery and join the Methodist Church. Come to think of it, you haint got anything in your business to sell, have you; that is, I mean you haint got anything but other folks' secrets to sell? And anybody else has got as much right to 'em as you have, so you couldn't get a dumb cent for your business, unless it was for your chance in with that newspaper. The best way to stand in with it, is to be able to tell the most stuff you can, true or false, before some other paper gets it; haint it?"

"Well," said he, "I thought I'd got a *clover*, but you seem to understand my position pretty thoroughly."

THE TRIBUNE REPORTER.

"Well, you *have* got a regular *clover*. When I left home I was in full blow, fresh, if not sweet, but on the train between Buffalo and Cleveland, some fellows saw me and wanted me for a button-hole bouquet, I suppose, and they picked me, and in Cleveland they picked my pockets, too. After I have been picked several more times, I'll be dried clover, I expect, a little too dusty to chew. I can just tell you one thing, no confounded brass band will ever pick me and my wife up again as a walkin' match."

After a few pleasant words in regard to one thing and another, and a request that I call on the *Tribune* before I left the city, he bade me good-night and stepped out. I seemed to be the show, somehow or other. I couldn't understand it. Here was a big crowd gazing at me. Two-thirds of 'em had keen eyes, curly hair and hook noses, and talked peculiar. They would say "Goot efening, mein frent," and so on. I asked the clerk what show troupe them fellows belonged to. (They was dressed up like dandies and had stove-pipe hats on.) Before the clerk had time to answer my question, a sort of rough and ready Western man standing beside me, said,—

"They belonged to a monstrous large troop that hailed from Jerusalem. Their show was the 'Abraham, Solomon & Isaacs Combination. They play a large variety of pieces. Their principal plays was 'Fritz, The Clothing Merchant of Berlin,' 'Honest Isaacs, The Jeweler of Ni Yark,' 'My Last Cigar, The Happy Dreamer,' a shenuvine long leaf Havana filled, Java wrapper und binder, effry vun varranted, made by imported Cuban workmen of our own growth on Uncle Moses Oppenheimer's plantation, what he got off his brother Jacob who failed in the gent's furnishing goots trade in Philadelphia, only turty dollars a thousand, 60 days' time, with plenty more time on more goots, with 'plenty goot security.'"

"Uncle Benjamin," said the stranger, "if you want to have a good sight of them fellows and other gentlemen, you just go up there and set in that little balcony, where you can have a splendid view of this grand office and lobby ;" and he pointed me up to the balcony.

I thanked him for his kindness and went to the ele—and slid up to the ninth floor. There being no street car on that hall, I had to walk around to the southern suburbs of the hotel, where I found Clarissa in No. 984, laying on the bed a resting. Says I, "Clarissa, if you have got rested, I want you to go with me down the elevator and sit in the balcony, where we can see everything going on in the office and lobby room, and it will pay us to see the people." She said she would be delighted to go; that anything of that kind would please her a great deal better than "fat cattle shows," and as for brass bands she never wanted to hear another as long as she lived.

She took a little swallow of peppermint and water, to keep the wind down in her stomach and scent her breath, and we went to the ele—and down to the parlor floor, then walked down those wonderful, massive marble stairs to the next floor, what they called the

"ABRAHAM, SOLOMON AND ISAACS COMBINATION."

"Entré Sol." I believe some one said it was a French word; and as we hadn't got our nigger waiter from the dining car to tell us the meaning of the word, and Clarissa's eyes being so poor she couldn't make it out, kind reader I'll have to leave it to you to find out what it means. At any rate, we was where the balcony was, and we got two easy chairs, drew them up to the iron rail fence, put up on purpose to keep folks from falling down, and seated ourselves.

We set there until ten o'clock, and it was very interesting to us, who had never seen anything but our plain simple country sights, and had known comparatively little if anything of the world at large. To us everything we saw was as new as to a new born babe.

The great room was a sight to us. Its elegant ceilings were supported by massive columns, and beautifully decorated in a most pleasing manner. On the farther walls was hanging a monstrous large oil painting, and several pictures of large buildings that was burned in the great fire. A great massive marble stairway was guarded by two bronze figures who held up lighted lamps, and the whole of this great room was made as light as day by electric lights. There was a crowd of men surging backward and forward in constant motion. Some leisurely wandering around gaping at things and folks in general; others in seeming warm discussion on some question; others entertaining a crowd of a half a dozen by some story, no doubt, that had a laugh ending to it. The strange intermingling of faces belonging to country merchants, cattle buyers, commercial drummers, lawyers, dignified clergymen (very few of the latter), reporters, board of trade men, young swell head dudes, with polished stove pipe hats, canes and single eye glasses, wise and knowing sheeneys puffing the everlasting cigar and moving around with an expression on their countenance conveying a strong desire to own the whole world, produced a picture of wonderful interest. Clarissa said she could enjoy herself every day for a month sitting there and studying human nature, if she had time, and could afford it. It was ten o'clock and we concluded we would retire, which we proceeded to do. We was tired enough to enjoy a good rest and sleep.

CHAPTER XX.

AFTER breakfast, Clarissa fixed herself up in the best she had with her, which was a black silk dress made up with pieces of navy blue velvet set in goring all around in different places on the skirt, and a goring piece on the outside of each sleeve, and trimmed with black and orange colored satin ribbon looped up into double bows, and artistically hung on around in different places where it would give the best effect, the same as corner pieces on a ceiling are put in the proper place to give the right appearance, or an air of richness to the balance of the decoration. Her bonnet was made of black and navy blue velvet and ornamented with a feather that fell off of an ostrich that died in the purple age of his life, and a cluster of blue forget-me-nots and honeysuckles. The milliner down to the village had quite an argument with her in regard to putting the flowers on, but Clarissa said them was always her favorite posies, and she didn't care what the milliner thought, she was going to have them on the bonnet. She had a large cape made of the finest kind of muskrat skins, and when she had got all dressed up and put on her gold bowed specs, she looked like a queen, or as I suppose a queen looks, for I never saw one—and I was real proud of her. I always have been proud of her, but now I was more than usually proud of her, as she was not only smart intellectually, but also moneyly, and she was my banker.

I said, "Clarissa, why do you spread yourself more than usual this morning; taint Sunday yet, and we haint going to church, be we?" "No; but I thought, Benjamin, we would go and find some of our friends this morning, and if they wanted us to visit them any we would stop paying board at the tavern, as it was quite expensive. But I don't do it on that account so much as I would like to see some of them, and then they can show us the city better than we can see it alone."

I said, "Well, I think that is a sensible idea; but where do you intend to go first?" "I thought I'd call on Mr. Harrison first. I heard yesterday that he was the Mayor."

"Well, if he is any dumb hypocrite like that mayor is in Syracuse, I don't want to see him."

She said she didn't believe he was, although she hadn't seen him since he was a young man, and she was a young girl, but he was a real likely young man, and everybody thought he was the soul of honor. He ought to be, for he came from as likely parents as ever breathed the air of heaven. The only thing that they ever said against him was that he was stuck up. That may possibly be against a person in the eyes of envious people, but in my opinion (she said) "I think it's a credit mark in favor of a young man or young woman to have self-respect enough to be above low and vulgar thoughts and conversation, and low and vulgar people. Of course, if they haven't got good principles and good brains to maintain their self-respect, but just assume it as a disguise to their real characters, then I despise it; but Mr. Harrison never assumed any such a position, it was perfectly natural for him. I'm almost afraid to call on him for fear he may not remember me, and will not care to renew our old acquaintance, but he can't any more than refuse to know me, and I shan't feel hard if he does."

Clarissa had her hand on the door knob as she finished her remarks, and I said I would second the motion, and go anywhere she wanted me to, but I reminded her that she hadn't counted out any money for me yet.

"Oh, yes;" said she, "excuse me, Benjamin, I had taken it out for you and put it in my muff, and forgot it; here it is, five dollars;

wont that be enough for to-day, in case we go a visiting?" I told her it would be plenty, and we started out.

Before we left the office we got our bearings for the City Hall, and left the Palmer. It was a lovely morning although there was a sharp wind blowing from the north, and although we couldn't see any brown and yellow leaves falling in fence corners, nor cows and calves humping up their backs on the sunny side of straw stacks—scenes that are familiar to us at this season of the year—we could see the beautiful clouds of smoke roll up above the monstrous buildings and giving the sun the appearance of a ball of fire, half hid by some great conflagration; and as we looked down Madison Street to the west, it seemed as though the end of the street had run into a cloud of smoke. In the place of the music of lowing cows and squealing pigs, we heard the never ending cry of the newsboy, boot-blacks, street fakirs of various kinds, the jingling bells of the street cars, and the roar and hum of a thousand and more vehicles of every description, rattlin' over the stony streets. There was so much to attract our attention that it seemed but a few minutes had passed before we reached the City Hall.

A policeman showed us Mr. Harrison's office. We went in; it was a fine room, all carpeted nice, and fixed up in good shape. Clarissa asked if Mr. Harrison was in, and a real smart looking young man answered that he was in his private office, the next room, opening out of this one, and asked if she would like to see him. She told him that she wouldn't have asked for him if she hadn't wanted to see him.

Said he, "Shall I take your card in to him?"

Clarissa told him he should not, for the reason that she hadn't got any printed yet.

He asked what name he should give the mayor.

She said: "Do you mean what my name is?"

He said, "Yes."

"Will you tell him it is Mrs. Benjamin Morgan, of Morganville,

Blank County, N. Y. She that was Clarissa Sunflower Snodgrass before she was married, and when he went to school."

The young man started for the other room, but before he got there, we heard some men reading something and laughing enough to bust 'em. In a few minutes a fine looking gentleman, heavy set, tall, with keen eyes and hair well sprinkled with gray, came out and approached us with a smile, and said,—

"Well, I declare; is this the lady I knew so well, long years ago, as Miss Clarissa Snodgrass?"

"Yes," she said, "I am the same, with the exception of the addition of a number of years, and a husband and family. This is my husband, Mr. Morgan, Mr. Harrison." I shook hands with him and he greeted us in a most cordial spirit. Said he,—

"Well, Mrs. Morgan, I am really delighted to see you. It brings back to my memory those early days in my history when I little dreamed that I should ever be the mayor of the great city of Chicago, or that you would visit me as Mrs. Benjamin Morgan. Please walk into my private office where we can have a little chat." and he led the way while we followed him into a beautiful room, finely furnished. He gave us seats in big easy chairs, and then said,—

"Well, well; I am surprised to see you, as I had lost track of you the last twenty years, but just before you come in, I was reading in the morning *Tribune* about your arrival in the city, and stopping at the Palmer House, and about your long walk around the city with the brass band."

Clarissa looked a little crestfallen, and wondered how on earth the paper got hold of that. She was surprised.

Mr. Harrison said "she needn't be surprised at all. Probably some of the *Tribune's* cheap reporters was following up the same band to take notes, and as he discovered you were strangers, he followed you to the hotel and got your names."

"But how did he know we was strangers?" she asked.

"Oh," said he, "them reporters know everything and everybody that lives here. Why, I tell you, I can't move but that they know it. If I go to church they will report it the next day, and for that reason I've quit going to church. If I drop in to see a friend of mine when on my way home, they know it and report it the next day. If I go to the polls election day, or the day after, they report it, and as likely as not make it out that I have voted all the Irish in the city two or three times. I get so annoyed by them —— —— —— reporters that I'd like to send every one of them down to Joliet and take Joe Mackin's place, and let poor Joe come home."

Clarissa spoke up and said, "That was what you was laughing about, wasn't it?"

CARTER'S PRIVATE OFFICE

He said it was, and picked up the paper and showed us the article. There it was, a half column, headed:

"*Fresh Arrival!* Uncle Ben Morgan and Clarissa, from Morganville, Blank County, N. Y."

Clarissa read it out loud, and there they had our whole trip yesterday to the Fat Cattle Show and the Palmer House business, all brought in, written up in a flourishing style, and while Clarissa was reading it, she couldn't help laughing right out although she was the maddest I ever saw her.

"Well," said the Mayor, "never mind the paper. I'll send my carriage after you to the Palmer House, at three o'clock this afternoon, and you come to my house and stay a few days, and we'll have a good visit." Just then some one called him. "You see," said he, "I am called here and there continually, by some one or other that think they want something."

"Yes," said Clarissa, "I know your time is taken up and you can't be bothered much. They told us at the hotel that they thought it very doubtful if we found you in your office, but if we didn't find you here, to go around to Mike McDonald's, and we would find you there; but I am glad we found you in, but now we will not take any more of your time." As we started to go he made us promise to go to his house in his carriage.

As we left, he went to the door with us, and bowed us out with a broad smile. When we got out on the sidewalk, I turned round to look up to the top of that City Hall building. It was the prettiest building I ever saw, prettier than Mr. Palmer's tavern. The great, round stone posts in front, beside the front door, was polished so you could see your face in them; and way up to the top was some stone men and women standing on top of some columns, dressed in old Bible style of clothes, and holding great flat stones on top of their heads. I was quite interested in looking at them, when the first thing I knew I was upset into a cart of oranges and peanuts. A dirty looking fellow had run a two-wheeled hand-cart loaded with that stuff, right against my back legs and I fell right into his cart and he went to swearing at me.

I said to him, "Look here, you dumb sassy scamp, if you do that again, I'll have a policeman arrest you."

Clarissa told me to come along and not pay any attention to him, but look what I was doing, and not be gaping at everything. I asked her how she expected I could see anything of the city, if I had to be looking out for everything and everybody in the road. She told me to look at that big window in the City Hall. I did so, and there was standing Mr. Harrison and another fellow who had been watching the whole performance. They was laughing enough to kill them.

We walked along down Clark Street till we come to the Dime Museum, when I invited Clarissa to go in with me. The low price was the principal inducement. We spent about two hours there, and saw an awful sight for the amount we paid. The last thing we saw, just before coming out, was a play on the stage, which they

"LOOK HERE, YOU DUMB SASSY SCAMP!"

called "Dante's Inferno, or The Devil's Home." The play was so exciting that for a few minutes it seemed real, and I forgot where I was. I spoke up and said, "Mr. Boss Devil, have you got four fellows there I left in the Cleveland depot t'other night, by the names of Smooth, Three, Kard and Montee?" He said he had, that they was his best men and was working for him all the time. I turned to Clarissa, and said—

"Let's get out as quick as we can or they'll have us," and as we left, everybody in the house was laughing at us, and the old Devil on the stage laughed louder than all the rest. After we was on the street again, Clarissa told me if I didn't stop making such a fool of myself and disgracing her, she would take the first train for California, and leave me to get along the best I could. I promised to try my best, and asked her as a favor, to pinch me real hard whenever she discovered I was about to make a break. She agreed, and we went to the Palmer and got dinner. While we were eating, I saw an awful pretty woman at one of the tables that seemed to attract an awful sight of attention. Ladies and gentlemen would go up and shake hands with her, and the men would leave a little bouquet at her plate until it was completely covered up with them. It made me envious, and I asked Clarissa to excuse me a minute. I had forgot something and would be right back.

I went out into the hall and found a waiter boy. I said to him, "Bub, look here; here is two dollars; you go out and buy three of the biggest bouquets you can find for fifty cents apiece, and bring 'em into the dining-room and come right to my table and bow and smile, and hand 'em to my wife, and speak right up loud, and say,—

"Mrs. Benjamin Morgan, these is the compliments of the editor of the *Tribune*, the editor of the *Times*, and Mr. Hizonor Harrison."

He said he would. I told him to hurry up, and get back in ten minutes if he could, and he might keep the other fifty cents. I went back to the table, and as I set down with a smile, Clarissa mistrusted I had been doing something.

I asked the waiter that took my order who that woman was that attracted so much attention.

He said it was Mrs. Langtry, the "Jersey Lily."

"Well," said I, "just wait a few minutes, and I'll show you a York State Rose." Clarissa pinched me. I told her that that pinch was in the wrong time, as she would presently discover.

The waiter had but just come in with our dinner, when t'other waiter come in with three monstrous big bouquets, any one of which was as big as all of Langtry's, and he handed one to Clarissa with a genteel bow, and said in a real loud voice,—

"Mrs. Benjamin Morgan, accept the compliments of the editor of the *Tribune*, and also this, with the compliments of the editor of the *Times*, and also this, with the compliments of Mr. Hizonor Harrison."

My bosom, for the first time since I arrived in Chicago, swelled with pride as I saw all eyes turned upon my Clarissa, whose face was crimson with natural blush, and Mrs. Langtry, as she gazed with envy at her, wore a white painted blush.

Clarissa was dumfounded. She couldn't understand what it

"CLARISSA WAS DUMFOUNDED."

meant. She didn't know why she should be made the recipient of compliments of the editors of the two greatest newspapers in America. I told her that the *Tribune* always recognized true merit wherever it was discovered, and if any person on earth possessed true merit, she did, and the *Tribune* had, no doubt, discovered that fact by means of its "reportorial staff." And the *Times* would never allow the *Tribune* to get ahead of it, and consequently had sent its compliments in to head off the *Tribune*. I told her I was proud of her, and I was glad to have the comparison drawn in such a public place between a pretty face and brains. The pretty face had lots of little bouquets from little men, while her intellectual capacity received big bouquets from big men.

After dinner we carried the bouquets to our room, and set down for a little talk. We had been seated but a few minutes, when there was a knock on the door, and as I opened it, a waiter handed me a letter addressed to my wife. She opened it. It read as follows:

MRS. BENJAMIN MORGAN AND HUSBAND:

Noticing your arrival in the city, by an article in this morning's *Tribune*, I desire to renew our acquaintance of years ago, and will be pleased to call upon you at such time as you may be pleased to name. I shall also be pleased to have you inspect my studio before you leave the city. Yours truly,

A. W. KINNEY, *Lakeside Building*.

Clarissa replied as follows:

MR. A. W. KINNEY:

Dear Sir,—Your note is just received. I thank you for your expression of a desire to renew our old acquaintance, and your invitation to call upon you. The latter we shall be pleased to do as soon as convenient, but I cannot name the time for you to call upon us, as we leave this tavern in a short time for Mr. Carter Harrison's residence, for a short visit. Very truly yours, MRS. B. MORGAN.

The boy had scarcely left the door before another boy handed another letter for "Mrs. Clarissa Morgan." It read as follows:

MRS. MORGAN:

I noticed in this morning's *Tribune* that you and your husband had arrived in our city, and are the guests of the Palmer. I shall be happy to have you visit me, and also to take in the Board of Trade before you leave the city. Please state where I may call for you at 2 P. M. on Monday next, with my private carriage.

Very truly yours, N. G. ROSSTER.

Clarissa replied as follows:

MR. N. G. ROSSTER:

Dear Friend,—I hope you will not think it presuming too much to address you by the title I used to consider you. I thank you for your kind invitation, and shall be pleased to accept. We leave this tavern in a few minutes for Mr. Carter Harrison's residence, for a short visit, and unless you hear from me in the intervening time, you will find us there at 2 P. M., Monday next. With many thanks, I am yours,

MRS. B. MORGAN.

Clarissa had not completed her answer to Mr. Rosster's letter before another boy called with a letter addressed to me. I opened it and read as follows:

Mr. Benjamin Morgan, *Palmer House, Chicago, Ill.:*

Dear Sir,—We noticed by this morning's *Tribune* that you had arrived in the city. We are also informed that you visited our museum this forenoon. We desire to meet you on a business matter. Will you please call at our office this P. M., between five and seven, or to-morrow morning, between nine and ten? We think we can make you a satisfactory offer. We are on the constant lookout for new attractions.

Very respectfully, yours,   Kohl & Middleton.

To this letter I replied:

Mr. Kohl and Mr. Middleton:

Each one of you Gentlemen—Your letter has been handed to me by one of Mr. Palmer's waiter boys, who is at this moment standing at my left-hand elbow, waiting for me to finish this letter. I can't conceive what on earth you can want of me. If you have got some kind of scheme on foot, and want me to go into it, you have been writing to the wrong one. I am no schemer, and no hypocrite, and I don't want anything to do with them as is. I have no desire to get acquainted with any one that will harbor and keep in their employ such confounded hypocrites as Smooth, Three, Kard and Montee, as your boss, the Devil, told me you did, when I was in there. I want nothing to do with anybody that plays Hell, as you do, morning and night, and, besides all the above and foregoing reasons, I haint got time to call on you, as we are going visiting to Mayor Harrison's. So you needn't write me any more about it. Yours,

Uncle Benjamin Morgan,
Morganville, Blank County, New York.

P. S.—If you want a feller that's good on schemes, to help the Devil in that play of yourn, I know a first-rate one for you. He lives down to the village, and his name is Jim Teeters. He has been helping the Methodists down there, but I guess they canget on without him. In fact, they was talking about turning him and Waddles out before we left home. Maybe you could get Waddles, too.

P. S.—Say, you haint got a feller working for you by the name of Bascom B. Bigler, have you? They called him 'Squire Bigler. He kind of got knocked out of his calculations down there last fall, and moved out here, hunting for a job. If you have got him to work, you might tell him Clarissa and I are here—right here in Chicago.

P. S.—Say, come to think of it, you needn't to tell him about our being here, for if he has seen the *Tribune* he knows it.

P. S.—I haven't time to write any more, as Mr. Harrison's horses and buggy are waiting for us down to the front door.

We dismissed the boys with the letters, and got our things together and went down the ele to the office, and paid our bill. The young man behind the counter said, "You haint going to leave us now, are you?" I told him we was just entering upon that act. He said he was sorry to have us leave, as we had been the main attraction in the house since our arrival. Just then he introduced us to a fine-looking old gentleman, by saying, "Mr. and Mrs. Morgan, let me make you acquainted with Mr. Palmer, the proprietor of this house."

Mr. Palmer said, "I am very glad to meet you. I was out at my private residence, on the North Side, when you arrived, and when I discovered by the article I read in the morning *Tribune* that you were the guests of my house, I hastened down here to meet you. I am real sorry you are going to leave; any time you will come in to a meal or stay all night while you remain in the city, you are welcome to do so, free of costs."

We severally and jointly thanked him for his kind invitation and welcome, and told him, as he had such a fine tavern and they was all so kind to us, we would make it our central point while we was in town, and bid him good-by.

CHAPTER XXI.

WE went out on Monroe Street, where an elegant carriage was waiting for us. A gentleman that was dressed up in fine style with a stove pipe hat on, showed us into the carriage and was just closing the door when I asked him if it was a nigh relative he had lost. He asked me what I meant.

"IS IT A NIGH RELATIVE YOU HAVE LOST?"

"Why," said I, "I merely wanted to know if 'twas a father or mother or son or daughter, or wife, you was called upon to mourn."

"Not either," said he; "what makes you think I have?"

"Why, that wide black band on your hat," said I, pointing to it.

He laughed and said that he was the coachman, and that was why he wore it, and closed the door and drove off to the City Hall, where the Mayor soon joined us. With a great big hearty smile of welcome he shook our hands with that peculiar kind of a shake that made me think that shaking hands was a science that he had studied all his life. Somehow or other there is no one that has got that kind of a shake hands business about them that seems to say, "You just stand by me and I'll be your friend," like an old politician.

We drove off at a rapid rate until we arrived at No. —, Ashland Avenue, where we alighted and was led into the house by Mr. Harrison, who introduced us to his excellent wife, who greeted us with a cordial spirit, and we was taken into a beautiful parlor. Time forbids any extended description of our visit of four days there. At 7 o'clock we had what they called dinner. Clarissa sat next to Mr. H., and received a good share of his attention. In reply to some of her questions, he said:

"He had been mayor of Chicago for a number of terms; that as one term was about to expire, the citizens of Chicago would come up almost *en masse* and beg him to accept the nomination again, and although he had repeatedly declined and refused the nomination, still they had persisted in electing him by tremendous majorities, and of course he had to act when he was elected; that the city had thrived and prospered and increased rapidly under his government, and he was considered 'The Best Mayor Chicago ever had;' that he had been invited to New York City to show them how to run a city government; that he supposed more than likely they would insist on making him mayor again at the next spring election, but he had got so tired of it, so tired of trying to run an honest government that he positively would not accept it, and he was going to write to the people of the city through the *Times*, over his own signature, not to nominate him next spring, for he would not serve,"

She said, "Supposing you are elected next spring, what will you do?"

"Well, if I had the power," he replied, "I would give the office to a friend of mine that wants it awful bad, and that needs it, Mr. Sidney Smith; but there is one objection to letting Sidney into the office, and that is this, he is a regular ferret, and about the first thing he will do will be to run over my past administration and see if he can find anything funny about it. He will try to examine into the records of the city council, and see if he can't discover some kind of a boodle scheme and kick up an unpleasant odor."

"Then why don't you give the office to some one else that wont cause so much trouble?" she asked.

"Well," he said, "you must understand that I can't give the office away. I haven't been mayor quite long enough to have that power, but if I had I could give it to Van Pelt. He is a particular friend of mine, and he would slide along smooth and not discover anything even if requested to by any number of the citizens, but I am afraid he wouldn't be a good mayor, and would be apt to split my party, which might spoil my chances for an election to Congress. I came pretty nigh asking Sid Smith to take it last spring, and when the people got to hear of it, they said I shouldn't do it, that the office belonged to me, and I belonged to it, and I should stay in it, so I staid.

"The fact is, Mrs. Morgan, I am absolutely married to Chicago."

"Was that your wife's name before you married her?" Clarissa asked.

"No, I didn't mean that," he said, "I meant that I thought so much of the city of Chicago that I felt as if it was a bride to me, and for that reason I say I am married to her."

"Well, then," I asked, "why dont you change the name and call it Harrisonburgh; it is the law for the wife to take the husband's name, ain't it?"

"Yes, that is the law, but there is just one difficulty in the way of that. While I think enough of Chicago to do all that, the city hasn't quite said yes to my *pop*, and I haven't quite *popped* yet."

We had an elegant dinner, and enough of the Mayor's personal history to serve as a double dessert.

After dinner was over the Mayor asked us to accompany him and his wife to the theater. It being Saturday night we could sleep as late the next morning as we pleased. We was glad to accept his invitation, as we never had been to a regular theater. So he had his private coachman, dressed in his private mourning hat, take us in his private carriage down to McVicker's Theater. We occupied his private box at the theater. I couldn't see as there was very much about the box that was private, as everybody that was in that great beautiful room could look right in onto us. I asked Mr. Harrison what made him call that a box; it didn't look a mite like a box, but more like a little bedroom than anything else. He couldn't explain it. Just after we got set down the band begun to play right down in front of us. Clarissa got up and said, "Mr. and Mrs. Harrison, I believe I'll have to go out, for I don't think my nerves will stand the strains of a brass band." Mrs. Harrison assured her that it was not a brass band, but a very fine orchestra, and that she would be delighted with the music; and she set down with a calm countenance and *was* really delighted with the music of the orchestra. The play was "Joshua Whitcomb, or The Farmer in Boston." Denman Thompson was to take the part of Uncle Josh. The curtain was pulled up, and the play begun. When he got along to where they had a dance, he pulled off his boots and commenced, but stopped sudden, and said:

"Ladies and gentlemen, I would like to dance this set through, but I followed a brass band all over the city this afternoon, and my corns are paining me more than usual. Therefore, you will please excuse my poor dancin'."

The whole house just hollered and yelled, and spatted their hands

EXPERIENCE WITH HYPOCRITES.

and stamped their feet, and then they yelled, "Uncle Ben Morgan!"

I got up and bowed, and said that was me, and asked them what they wanted. Clarissa pinched me horribly. I sat down immediately. The Mayor laughed, and so did Mrs. Mayor, while Denman just roared a minute, and then said he didn't know his old neighbor, Uncle Ben Morgan, was there before, but that he would hunt him up after the show was over.

We enjoyed the theater immensely. It was mighty good, and I made up my mind that if Uncle Josh couldn't clean out that miserable drunken cuss, that I'd just get over onto the stage and help

"I WAS JUST STEPPING OVER THE BALUSTRADE."

him. Once I was afraid he'd be too much for Uncle Josh, and I got up and was just stepping over the balustrade in front of our box onto the stage, to give that darned cuss a belt, while Uncle Josh was praying up in that miserable attic, when Mr. Harrison pulled me back, and said that was part of the play—that it would all come out right. He never saw a play that didn't come out right in the end. Clarissa spoke up, and said, "Our lives are just like a drama; they are composed of *main* and by-plays; that she believed in the end they would come out all right. We might not be able to understand it all, but the great Manager of all human plays would see the end was all right, and that justice was measured with knowledge and consistency." The Mayor complimented her on her philosophy, and said, "Mrs. Morgan, that thought is very consoling to me. When I try to close up the dens of vice and iniquity that exist in our proud city like so many cesspools, breeding corruption and moral death, I am cursed and lied about by some of my best political supporters and workers; and when I try to let them alone, and run as they please, then I am lied about and cursed by all the newspapers in the city. I am constantly harassed by some thing, or some one. And the fact that it is all a drama, and the great Author of the play will bring it out all right in the end, is a consolation that I prize next to my salary and perquisites."

The play ended all right. Hypocrisy was exposed and justice done, and we went home well pleased with our second day's experience in Chicago.

CHAPTER XXII.

SUNDAY morning the bright sunbeams found their way through the open blinds and rich lace curtains, and told us it was high time for us to get up. The room we occupied was large and richly furnished. It was heated by steam, and everything about it had an inviting appearance of comfort. The door to a little room

"ONE RUN COLD, T'OTHER RUN HOT."

adjoining ours was open, and while I was hunting for a place to wash my face, I peeked in there, and saw a fine marble-top wash-sink with a marble basin, and two faucets. I went in and turned on the faucets, and one run cold water and t'other run hot. I told Clarissa that I didn't believe the folks would care if we washed there, and I was going to, at any rate, and run the risk. Along the side of the room was a long zinc-lined coffin, without any cover. I asked Clarissa what she supposed they kept a coffin there for. She examined it closely, and said it wasn't a coffin, but it was a washing tub, and she was going to take a bath in it. I told her she had better go downstairs and ask Mr. Harrison if it was all right, and not make any mistake. She said she wouldn't make a fool of herself by doing that; she knew what it was for, as she had read a good deal about such things, and her cousin Buzzbee, in Syracuse, had one just like it in her private bedroom. So she turned on the water, and let the tub fill up. She had her bath, and enjoyed it so much, that when she got through I tried it, and I didn't blame Clarissa a mite for enjoying it. I thought it was not only a good thing, but 'twas lots of fun. I never had a bath before in my life. I don't mean to say I never got washed all over before, for I make a practice of going in swimming down in the creek, in my west pasture, two or three times every summer; but I never had a zinc-lined tub, hot and cold water wash before. When I get home I'm going to cut our buttery in two, and make just such a tub in one part of it, so we can go in swimming in the winter as well as summer. After we was dressed up we went down to the parlor, where Mr. and Mrs. Mayor was waiting for us.

After breakfast the Mayor set down and entertained us an hour, with a description of Chicago and its wonderful prosperity under his reign. He told us that he had to work against strong odds in carrying out his policy; that the *Tribune* had always been fighting him and opposing him and misrepresenting him, and all the papers occasionally threw up something mean about him. "But," said he, "Mrs. Morgan, you know I come from the President Harrison stock on one side, and the Virginia Randolphs on 'tother, and the blood that runs in my veins is not the kind that is easily daunted;

and I was born in Kentucky, where people of honor live. I graduated from Yale College in 1845, and the class that graduated then were all gentlemen, that would not, under any circumstances, betray a friend. I traveled a long time in company with Bayard Taylor through Europe and Syria and Asia Minor, and have consequently seen enough of the world to know that no man ever amounts to very much in this world without being opposed and lied about. So I don't pay any attention to all these criticisms and slanders, but intend to go right ahead and work for the prosperity and growth of Chicago, and in being elected its mayor, until the city shall have one million people living in it. Then will I be content to lay aside the official robes of Burgomaster, and will devote the remainder of my time in getting some of my friends elected mayor who will carry out my line of policy."

His recitation of his life in Chicago sounded like a novel, and I'll leave it to the reader to imagine who the hero was.

The church bells was ringing in all directions. Clarissa manifested a desire to go to meeting somewhere. When Mr. Harrison asked her who she would like to hear, she said she had read a great deal about Professor Swing, and she would like to hear him, if it wasn't too far off. He said that he hadn't been to church for a long time, but he would take us down to Central Music Hall and we would hear the Professor. Mr. and Mrs. Mayor and Clarissa and I was seated in their private carriage five minutes later, and drove to Central Music Hall. They pointed out all the prominent buildings on the way down, and it was a pleasant ride. We entered the hall, and while there was a great many people waiting for seats, we was immediately shown to very desirable seats. Soon after we was seated, soft, low and pensive strains of music greeted our ears, coming, seemingly, from a great distance. First, the rich, deep diapason of dying thunder seemed to fill the entire room, and I looked all around to see where it came from. Presently the mellow strains of a baritone and alto horn seemed to unite their notes, while the cornet, clarinet, bassoon and piccolo came in to fill the full measure of harmony. Louder and nearer came the grand combination, until it swelled, it seemed to me, into a mountain-wave rolling into the great room from all sides, completely engulfing us in a sea of harmonious sonds! I was puzzled. I looked in every direction to find out the cause. I could not discover any one that I could charge with taking a part in it. I hated to ask a question there, but I hated still more to be in ignorance of what I might know by simply asking a question. So I asked Mr. H. where that music come from. He told me it was the organ. I told him I never heard one before. He showed me about it. The magnificent instrument was divided into two parts, and one half was on one side of the stage and 'tother on 'tother side, while the player set up in the gallery over the stage, behind a red curtain. It is a beautiful instrument, and in a beautiful room. The continual changes and variations of that grand organ was enough to make one feel religious, if they had never thought of it before, and although when we first went in, I thought we was in another theater,—for it looked a good deal like the one we was in last night,—when the music filled the house, and no doubt filled the very hearts of all the people in it, I felt we was in a place dedicated to the Author of all harmony, and a sacred feeling seemed to possess me.

In about twenty minutes after we entered the hall, a little side door on the stage opened and in walked a small man, smooth-faced, and very homely, and seated himself beside a small pulpit or Bible stand. Another gentleman walked in and sat a little to the left. The latter was the chorister, who called attention to the printed hymns that was in every seat. The tunes was all old-fashioned, and easy to sing. The organ player played the tune through once, then the entire congregation stood up, and while the chorister led, everybody seemed to sing. Clarissa sung just as well as any of them. I tried to sing. I don't know why I attempted the trick, but that organ seemed to pick me up and say to me, "Come, take a part, and I'll carry you through."

After the singing the long-haired, beardless, homely man arose and offered a prayer that embraced more good sense than any petition I ever heard from the lips of a minister. The gratitude of thankful hearts for mercies past, and future blessings asked, poured forth from his lips as sweetly and smoothly as does a stream of crystal water glide along 'mid flowery banks, seemingly thankful for being confined in a course that led it on to the sea. Then followed his sermon, and as he proceeded every sentence seemed to add to the

CARTER CROSSING THE DESERT.

stature of the man; and his eloquence robbed him of the homely looks, and clothed him with manly beauty; and when he closed his discourse, to me of all ministers I ever heard, he was the greatest; and of all the public speakers I ever heard, he was the most eloquent. His greatness did not consist of his advising God what to do as Jonas Danberry does when he wants God to bust a hole in the roof of houses, but in getting into the lives of people, and trying to make them sweet, and as flowers are the adornments of beauty in nature and the emblems of the beauty of holiness, so the human heart should adorn itself with holiness.

He exposed the hypocrisy practiced by men in high positions, and preached the doctrine of honesty and purity in politics and business, and he seemed to want to lift all mankind up to that *ideal man* of perfection—Christ. His eloquence did not consist of roaring like a lion one minute and from sheer exhaustion whispering the next; exhorting men to be terrible bold soldiers of the cross ready to stab anybody that didn't believe a certain way; and then manufacturing crocodile tears in pursuing an imaginary sinner down to the grave, and seeing him tumble into the jaws of the dragon, leaving a large circle of friends to mourn his never ending torture; nor in pawing the air one minute with both arms and hands and one foot, and then with clenched fist spoiling the Bible and busting the pulpit by terrible blows, as Danberry and Jones, and most all ministers do that I ever heard down to the village and out in the school-houses around there. But his eloquence is in his plain language, every word of which is fitted in the right place to frame sentences, full of thought and logic, and so simply uttered that every word was easily understood. Sweet flowers and refreshing draughts from a fountain overflowing with knowledge are handed you along with the sermon.

I felt after the services was over that I had been to church, to a lecture, to a school-room, working in a flower garden and drinking from a spring of sparkling cold water, all at the same time; and I told Mr. Harrison that it was the best treat I ever had. I told the mayor that he must excuse my ignorance and green manners; I meant all right, but I had never seen anything of the world in my whole life, so to speak, until the last ten days; and I thoroughly appreciated everything new that I saw, and I appreciated that grand organ music, but I appreciated the value of such men as Professor David Swing in a community more than all, and if I was living in

Chicago, and was the mayor, I would make it a point to hear such men every Sunday, for it would help me to be a better mayor.

"Oh, well," said Mr. Harrison, "if you lived here as long as I have, and had as much on your hands to attend to, you'd want to take a rest on Sunday; besides, Chicago is chuck full of such smart men as Swing; may not be quite as flowery and highly educated as he is, but nevertheless very smart men."

When we reached the mayor's home we set down in the parlor, and Clarissa picked up the Sunday *Tribune* and about the first thing she saw on the first page was an article headed: "Mr. and Mrs. Benjamin Morgan, the guests of Mayor Carter Harrison. They visit McVicker's Theater, and add to the interest of the play." She read it through and laughed, but was a little disgusted. I asked Mr. Harrison if he thought it was possible for us to do anything in that big city without the reporters getting hold of it. He told me he thought it extremely doubtful.

That afternoon they took us riding all over the city, and showed us the water works, the cable car engine works, the Cook County Hospital, the Chicago Library, and several places of interest. In the evening several of his friends called. We got acquainted with John Van Pelt. Clarissa used to know him when he didn't amount to much. But he had forgotten her. She thinks he don't amount to much more now than he used to, except he may have more money, but she says money don't make brains. Daniel Wren, one of Chicago's greatest men, according to Fairbanks, and Mr. McCarthy (I believe they called him Buck), a gentleman they said was in the wire-pulling business for the machine, was introduced to us as Mr. Harrison's particular friends. Then a fellow called at the door and asked if Mr. and Mrs. Morgan was in. Mr. Harrison's hired girl went to the door, and when the fellow asked for us, she said, "Faith, an' how should I know? this is the mayor's home. I niver seed the Morganses. I'll go ax the ould man if them folks be here," and she shut the door in his face and come to the parlor door, and

said, "Mr. Harrison, they be a gentleman as wants to know if th
Morganses be in. I told him I'd ax you." "Well, you tell him,
they are here, but ask for his card," he replied. Bridget went
back to the door and said, "Yis, the Morganses be in here; what do
you want of 'em?" The stranger said he wanted to interview them.
"Well, the mayor wants your pack of cards before you come in."
He said he hadn't brought 'em with him, as it was Sunday, but
that he was a *Times* reporter. "Well, thin," she said, "you can
just stay out there till I ax the boss if you kin git in," and back
Bridget came to the parlor door, and said, "Mr. Harrison, faith,
and he said he left his pack of cards at home; it being Sunday he
didn't think you'd want him to bring them along, but his name is
Mr. Reporter of the *Times* and wants to interview the Morganses."
Mr. Harrison asked us if we wanted to be interviewed. I told him
I'd rather go to bed, but Clarissa said she'd like to tell him some
things. Mr. Harrison told Bridget to show him into the library,
and Mrs. Morgan would meet him there in a few minutes.

Clarissa met him in the library room. He bowed a very polite
bow, and introduced himself to her as Mr. Gimlet, a reporter for
the Chicago *Times*, and said as our arrival had caused quite a little
sensation in newspaper circles, in consequence of the notice published in the *Tribune*, he desired to gain a little of our history, that
he might publish it in the *Times*, as it was a little galling to the
pride of that great paper not to be up to the *Tribune*. "Now, Mrs.
Morgan, if you will be so kind as to tell me who you are, who you
was and who you expect to be, providing you anticipate any change,
how old you are, and what year, month and day you was born in
(I'm not particular about the hour), where you was born, raised and
educated; where you married your present companion; how long
you have lived in peace and harmony together, and how many scions
have been added to your family tree; what are their respective ages
and sex; from whence come ye, and whither do ye go? and any
and all other information that you may see fit to add that you think

may be of interest to the public, you can answer the questions in your own way. I can write as fast as a train can run."

I felt a little nervous to have Clarissa in that room with that fellow; not that I didn't have perfect confidence in her, but I was afraid he would annoy her. So I slipped into the library room just in time to hear his questions. There he sat with a block of paper

"READY AND ANXIOUS TO BORE A HOLE."

and pencil in his hands, the very picture of a gimlet, ready and anxious to bore a hole. Clarissa sat like a stone statue during his storm of questions. After he had come to a full period, Clarissa arose like a queen upon her throne, adjusted her specs, took a searching glance at him, and then said: "Mr. Gimlet, you seem very anxious to write something; so you may write, in reply to your many and several impudent questions, that I was born at a time, and in a country, when and where folks thought it was all they could do to mind their own business, and let other folks' business alone. The principal thing I have learned since I have had a visible existence in this world is, that those people as have nothing else to do but to hunt up other folks' business and learn their secrets, turn out to be liars, backbiters, slanderers and black-mailers. They have all the essential elements of thorough hypocrites, and I want nothing to do with 'em. You can tell your newspaper that Mrs. Morgan and her husband, Benjamin, are two people that mind their own business, and keep their noses out of other folks' affairs. That they don't pretend to be highly educated and learned in the ways of the world, but they manage to paddle their own ship. If they see fit to take an afternoon walk with a brass band, it is their own affair and nobody else's. You are welcome to this amount of information, and now you are more welcome to go out the same way you come in," and she pointed to the door with a firm command in her appearance, while he gathered himself up in an awkward manner and twisted himself out of the door, with an attempt to apologize for his intrusion.

I felt proud of her once more, for she proved herself equal to the occasion. He had met with a Waterloo, but was allowed to retreat with his right and left wings badly crippled, while his main column was completely shattered. It was a victory of good common sense and self-respect over *Chicago brass.*

The interview ended, we returned to the parlor, where I related, as best I could, the encounter and the result. Mr. Harrison was wonderfully pleased, and said he wished every reporter in the city could get just such a dose every time they met some one they wanted to pump. He said they had always been like a cancer to him, gnawing and gnawing away at his life blood.

Mr. Wren, who was talking to Mrs. Harrison, said, "Carter, you hadn't ought to pay any attention to 'em. They have buzzed about me ever since I have been a commissioner, but I don't pay any more attention to 'em than I do to so many mosquitoes humming around my ears," and he shook 350 pounds of human flesh in an attempt to laugh, while John E. Van Pelt said mosquitoes was dreadful annoying, for, while they was buzzing around, that they was mighty sure to light and bite, and his forced grin clearly showed that something had sucked away his life blood, until ninety on the scales would be a hard thing for him to turn. I asked them if skeeters was very thick in Chicago. He said the kind we had in the library room was most mighty plentiful; he dreaded the winter from them kind more'n he did the summer from the swamp mosquitoes, for he could keep the latter out of his house by bars, while it was impossible to keep the former out of his secrets and his business transactions.

Mr. Harrison said, "Never mind, John; don't cry till you're hurt." Wren smiled all over, and said, "Coming events cast their shadows away in front of 'em." I couldn't understand very much what they was drivin' at, and, being tired, Clarissa and I thought we would retire, so we went off up-stairs to bed.

CHAPTER XXIII.

THAT night there was a heavy snowstorm, and Monday morning Mr. Harrison had his private coachman bring around his private sleigh, and they took us down to the City Hall, where the *great man* left us with an *au resivoir* which I didn't know what it meant, and the driver took Mrs. Harrison and the rest of us all around the city. We went to Mr. Lincoln's park, and then to South Park, and then to Mr. Garfield's park, and we see more city than I ever dreamed there was.

By the time we got home it was one o'clock. After lunch we was setting in the private parlor, when the door bell rang, and Mr. N. G. Rosster presented his card, with a request to see Clarissa and me. He was shown into the parlor, and although Clarissa hadn't seen him for nigh onto a quarter of a century, he recognized her to once, and seemed glad to meet her. After an introduction to me and Mrs. Harrison, he said he had called for us to go to his house.

Mrs. Harrison seemed sorry to have us go, for she said she had enjoyed our visit so much. She had been on the laugh most of the time, and Carter had said that he had felt more chirked up since we come there than he had at any time since they arrived here on their wedding return, and urged us to make them a visit on our return from Calfornia.

We left their beautiful Ashland Avenue residence with pleasant memories of a delightful visit and wishes for the prosperity of the Harrisons, and the hope that Chicago would make him its mayor for life.

"WE WENT TO MR. LINCOLN'S PARK."

Seated in the magnificent private sleigh of Mr. Rosster, we drove down to State Street, thence south to his residence. We thought we had seen some fine houses, but Mr. Rosster's residence beat anything we had yet seen. It was beautiful outside, but it was a perfect marvel of beauty and richness inside. In all its appointments comfort seemed to have been the great aim, and the mark had been hit right square in the center.

We had a delightful visit in the afternoon, and in the evening we went to the opera—that is what they called it—at the Chicago Opera House. The theater was full. We had some preserved seats that was kept empty on purpose for us, as we didn't get there till pretty late.

Mr. Rosster gave Clarissa a pair of spy-glasses, and told her to look at the folks on the stage through them after the curtain was pulled up, and she could tell better how they looked. Mrs. Rosster had a pair, too. Then they bought some books of some boys that went through the crowd selling 'em. They called them librettoes. I asked him what he wanted of them. He said that was the opera, and by reading it we would understand the play. In a few minutes the curtain pulled up, and there was fifteen or twenty men and women, all dressed up in fantastics representing people from other countries and in other times, and while the orchestra played furiously, they all broke out singing, and done their level best to drown the orchestra. All the way through they made the most fearful work in trying to sing I ever saw. Sometimes a feller would have his hand on his heart, and then on his head, and some other feller would point a pistol and a sword at some one else, and threaten to kill them, and all the way through it was just a mixedupness.

I tried to read the book, and when I done that I couldn't see 'em play, and when I looked up to see 'em play I lost my place in the book. So between the book and the stage I got so mixed up I couldn't understand a single word. I just wish Melancthon Stevens could have had hold of 'em and trained 'em; he'd learned 'em so they could sing so folks could tell what they was singing, for Melancthon prides himself on learning his pupils to pronounce their words while singing, so folks can understand them.

After the show was out, I could hear lots of the ladies and gentlemen say that it was "Perfectly splendid;" "It was grand!" and I know well enough they was shamming, for I don't believe there was one in the house that knew half they sung or said. I don't want any more opera for me. I'll take the old fashioned singing school, with its do-re-me-faw-sol-la-se-do, than the teedle-teedle-teedle; tidle-tidle-tidle-tidle; twadle-twadle-twadle; bubble-bubble-bubble; *bum*-bum-bum, etc.

Clarissa told me, after we went to bed, that she tried to look through them spy-glasses, but her specs bothered her so she couldn't see anything with them. She didn't want to let Mr. and Mrs. Rosster know but that she enjoyed the opera, as they was so kind to take us, but really it was tortures to her.

The next morning Mr. Rosster took us down to the Board of Trade and showed us all through the building, and then took us into the *Exchange Hall*, where all the buying and selling is done.

Of all the din and racket and roar I ever heard, that place beats them all. If every lunatic in the State of New York was turned loose in one big room they couldn't make a worse noise. There are a lot of steps built up around an open space on the floor, and they call that the wheat bin; and then a little south of them is another circle of steps they call the corn bin, and west of the wheat bin is another they call the pork bin, and the men that want to buy or sell wheat, or corn, or pork, get into these bins, and on the steps, and when the time comes to open the board, which means to commence trading, they begin to yell at each other as loud as they can holler, and they'll shake their hands right in each other's faces. Sometimes they'll shake one finger at a fellow; sometimes two fingers, then the whole hand, and sometimes both hands. I thought they had got into some terrible fuss, and I told Mr. Rosster that I guessed I'd go. "What for?" said he. "'Cause I never was a hand for a fight, nohow, in my life," I replied. I thought there was going to be a tremendous fight sure, but he explained it all to me and showed me how that when one fellow hollered to another, and threw one finger out toward him, he wanted to sell 5,000 bushels, and when he threw out two fingers, he wanted to sell 10,000, three fingers, 30,000; the whole hand, 50,000 bushels, and if the other fellow held his hand toward himself with the same fingers up, it showed he would buy the corresponding amounts.

After Mr. Rosster explained the whole process, I said, "Well,

"SOMETIMES THEY'LL SHAKE ONE FINGER, SOMETIMES TWO."

Mr. Rosster, I think I understand it; it's just like that game them fellows learned me on the train between Buffalo and Cleveland. They called it poker. The fellow that holds the best hand takes the pot, but once in a while a fellow that didn't hold any kind of a hand won the collaterals by a scheme that is practiced extensively in all departments, called bluff. A fellow that can handle the cards fine they tell me can so manipulate the dealing of 'em as to bring the winning cards into his own or his partner's hand. And, so far as

I can see, it is just so here. A few shrewd, long-headed fellows have been operating on the board so long that they understand just how to manipulate the deal, and they generally take the pot. They don't do it very often, as they would scare away the game, but as often as the pile is big and fat, they manage to call it in." Mr. Rosster said, "Well, Mr. Morgan, you have hit it pretty close; but we are no more gamblers here than you farmers are. You risk your time, hard labor and seed against the elements, with the hope and expectation of winning a good crop, and frequently you lose it all. It's a game of chance with you, and so dealing in the grain *after it is raised*, is a game of chance in which the members of the Board of Trade take their risks. These old boys that have been here for a long time, have grown wealthy; they are scientific shearers, and know how to take a fleece off of a lamb in quick time. Why! all these elegant residences you see, riding through the city, that belong to the Board of Trade men, and even this great costly temple built for purposes of trade, is virtually lambs' wool, for the rich fleeces removed from the tender lambs have built them all. The successful shearers are known as great financial men, and receive the fat of the land, but the poor, tender lambs, chilled by the frost of a cold world, crawl into some fence corner and die, and are heard of no more."

After leaving Mr. Rosster's we went to the Palmer House to stay one night before we left the city. Mr. Palmer was there behind the counter and seemed dreadful glad to see us back again. The clerk handed me a pen, and I wasn't afraid to step up, and in my best manner write, "Mr. and Mrs. Benjamin Morgan, Morganville, N. Y." They gave us one of their fine parlor bedrooms, on the same floor the dining-room is on. As we was about starting to our room, the clerk took out a great big bunch of letters and looked them all through, and handed me two. One was directed to me, and one was to Clarissa. After we had got seated in our room, I opened my letter and read it. The following is an exact copy of it:

"Deer pa

"we havunt had a letter from yoU sense You left hum morne tu weeks ago and we begin tu feel, Alarmed at your not writing, Tu us i got a paper. called the Chicago tribune. that sum wun sent tu ben brown down tu the villege and he let me take it, and i brot it hum fur mary tu read, thay wuz a long peece printed in it about you and ma, and the brass band. bigolly I wish id ben thar, fur i like brass BanDs and pi bettern ennything and every buddy In the naburhud haz red it and last nite when i wuz down tu waddles Korners, skule house tu the liseeum thay wanted me tu speek a peece or reed a seleckshun, so i red that peece about you, and youd jest ort tu hav ben thar, the house wuz crowded full, and when I red that, i never hurd such a rore uv laff in my life mary wuz hoppin mad coze i red it, and sed she never wuld let me dun it if she had noed i wuz goin tu, but i tell'd her i wuz glad you had so much fun in that big sitty. and i wanted tu let em no what a good time you wuz havin, and make our jellyus naburs feel mad a

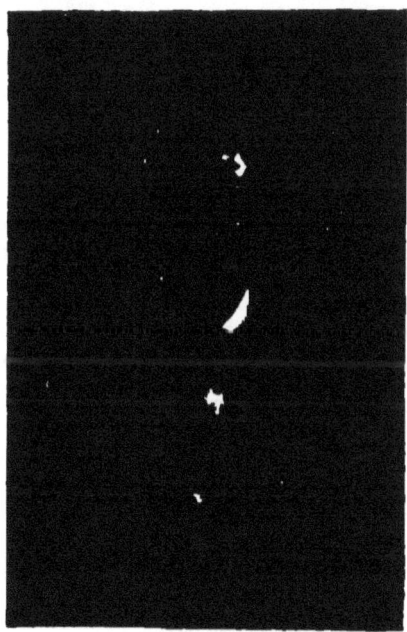

EBENEZER PLUNKETT.

little while, jim teeters haz got hiz skrape fixt up, and got out uv Jail and the methodist church and hez sold out hiz grosery tu eb plunkiT whu tuk, Possesshun last friday and give mary a grate big bagful uv Candy Last saturday and left the villege fur sum place out west thay say he, Haz gone tu Chicago and dassent never cum back hear fur fear the methodists will lick him and ebeneezer iz having a good trade and a good time with mary. i'll bet fore cents tha'll be married tu each uthur before you git hum if you dont hurry for thay act jest as if thay'd di putty soon if thay wuznt, the hired man and the brindul steer had a runaway and the steer got the best uv jim and twisted hiz horn over so it lops rite down over hiz i. i dont see how he did it, but jim sed he bellered like thunder sara smuggins spraned hur left fut in the same place. She did last spring slip on the ice out by the pump, george Waddles haz had hiz trial and the juge fined him 3000 dollars and cost and told him if he didnt pay in ten days he'd send him tu *sing sing* fur 2 years, and you no that wuld be darn tuff on george, fur he cant sing a tune thru rite alone tu save hiz gizzard and fur him tu sing sing fur tu years if i wuz he which i am glad i aint, i'd rathur stay in jail. pleeze rite tu us and send us sum more papers. if they say sumthin funny about you, Sa dad dont let enny uv them sharpers git your munny, eb and i am both afraid uv it, he is the fraidest. Tell ma if you see hur that i am awful humsick without hur, and i wish she wuz hear, and kiss hur fur me Mary and the horses are all rite, you neednt worry about ennything about hum, az i'll take care uv every thing,

Your sun   Abe.

"P. S. ebeneezer jest drove up and hollered for Mary tu cum out coze he had a skittish horse and culdnt stop longenuff tu get out."

After I had read Abe's letter, Clarissa read her'n; it was from Mary, and run as to wit:

"MORGANVILLE, BLANK Co., N. Y., Nov. 25, 1886.

"DEAR MA:

"I don't see why you don't write to me. I have been down to the village or sent down by the neighbors every day for the past week, in hopes of getting a letter from you, but each and every trip has been rewarded by disappointment. Had it not been for the Chicago *Tribune* sent to Mr. Brown, and which Abe (the idiot) has made public property all over the county, I would have no knowledge of your whereabouts. I felt provoked at Abe for reading that article at the lyceum the other evening, for it made me real ashamed to think you had become a show for the city of Chicago to laugh at. I know it is not your fault, but Pa's. He ought to have known better, but as you are having a nice time to make up for it, I don't know that I am very sorry after all. I want your advice on a very important subject. Ebenezer has bought out Jim Teeter's store and taken possession, and he is up here to see me every night, and teasing me to go in partnership with him. He says he can't run it alone successfully. That while his body is there in the store, his head is down here with me all the time; and if I would only go in partnership with him right away and move down there, then he could have his head and body together in the store, and could make a grand success in business. He says if I will go in with him he will furnish all the capital and pay the minister besides. Now, Ma, I never had such a splendid chance to go into business, and I want to take his offer. It is a life long partnership, and Eb is so anxious he can't wait without injuring his trade considerable, and I don't want his trade injured, so I want to know if I hadn't best to say yes, and let him set the time. Now, please tell me I had better do so. We can have the celebrating party after you get home. I can get Dolly Doolittle to come and keep house for Abe and the hired man until you get home. I had some photographs taken for Ebenezer. I send you one. I had it taken with my summer clothes on, just as I was dressed when I went to Nancy Boyle's wedding. Eb wanted it that way. We had a Thanksgiving party here last Thursday, and Eb took Pa's place at the table, and they cracked lots of jokes at his and my expense. I just felt as if I would like to be Eb's partner, and feel that way more'n ever, and I wish you would write me a good letter so I can show it to Ebenezer. It will tickle him half to death. Then I would have lots of pleasure in showing him what a good nurse I can be in curing him up. I shall take it for granted that you will write as I want you to, for you are such a dear good mamma. So I will now ask your advice as to how I shall make my wedding clothes, and what to get. I know you have such good taste in dress, and then you have seen the folks in the big cities and know how they dress on such occasions. I don't want anything very extravagant. Pa left money enough with me for all I want. I can get Sarah Smuggins to make my outside dress, and I guess I can make the rest of the things myself. Eb says I needn't get any furniture or bedclothes, for he will buy everything we need in that line as a part of the capital stock in the new firm's business. I do need some new stockings, as mine are all worn out, and I have darned them so much that they are a darned lot to look at. They have got a real pretty green silk at Brown's store, I think would be just the thing. I can trim it in cardinal red velvet for the wedding, and this winter, and next

MARY.

summer I could take off the velvet and put on black lace, so it will do for my nice dress a long time. I shall wait your answer, however, before I buy anything, and will be governed by your advice largely, but oh, do say yes, and I'll love you ever so much if you will. Tell Pa not to chase up the street cars until he has tired out all the brass band wagons in the city, and that I love him still with all his failings, for he is a 'dear good honest and kind old Pa.   Your loving daughter,   MARY.

"P. S. Eb is here and wants his love to you and Pa put in this letter, and here it is:

"I luv to make munny,
 I like my pa;
I luv to eat honey,
 I luv my ma.
But I luv my Mary
 And hur good ma,
More muchly than 'nary
 Mun' hun' and Pa.

"It's the dream uv my life,
 A muthur-in-law;
And Mary for my wife
 With hur good sweet jaw
To assist in the strife
 With the world so raw,
And brass band, drum and fife
 And Mary's pa, Pa-w.

"I've just bot out Teeters
 Munny tu make;
With Mary and meeters,
 Hunny and cake,
We'll ketch the old skeeters,
 We're bound tu take,
We'll show them two sweeters
 That's wide awake.

"So tu give us a start,
 A cup full of bliss
That'll gladden Mary's hart,
 Pleese du say Yis.
And axcept on my part
 Fur all uv this,
The esteem uv my hart
 And a big kiss."

CHAPTER XXIV.

CLARISSA was visibly affected by Mary's earnest letter. I could see the rain water drip off the end of her nose occasionally, like sap from a spile, but when she came to Eb's poetry I thought she'd bust, and when she had finished the letter, she removed her specs and wiped her weeping eyes, while she looked toward the ceiling for mansions in the skies, and after she had regained her *normal* (normal is a medicated term and used only by doctors, but I borrow it for this particular purpose) condition, she spoke as follows, to wit: "Benjamin, you have heard Mary's letter; what do you think of it?" I said I thought it was a dumb good letter, and I was awful glad she had wrote it.

"But that haint what I mean," she said; "I want to know what you think about her request, and about her marrying Eb before we get home."

"I don't know; what do you think?" said I.

"Well, we've known all along that that's been their intentions, but I didn't expect they'd want to marry before next summer. I am surprised at Eb; he is worth more'n I had any idea, and he is smarter than any one in that neighborhood, and his going into business in the village will give Mary a good position in society at the very start, and looking it all over, I think it's best to do as Mary suggests."

I said I fully agreed with her, and that long ago, and now since she had expressed her opinion, I was fully convinced that Mary's head was level, and I asked Clarissa to write Mary a good letter, and slip a fifty-dollar bill into it for her to buy stockings, with my compliments and good wishes for a successful trade, but to be sure to tell Ebenezer to have nothing to do with them hay-scales, as it is a sign of bad luck, but to be *honest* and just, and give *down* weight if he has to charge a little extra for it. Tell Mary she needn't worry about me; my legs are good for a few more days in Chicago, and I have just as much to laugh at here as the folks have to laugh at me about. Tell her I am the same honest pa I always was, and the most honest pa she ever had.

Clarissa wrote as follows:—

"Palmer House, Spare-bed-room.
"CHICAGO CITY, Nov. 28th, 1886.

"My Dear Daughter:

I am glad to get your letter, and altho' I am wonderfully surprised at your sudden decision, and earnest desire, I am, after thinking it all over and looking at it in all its bearings, satisfied to have you do as you wish to in the matter. Ebenezer is a smart young man, and I believe will make you a good reliable husband. I am surprised to find he is a poet. I am sorry I have not time to write you a long letter and give you full directions in all matters pertaining to your contemplated partnership. We have an engagement to go to the Theater with Honorable John Wentworth this P. M. and I have no time to spare now, but will write again in a few days. For the present I will suggest that you have your silk dress cut and made in the Queen Ann style. I see everything here is running that way. They cut and build their houses, and bedsteads, and bureaus and chairs and looking-glass frames and dresses and cloaks and bonnets, Queen Ann style. I'll send you a book of Butterick's patterns to aid you in selecting your style of dress. One thing, don't, under any circumstance, have it cut goring, for that is all out of fashion. I inclose you a present from your pa, a fifty-dollar bill, for you to buy stockings and sundry things to go into them, with his compliments and good wishes for your trade. Hoping you will under the pressing circumstances of the present, excuse my short letter, I will close with these touching lines—

"I want you to love one and t'other
Better than trade and money;
I want you to love your mother
Better than cake and honey.

"Remember, while it is sunshine,
That there may be cloudy days,
And dont turn love into moonshine
But be true in all your ways.

"Your own Mother, Clarissa."

The letters read and Mary's answered, we was ready for supper, and supper was ready for us. As we entered the dining-room we seemed to be the observed of all observers, and the African waiters was awful polite to us, and they was all grinning. Clarissa was more nicely dressed than when we was at the Palmer a few days before, as she had been into Marsh Field's big store and bought her a brand new silk dress ready made. It was right in the height of fashion. She got it at a bargain, as it was made for a wealthy Board of Trade man's wife, but before they got it done he had gone

CLARISSA'S QUEEN ANN DRESS.

long on so much stuff, that he got short of cash and was completely, teetotally, and now and forevermore busted, and consequently the dress was on their hands, and they was willing to sell it for what it cost to make it and throw in the price of the material. They told her to try it on and if it fitted, she might have it for twenty-five dollars. She tried it on and it fitted her better by a considerable sight than if it had been made for her. It was black crow grain silk and shiny satin. There was one thing about it that bothered Clarissa muchly, and that was a wire basket or chicken-coop arrangement in the back end of the skirt, to make it have the appearance of a city lot, narrow in front but running back a good ways. She never had anything of the kind on before. She wore it this afternoon the first time, and when she sat down to the table in the dining-room, it took her as much as five minutes to sit down comfortable like without doing damage to the rear attachment to her new Queen Ann dress. I don't generally try to listen to other folks' conversation, but I couldn't very well help hearing the following talk going on between some women that was sitting at the table right back of us. It run about as follows, to wit:

"Say, Mrs. Blatty, isn't that the woman that was here last week and received them bouquets?"

"Yes, Mrs. Teller, that's that Benjamin Morgan and his wife, Clarissa, the *Tribune* had so much fun about."

"She is considerable dressed up to what she was then," said Mrs. Smeller. "Yes; but say, just look at that dress closely and see if you don't believe that that is the very identical dress that Marshall Field & Co. made for Mrs. Buncum."

"Well, as true as you live, it is the same one, or one made exactly like it."

"Why didn't Mrs. Buncum take it?"

"Why, didn't you know he had failed, and lost every cent he had?"

"No, I hadn't heard of it."

"Well, it's so, and he is so badly involved that he can never recover, and she couldn't pay for the dress. I was along with her when she ordered it, and it was to be $200."

"Well, I'm glad of it. She used to fly high and outdo all of us, here. I always knew she was a coarse, low-bred thing."

"Why, Mrs. Teller, how can you say that, when you and she was bosom friends while they was boarding here, and you copied after her in a great many things? I think she was a lady in every sense of the word, and I am truly sorry for her, and I am going to ascertain her whereabouts and call on her, and offer what assistance I can, without giving offence."

"Mrs. Porter, I'm glad you think so much of her. I can't afford to associate with any one that haint able to keep up to style."

Clarissa had heard every word, and her firm principles of right and honesty got the better of her sense of propriety, and she wheeled round in her chair and addressed the last lady that spoke, who happened to be right back of her, as follows: "Ladies, please excuse me for interrupting your conversation, but I can't sit in the hearing of hypocrites without giving them a piece of my reproving mind. I want to say that any woman that is not a natural lady, and has not the essential elements in her of true womanhood, can't afford to associate with anybody that can't prop them up and carry 'em along, but a true woman can not only afford to continue to associate with her friends in adversity as well as prosperity, but they can better afford to do so than otherwise, for they elevate themselves to a higher position in their sex, and reflect more of the image of their Creator by such a course of life. Now, I don't think it is any of your particular business where I got my dress, so long as it is paid for, and don't come out of you, but since you have made known to me the unfortunate lady's circumstances, I shall find out where she is and send the dress to her, with the compliments of an honest woman who feels sorry for them as is unfortunate. I can afford to do it, while you possibly can afford to cut her acquaintance. I don't know but you may be a millionaire, but one thing I'll prophesy, and that is you will see poverty before you die."

If a camphene lamp had bursted on that table it wouldn't have cleaned them women out quicker than Clarissa's shot of burning words. All but the one they called Mrs. Porter left the room with horror-stricken and scornful complexions on their countenances. She came up to Clarissa and said, "Although I am a stranger to you, yet I feel truly gratified to meet you as a representative of the true worth in woman, honesty and charity, and although it may shock some of the boarders at this hotel to hear such plain remarks, especially in the dining-room, it will do them some good, and may be the means of stopping some of the backbiting that is of too frequent occurrence. I shall be pleased to have you call at my room, No. —, third floor, before you leave the city." Clarissa thanked her for her kind invitation, and said she would try to do so if she could get the time.

By this time the African waiter came in with our supper, and we paid special attention to taking care of it. I was pretty hungry; in fact, I am always hungry when it comes anywhere near meal time. After we had returned to our room, we engaged in a talk about the dining-room episode. I told Clarissa I was just on the point of asking that Mrs. Teller if she wanted to know where I bought my clothes, when she opened on them, and I was glad she did it, but just as likely as not they would have the whole affair in the paper the next morning. While we were talking the Hon. J. Wentworth called and introduced himself to Clarissa by saying, "I don't know but you may have forgotten me, as it has been a good many years since I have seen you, but I used to know your father, Mr. Amasa Snodgrass, intimately when I was a young man in New Hampshire, and I knew you when a young lady." Clarissa met him in a cordial spirit and said she remembered him as well as though their acquaintance had continued up to yesterday, and in fact, it would be quite impossible for her to ever forget such a *long* acquaintance.

He said after noticing our arrival, he had recalled her to mind and thought he would renew the old acquaintance and also get acquainted with Mr. Morgan, therefore sent his card and invitation to us this morning. Clarissa then introduced me to him.

He sat down and for an hour he was the most entertaining gentleman I ever met. He is quite old in body, but young and vigorous in mind, and chuck full of wit and humor. He gave us a complete history of Chicago, and well he could, as he has been identified with its birth and wonderful growth. His description of its physical and political growth sounded like a thrilling novel; his reference to scores of men—whose names are as familiar all over the United States as household words—and a summing up of their hypocritical characters, made me feel that the great Chicago was born in sin (of poor parents that was naturally well-meaning but

"BECAUSE IT'S THE ONLY BUILDING I KNOW OF IN THE CITY THAT HAINT GOT A MORTGAGE ON IT."

wanted to make money so bad that they had left their honest clothes back yonder where they came from) and was cradled in iniquity, but when it got strong enough to get out of its cradle and go alone, it had become better, and had been growing better ever since, until now it was full as good as some of its neighbors, especially Cincinnati and New York.

He told us that Chicago was a good deal like an animal that once in about so often, when its coat of corruption got too long and had a strong odor, would shake itself and shed it, and come out with a clean, slick coat. It done this when the Colvin government had become a sickening sight to honest people. "And," said he, "I prophesy that about next spring she'll shed her coat again, for Harrisonism is getting to smell pretty loud."

If I had time I could make quite a book on the play of "high-spy" by Chicago politicians, from what little I have heard since I've been here, but it wouldn't be new nor interesting, as everybody knows all about it, for what the *Tribune* don't tell on one side the *Times* does; so, after all, the city is a good deal like a Christian ought to be, "read and known of all men."

As the little clock on the mantel struck quarter to eight, Mr. Wentworth said it was time to go. We went to the Grand, right opposite the Court House and City Hall. As we were passing in front of the courthouse Mr. Wentworth said that was the greatest curiosity in the city, pointing to it. I asked him how so? He said, "Because it's the only building I know of in the city that haint got a mortgage on it." I told him he must be trying to sell us some cod, or mackerel, but I didn't take it in.

We went into the theater and had some nice seats in the front row in the first balcony. That night we took the biggest trip that's recorded in the pages of history, either sacred or profane. We went round the world in eighty days. The coolest man I ever met in my life was that ar Phineas Fogg. I suggested to Mr. Wentworth that they ought to elect him Mayor of Chicago; I believe he'd clean out them anarchists completely. When the party was coming east from San Francisco on the Union Pacific Railroad, and got into them robbers' gang and Indians, it made Clarissa a little nervous, and she said she was almost afraid to go over that road; but Mr. Wentworth assured her that that was only in the play. A novel couldn't be got up without having all the circumstances just right to show off the hero or heroine, or both, in the strongest light, and if the circumstances never did exist, the writer had to make them exist, and right there lay the strength and power of our great writers—the ability to create what never did and in all human probabilities never could, exist. That's the reason Charles Dickens is so great, and one reason why he went home disgusted with America on his first visit, was that he found his extreme ideas more nearly realized here than he thought they could be in any country, and when he wrote his next book 'twas harder work for him to make new characters and new circumstances; that's what ailed Charles Reade, and a host of others.

Clarissa regained her usual calm habit after his explanation. The trip completed, the money won, and the curtain dropped, we went home, bidding good-night in the office of the Palmer House to the greatest man by some inches, that Chicago can lay claim to as her own.

We ascended the grand marble stairs to the parlor floor and wended our way to the spare bedroom we occupied. The next day we visited the Home of the Friendless, the Public Library, the Battle of Shiloh, the Fat Cattle Show, the Chicago Waterworks, and called on some old friends we had run across. All of which we have not time to speak of, as the train we want to go on leaves at 10:20 A. M. to-morrow morning.

By the time we reached the Palmer it was 6 o'clock in the evening, and we was considerably wearied, if not more so. But an hour in the supper room and the grand meal we ate rested us so that after supper we went down to the "Entré Sol" and sat in the little balcony and watched the moving, restless crowd in the office room. We had not been sitting there long till we saw 'Squire B. B. Bigler and Jim Teeters walk in from the State Street entrance, and go up to the counter and register. Teeters had a satchel and a plug hat on, and evidently had just arrived, but Bigler didn't have any, and kinder acted as though he'd been in there before. I kinder thought

I'd like to find out about things at home, and know something about what they were here for, so I hollered out, "Squire Bigler." I hollered three times before he looked up, but the whole crowd looked up as if they was surprised, but I didn't care for that; I was too tired to go down there, and I wanted him to come up. When I got his attention he seemed wonderfully pleased, and he and Teeters come up where we was. He shook hands with me and Clarissa as if he was our son, and said he had been trying to find us ever since he read in the *Tribune* about our arrival. He said he had been in Chicago pretty nigh a month. He come here right from our neigh-

"I HOLLERED, 'SQUIRE BIGLER.'"

borhood. He said his defeat in the election last fall was just the best thing that ever happened to him, for now he had got a position as assistant to the general solicitor of one of the largest railroads that runs from Chicago westward. He gets good pay, and a chance to make considerable outside, and already he had got a big deal on hand for three or four silver mines in Colorado, and if he made the deals he would clear $150,000.

He was awful glad to see us, and wanted us to come and see

him before we left, but we told him we was going to leave in the morning. He told us if we went to Denver to be sure to stop at the St. James Hotel and he would be very apt to meet us there, as he was going out there the latter part of next week. He hadn't sent for his wife yet, as he was waiting to get a house to move into that he had the promise of.

Teeters came up and shook hands with us and took a seat and waited till Bigler got through before he said anything. He looked and acted cheap enough. He told us all about things around the village, and about selling out, and said he left there yesterday morning, and had just come in. He said Waddles had got out of jail, but had to pay about $1,875 and costs; he was now trying to sell out, and if he succeeded he was going to move to Chicago.

After Clarissa and I went to bed I told her that I didn't wonder at what Mr. Wentworth said about the city in its early days. If three such men as Waddles, Teeters and Bigler should move to Chicago from every neighborhood in the United States it would be the largest city in the world, and the most hypocritical. It was a good thing there was honest women and mothers here, and that children was born regularly every year, otherwise it would perish from the face of the earth. One thing I am glad on, that is my reasoning is not true in facts, for where one swindler moves to this city, five good, likely, well-meaning and honest people come along to keep them down.

Clarissa signified a desire on her part for me to shut my mouth and go to sleep, so she could sleep and rest. As her desire is law to me, I at once obeyed.

The usual roar and rattle of wagons and the endless cry of the newsboys awoke us at an early hour, and Clarissa packed our things and had everything ready for us to leave before we went to breakfast.

CHAPTER XXV.

AFTER breakfast we had our baggage taken to the Chicago & Northwestern Railway depot, and after urging Mr. Palmer to make it convenient to make us a visit if he ever come our way, we bid him and his smart young clerks good-by and walked over to the depot. We preferred to walk so we could step into Mr. Harrison's office on our way and bid him good-by. We found Mr. Harrison in, and as he shook our hands cordially he urged us to return via Chicago and give him a visit, so he might know how we got along. We expressed our gratitude for his kind treatment and attention, and told him if ever he came to the village, although I wasn't its mayor—for two reasons, first, the village wasn't big enough to have a mayor, and second, I lived eight or ten miles out of it—I would do all in my power to return his kindness. We walked on to the depot. We got there about twenty minutes before the train left, and I had plenty of time to get my baggage checked.

We finally got on the train, and I secured two down-stair bedrooms in the sleeping car, right opposite each other. I had made up my mind to get as good accommodations for Clarissa on the whole of this trip as I could, whether Ketchem, Holdem & Skinem paid it or not, as it would, in all probability, be the last trip of the kind we would ever take.

As the train pulled out of the depot and we were leaving the city of Chicago, I felt a pang of regret, as we had passed several days, with the exception of the first, most pleasantly within its limits. It had been both a school and playhouse for us. We was constantly learning something new, and being amused at the same time. The fact that we two green country folks had, at the very outstart of our great Western trip, visited the greatest city on the American Continent, had met many of its most prominent citizens and been received by them in a most cordial and friendly manner, made our departure in one sense regretful.

I am well satisfied, although unacquainted personally with other cities, that for push, vigorous prosecution of business, friendly feeling, and power to manage its own affairs, ability to rise above all disasters and obstacles, nerve and pluck, it is the greatest city in America, and it's only a question of time when she will be the greatest in population, as she has got plenty of room to grow. I am fully satisfied that Jim Teeters' project of hiring the river there and shedding it over for bathhouses won't work worth a cent, for three reasons: First, he'll never have money enough to do it; second, he never can get the water clean enough and smell sweet enough to answer the purpose, and third, almost every house has got a bathtub in it, and the folks you meet on the street are as clean a looking lot as can be found anywhere.

Clarissa had provided herself with some good books to read on the way, and after we was well out of the city she brought out a book from her satchel called "Shadows of the Future." I asked her where she got it. She told me Mr. Harrison give it to her and told her he studied it considerable, and as he knew it pretty nigh by heart he could spare it as well as not. Nothing worth noting took place during the day until we arrived at Boone, where our train was detained about ten hours on account of an accident on the road ahead of us. We walked around the town and dropped into several stores and other places, and found a thriving, wide-awake town, with some large business houses. Doctors and drugstores seemed to be the most numerous, and seemed to have the most to do. The furniture dealer and undertaker seemed to have the next best business. I talked with one or two lawyers. They said business was a good deal better since the State had passed a law known as the Pharmacy Act. They had a chance to work up all the business they wanted If they didn't get it one way they could make it another. I met a lawyer there that knew Squire Bigler intimately. We didn't disagree in our opinion of him. We went into the Wells House and found one of the most complete taverns I ever saw. The landlord saw we was strangers, and asked us who we was, etc. Of course I knew he didn't want to pry into our private affairs, but still I saw he had a sort of a lingering, longing, gnawing appetite, that most all tavern keepers have, to know who you be? where you come from? where are you going? how long are you going to stop with me? how much money have you got, and how much of it can I get? So I told him my name was Uncle Benjamin Morgan, of Morganville, Blank County, New York, and this here woman was my wife, Clarissa; that if he took the Chicago *Tribune* he had heard of us; that we was on our way to California, was blocked here by a accident on the road ahead of us, and we thought we'd look around a little. He was awful polite to us, and showed us all around, and then insisted on our taking dinner with him, which we did. When we come out into the office we noticed hanging on the walls in a gilt frame, the following:

"DIRECTORY FOR THE USE OF TIRED, WEARY AND SICK FOLKS.

"If you wish a doctor in Boone to find,
The first in the block is Dock Ensign ;
Next below according to our plan,
Is our railroad doctor, Alleman ;
Go up the next stairway not fearing,
And you'll find within Dr. Deering.
Then comes the one on which we wager,
The jolly good Doctor Stockslager ;
Continuing on, the next below
Is the ladies' favorite, Doctor Rowe ;
And in the same room without a jar,
Dwells the scientific Dock DeTarr ;
Within the next four walls' inclosure
Is to be found the oldest, Moser;
But if little pills you are stuck on,
At the next door you'll find Huntington.

EXPERIENCE WITH HYPOCRITES.

"With drugstores all of which are alive,
Our city is blest with numbers five ;
The first that keeps stuff colic to squelch,
Is owned and operated by Welsh ;
The next across the way you peek in,
Is J. Peterson and McMechin ;
The next, where you can stop your wailin'
Belongs to one Henry Thormalin ;
As you go down, not very far,
Is the establishment of DeTarr ;

WELLS HOUSE.

Step across the street and walk in
To the store of Draper & Laughlin ;
When through with doctors and druggists, you lie
On your sick bed, waiting to die,
You want a coffin to hold your arms,
You can get what you want, at G. W. Barnes.

"BUT IF YOU TAKE YOUR MEALS AT THE WELLS HOUSE, YOU WILL HAVE NO USE FOR EITHER OF THE ABOVE."

I merely introduce the above directory to show the novelty and ingenuity of Western men; every man, woman and child in Morganville, Blank County, New York, or down to the village would have died, buried themselves, been resurrected, brought before the Judge and received final sentence before they'd ever thought of such a scheme to get folks to eat at their tavern, but these Westerners are right up to the front in everything, while we old fogies down on our little potato patches, grubbing along with old dull hoes, don't know half as much as we ought to. I shall always remember the village of Boone, with its doctors, drugstores and magnificent hotels. Our train was ready to start and we was aboard and ready, and we shook the dust of Boone off of our car wheels as we made a dive for the Des Moines River at a fearful down grade rush, and climbed out of its valley at equally as hard a grade on the opposite side.

As we pass through the State of Iowa one cannot help being impressed with its beauty, although November is not a favorable season of the year to see beauty in landscape. Yet its undulating surface, with broad prairies and numerous streams, makes it look beautiful, even in the bleak and desolate November. I learned that Iowa derives its name from the Indians, and in their language it means "the beautiful land." It was originally part of the large territory of Louisiana, ceded to the United States in 1803. The first white man that settled within its borders was Julian Dubuque, a Canadian Frenchman, who in 1788 got a grant of a big tract, including the present city of Dubuque and the rich mineral lands nigh to it. It was admitted as a State into the Union December 28, 1846. The first Constitution was adopted August 3, 1857. Every Iowan brags about his State unless he is in the liquor business, either as a buyer and consumer, or as a seller. Then he curses it. We passed the two Missis in the night, therefore I am unable to tell how they looked or describe their winter clothes, but they tell me that Sippy is more graceful and has a cleaner complexion than "Soury." I know the bridge over Soury is a wonderful structure of iron, supported by monstrous great iron pins that go right down into Soury's bosom, and I'm told by some people that got on at Omaha that them iron pegs go clean through Soury and fasten themselves upon her grandparent called *sub-strata*, but I don't pretend to believe all I hear these Omaha folks say, for all of 'em that got on our train tell such big stories that they smell fishy. For instance, out of the ten Omahaians that come into our car at that city there was only one that didn't tell some whopper about Omaha, and he seemed kind and didn't speak a word during the whole

"UNLESS HE IS IN THE LIQUOR BUSINESS, THEN HE CUSSES IT."

day we was spinning along on the Union Pacific, and such statements as these was the burden of their remarks: "Yes, sir; Tom, I tell you that Omaha in ten years from now will be a bigger city than Chicago." "Well now, Bill, you just bet your bottom dollar she will. You know that Phil Armour is going to move his packing houses here from Chicago, and that will double her in less 'an five years. I just wish them are Eastern strikers would just go ahead with their strikes, for just as fast as they do the manufacturers will just close up their establishments and find a location out West to move to, and I'm just tellin' you, boys, that if we work our pins right, we can get every one of 'em to Omaha."

"Now you're shouting, old boy; why, last week Studebaker, from South Bend, Indiana, was in Omaha trying to buy seventy-five acres of land to move his big wagon factory on; he went and looked at the land down on the flats, and to-day you can't buy a lot 40x120 down there within half a mile of the piece he looked at for less than five hundred dollars, and two weeks ago they would have been dumb glad to sold 'em at five dollars apiece; why, I've got two lots right opposite the Cuzzins' House that I tried to sell a year ago at $1,000, and to-day I wouldn't thank a man to offer me less than $75,000 for 'em."

"Well, George, my advice to you is not to sell 'em for any such money as that. You just hang onto them and in ten years from now, with the present rapid growth of our king city, they'll make you a clean half a million."

"I believe you, Ben, and I guess I'll hang."

"There is one thing, boys, you haint mentioned yet," said a big bushy-headed fellow that had been silent up to the present, "and it's a very significant indication of Omaha's wonderful future, and that is this, Colonel Sellers is down in Kentucky organizing a colony of rich Kentucks, and is going to bring them up to Omaha, and go out to the northwest part of the city and build a large addition. They will go into various kinds of manufacturing business, and that alone will double Omaha in less than one year. I received a letter from the Colonel last week, in which he states that everything is all ready, and the organization is complete except one thing, and that is the signing of the articles of agreement. That just as soon as the parties have all signed they will make immediate preparations to move, that he expects to have all the signatures within two or three days. Why, everybody over in Council Bluffs is putting runners under their houses, and just as soon as the river is frozen over solid, you'll see more Council Bluffs' residents sliding over to Omaha than there are bees in a hive."

The remarks of the last gentleman seemed to be the Bartholdi story of the party. A dead lull seemed to rest upon us all. I had become so interested in their descriptions of the future of Omaha that the suspense caused by this lull was more'n I could bear, so I went over and set down beside the man that had not thus far uttered a word, and I spoke in a quiet way to him so as not to attract too much attention, and asked him if he could give me a correct idea of

OMAHA WITH COLONEL SELLERS' ADDITION.

the size of Omaha, its population, facilities and future prospects. He turned his face to me, and with a grin that closely resembled a cross between that of a monkey and a son of the lost tribe of Israel shook his head and give me to understand that he did not understand me, when I repeated my question more clearly and in a louder voice, and in reply received the same shake of the head, and the same idiotic smile. I repeated the question four times, increasing the power of vocalization each succeeding time, when one of the gentlemen in the party said, as he spoke between his laughs, "Ha, ha, ha; say, he, he, he, stranger, ho, ho, ho, that ar feller. hu, hu, hu, is deaf and dumb. Wha, wha, wha."

I said, "*Thanks*," and I said to Clarissa when I returned to our seat, "*God bless Omaha.*" "What for?" she asked. "Why," said I, "she has got one citizen that can't *lie!* That fellow over there is deaf and dumb."

The fellow that told the Bartholdi story overheard my remark and said, "Stranger, perhaps you don't believe what we have said concerning Omaha, and I am not surprised at all, as I can scarcely believe it myself." I said, "I thought so when I heard you." "Wait

THE FELLOW THAT COULDN'T LIE.

till I finish my remarks," said he, "but I know it is just as I have stated."

"Well," said I, "I am surprised that we folks back in New York State haven't heard of your wonderful city. I remember reading about Omaha in our village paper about twenty years ago, as a pioneer village where the Union Pacific Railroad started from, but hadn't any idea before now that the sun rose in a town on the Missouri River, or that it had its golden bed there, but I don't know much about geography, and if Clarissa says it is so, I'll believe it," and I turned to Clarissa and asked her how it was.

She replied with considerable indignification that "the sun didn't rise nor set in any town, city or country." She said she had very often heard of Omaha, but she didn't think it had any such a wonderful future before it, for if it had, Carter Harrison would have said something about it, and would, in all probability, be figuring on his prospects of being its mayor some future day, after he has got Chicago on a good social and financial basis. She might, however, discover something in her book of "Shadows of the Future." She hadn't read but a few pages yet. If she did, she would call my attention to it.

The Omaha gentlemen soon after arranged themselves into card parties and went to playing for fun, to pass away the time. They asked me to take a hand with them, but I told them I didn't know anything about cards, and didn't want to, but that I didn't have any objections to Omaha making millions and having all the fun they wanted; for which they thanked me. The remainder of the trip, until we arrived at Cheyenne, was rather dry and monotonous within the cars and still more monotonous and uninteresting without. The broad plains, shorn of every evidence of vegetation, seemed like an immense corpse, while the whistling, chilly wind sounded like a funeral requiem. Before arriving at Cheyenne, I told the conductor that I'd like a lay off check for a few days, as we wanted to go down through Colorado.

We left Cheyenne on the afternoon train on the Denver Road and arrived in Denver in the evening. When the conductor called on me for tickets, I handed him what I got in Syracuse, and he said that was no good to him; there was nothing among them that entitled me to ride on his road. Then I pulled out the advertisement and showed it to him. He smiled and shook his head, and said that he had quite a number on his trains during the past ten days, in the same fix. That I would have to pay my fare on his road; that he would give me a receipt for the amount I paid him, and I could present it to the company's office in San Francisco, and would no doubt draw it back, if the company was good for it. "Another Christian act!" I remarked. I paid him, or rather Clarissa paid him (for she had the money).

When we arrived in Denver we went to the St. James Hotel, and after supper, which was about nine o'clock, Clarissa went to her room which was a front bedroom on the third floor, and I went out into the office to sit down a few minutes. I am not as quick about learning new things as some, but I am gradually, as the boys say, "gettin' onto 'em." Clarissa has instructed me in the use of kindlin' wood, and now I can take a double handful of the little splinters and sit down in a hotel office and jab my teeth with 'em and throw them around on the floor with pretty nigh as good grace and style as the average high toned boarder.

I was sitting in the office of the St. James, my feet braced against the window casing, and leaning back in a comfortable old-fashioned splint-bottomed arm chair, and scattering the broken wood picks to the right and left in a professional manner, and thinking about what a wonderful traveler Uncle Ben was getting to be, and what sights he had seen, and what stories he would be able to tell the folks down around Morganville and the village—the biggest story of the lot I could tell 'em, as things run in my mind, being the Omaha boom, when some one slapped me on the shoulder, and said, "Uncle Ben, how are you?" Whether it was the suddenness of the shock, which seemed to electrify me, or the slipping of my chair, that caused me to double up like a jack-knife and plant my seat of government on the floor, with a dull thud, while head, heels and arms were confusedly mixed with the arm-chair, I am at present unable to tell, but upon recovering a position becoming to one of my years, I confronted the form and person of Squire Bigler, who seemed delighted to see me and begged my pardon for the accident, of which

EXPERIENCE WITH HYPOCRITES. 277

he had been the innocent cause. He drew up his chair and both of us being seated in a sensible manner, he went on to tell me when he come in, and his plans, etc.

Said he, "Uncle Ben, you know what I told you in Chicago?" "Yes." "Well, I am on my way to Leadville, where I have got some large mining interests to look after, and I am going to make a fortune out of it. Besides this, Uncle Ben, I have got the biggest scheme on foot for big money that there is out. I'm going to get a few fellers that I know that have got money, and organize a big cattle company. I will get the feller that will put in the most

"UNCLE BEN, HOW ARE YOU?"

money elected President, and the other fellers as directors, and get myself elected as Secretary and Treasurer. We can get plenty of men that are looking for places to put their money where it will bring them from 25 to 50 per cent. interest, to invest. We can put in one dollar on the hundred of the capital stock, cash, and then operate our scheme altogether on the money these outside parties invest. We can get any quantity of land in this State for grazing purposes, and not cost us a cent. And when we are organized we will get up flaming circulars and send them all over the United States, and in two years we can make a mint of money. Now, Uncle Ben, if you'll go into this along with me I'll assure you that you'll make a splendid fortune in less than two years." He went on for more'n an hour telling about his schemes and urging me to take a hand with him. I thought to myself, "I know the Squire just as well as if I'd made him," and with this knowledge I decided that Uncle Ben Morgan would be better off in two years hence to have nothing to do with Bigler. So I said to him:

"Mr. Bigler, your scheme looks very plausible, but I wasn't born on Friday, and under the scheming star. I've worked hard for what I've got, and by hard work, economy and strict honesty I have managed to get enough ahead to take care of me and Clarissa as long as we live, and leave something to the children, and I will let well enough alone and not take a hand in any schemes. I went into a little scheme on my way out here, between Buffalo and Cleveland, and I have concluded to let schemes of all kinds alone. But," said I, "Bigler, you go on with your scheme, and when you get in operation you write to me and send me one of your circulars and a statement of your organization, and I'll show it to some of the folks around home."

After he had further developed his plans and showed to me more'n ever that he was a heartless hypocrite, I told him I was tired and going to bed, which I did.

After I was undressed and ready to get into bed I tried to blow out the electric light. I fooled around the dumb glass thing for a long time, but I couldn't find a hole in the thing to get the wind into it, so I had to call a waiter to put it out for me. When I got into bed I told Clarissa about meeting Bigler, and our talk. She said that Bigler would turn out like Teeters, a first-class swindler, unless he changed his course, and she didn't think he would be apt to do that, as he has pursued a crooked line of policy all his life.

CHAPTER XXVI.

THE next morning we took a fine carriage and driver, and went all over the capital city of Colorado. We was delighted with its splendid streets. They are as hard as the best paved streets of Chicago, and much smoother. It is indeed a beautiful city—alike beautiful on account of its magnificent public buildings and private residences, its cleanliness and its location. The great Rocky Mountains raise their rugged peaks but a few miles to the west, like a huge wall to protect it from invasion by a foreign foe, while the plains stretch off to the east beyond human vision.

One can almost imagine three camels, with their riders—one from the plains of New Mexico, one from the Northland, and one from the foothills of the Sierra Madre—converging at a given point in the east, being led thither by a star, so similar is this location to some of those places in Judea made famous in Bible story.

Although it was the first day of December, yet the air was soft, mild and dry, and the ground free from snow, but the tops of the distant mountains sparkled like hotel clerks' breastpins in the morning sun with their covering of snow and frost, and occasionally I could see flashing clouds of crimson light fly up to the blue sky above, just like I have seen a real genuine blush fly up on a girl's cheek at a corn-husking when she found a red ear and her fellow paid her for it in the customary currency used at corn-huskings. We visited Capital Hill, and every other prominent point in the city, and then we went out to the great silver smelting and production works managed by Professor (Senator) Hill. He happened to be there, and I introduced ourselves to him, and explained to him who we was and where we was from, and told him how anxious we was to learn what we could on our trip. He said he read about us in the Chicago *Tribune* about ten days ago. He seemed pleased to think we had called on him, and he took particular pains to show us all through the great works, and explained the entire process of getting the gold and silver out of the rock and separating it from the vulgar (Clarissa says that is the proper term for base, as it means the same thing. I use it here because I want to be proper) metals and refining it, and bringing it out pure and unadulterated in great bricks.

I'll be dumbed if I wasn't educated more in the two hours I spent with Senator Hill in them works than I ever was in the seven winters I went to schools kept by young men that didn't know but mighty little after all; but they wasn't to blame for what they didn't know, for, in all probability, they never had a chance to know much.

I tell you what it is, if anybody wants to know some of the practical things in this world that's worth knowing, they should just take a trip and travel once in awhile, and when they see things they don't understand, just ask about it, even at the risk of being impudent; it's better to be a bold, or even impudent, seeker after information you don't possess, but have a hankering for, than to be a cowardly fool—and they will learn more that will be of satisfaction to 'em than they can in any way for the same amount of money and time.

Now, Clarissa and I learned in two hours at them great works what has caused the brains of the best heads years and years of hard study and work, and the expenditure of immense sums of money in experimenting. I find I am running away from what I started on, so I'll do what the railroad boys say, shut off and reverse.

Had I the time, I would enter into particulars and say considerable about Denver and its many institutions, its mint, its banks of various kinds, not omitting them as was organized and established by King Pharaoh, and which have never lost their popularity; especially in the Western cities, they tell me that they are quite numerous. I think it was a blessing to Moses that Pharaoh's daughter hid him from the old man, as, in all probability, had the old king discovered what a smart lad his daughter had found, he would have made him his principal dealer. But it is sad, however, to be made aware of the painful fact that Moses' nigh relatives are very fond of Pha-

"GET IN BACK OF ME, YOU GOLDEN TEMPTER."

raoh's game, and spend much of their time nights in trying to beat the banker or amusing themselves with his fire *poker*. Sometimes they get their hands on the hot end of it and get burnt, sometimes to the extent of several hundred dollars' worth. However, there are other kinds of people besides the sons of Abraham, Isaac and Jacob that do business at the old king's bank.

When we returned to the hotel for supper it was 5:30 P. M. (which means Post Master under the last administration), and we was glad to take a little rest in the parlor before supper was called. While setting there Mr. Bigler came in and greeted Clarissa with a real warm spirit and shake of hands. We went in to supper together, and really it was pleasant to have his company, for he can act the finished gentleman in a most agreeable manner. He asked us to go to the theater with him, and we accepted his invitation.

We went to Tabor's Opera House, and saw the play of Three-eyed Richard. The building is a very fine, massive structure, and the theater room is nicer and more grand than any I saw in Chicago. We both of us liked the play very much, but I never knew there was such a confounded old rascal as that humpbacked old villain, Richard. I don't know but that, after all, some of these days I'll be compelled to disagree with Clarissa on the point of hell, for if there isn't a hell, I think there ought to be for just such villains as this feller was, and several others I have met since I started out on this trip.

The next day I was walking leisurely down the streets, swinging the gold-headed cane that Clarissa made me a present of, and looking at everything I saw, and if I was stopped and interviewed once on the subject of *mines* and *mining* stock, and asked to buy, I was a dozen times. Before I returned to the hotel for dinner I was so confused that both of my arms was lame and paining me. The wonderful fortunes that I could make in a very short time by the investment of a little money was appalling, and stronger minds than mine have tumbled down before such temptations. But I have managed to say, "Get in back of me, you golden tempter; I don't want to be contaminated by you."

I don't know what it is about me that conveys the idea to so many strangers that I have money to invest in every scheme that comes up, unless it is my gold-headed cane and calfskin boots, and honest countenance. I was offered stock in the Dives, Pelican, Vulture, Blackhawk, Old Crow, Mudhen, Bluejay, Robin, Peacock, Turkey, Rattlesnake, Busted, Big Silver and Little Silver, Tom Cat, and every other animal name you can think, any one of which would, according to the seller's story, make me a millionaire.

The thought of so suddenly and in such a short time being made the richest man in America, and having such a burden thrust upon me was revolting to my nature, so I persistently declined being made rich on such short notice, and in such a short time.

The two days I was in Denver I discovered that while the Denverites are a very intelligent class of people and are full of tact and push, the uppermost and controlling thought which seems to line their clouds of speculation by day, and gild their dreams by night, is money, money, money. I merely judge by those I met with; perhaps the masses there are no more greedy than the rest of mankind.

We made the tour of Central City, Georgetown, Leadville, Canyon City, Pueblo, Colorado Springs, Manitou, Pike's Peak, the Garden of the Gods, and back to Denver. Of all the sights in nature I ever dreamed of, the most wonderful we saw on this trip.

There is sufficient to fill a large volume and be of intense interest to the average reader, if written by one skilled in such art, but I have only time at present to say but little about it. In rattling up the mountains and twisting through the canyons and gorges, you are apt to get a little dusty and smoked, and I would advise you when you get to Idaho Springs, to go down and visit one of the tall representatives of Blank County, New York, Harrison Montague, and wash off and swim in his big bathhouse. It is the most delightful bathing place in the whole world, so far as I've seen. The water comes from original headquarters, at just the right temperature.

Colorado is a high State. The ground is high, the air is high, the mountains are high, the people are high, they look high, they think high, they walk high, and they talk high. Everything you look at is high. If you want to buy anything it is high, everywhere you go you have to pay high for it. Clarissa seemed to fill up with the spirit and air of the country, and she got high notions, and felt younger than I had ever known her to since I courted her; and when we was driving through the Garden of the Gods, she was completely enthused with the spirit of rapture and admiration, and as we passed Cathedral Rock, at the very entrance to this wonderful garden, she expressed a desire to climb up to the top of its lofty pinnacle and view the wondrous land we was entering into, as the eagle does from his superior heights, but we drove on, and she didn't climb.

When we come to the balanced rock the driver stopped the carriage and told us we could get out and go around the rock and take our time to see this wonderful piece of work that was supposed to have been begun by one of the ancient gods, who was driven out of the garden and murdered before he had completed his job. Jealousy on the part of the other gods is supposed to have been the principal cause of the dark and foul deed.

He showed us all over the sides of the rock, where visitors had inscribed their names. As high up as we could see through our spy-glasses we could see names chiseled into its sides. Clarissa said she wished she could get up higher than any of them and cut her name, then she could always feel that Mary and Abraham's mother had her name as high as any mortals in this mundane (I don't exactly know what that word means, but some big writers have used it more or less frequently, and I guess I can) sphere, and it would be a source of pride, when she had departed from mortal scenes, for them to tell to their posterity and others, that their mother's name was recorded on high in one of the tablets of the gods—in Colorado. The driver, seeing she had a strong desire to do what so many others had done, thought he would assist her.

He found, hid behind another big rock, a crude ladder, made of poles and sticks tied onto it with strips of rawhide. It looked very old, but he thought it would be safe. It had the appearance of having been made at the same time the rock was. The ladder was

EXPERIENCE WITH HYPOCRITES.

brought forth and placed against the rock, when, to her disappointment, it did not reach as high as she wanted to go by several feet. But the driver brought his ingenuity to bear upon the case, and got a couple more poles and tied on the bottom of the ladder, and tied some more sticks across them and got it long enough to reach about a foot higher than the highest name we could see. Clarissa is possessed of not only considerable nerve, but lots of inventive genius, and on this occasion she displayed both. She pinned her skirts tight around each ankle in such a way that a passing observer would have sworn (if in the habit of swearing) that she had on a pair of zouave pantaloons.

When she had completed her toilet she proceeded to climb. Cautiously she stepped upon each succeeding higher stick, while the driver and I held the foot of the rickety ladder to keep it steady. She finally, amid squeaks and squawks and twistings of the

"SHE WISHED SHE COULD GET UP HIGHER."

ladder, reached the top stick, and the snriek of disappointment she uttered as she caught a glimpse, on the very summit of the rock, about twenty-five feet beyond her, the name, "H. A. W. Tabor, Governor of Colorado," was truly heartrending. But she opened my old jack-knife I had loaned her for the occasion, and proceeded to cut. She had cut the letters C L A, when the splicing strings the driver had tied the poles on with broke, and down came Clarissa and the ladder. As good fortune would have it, I and the driver caught her on the fly. It was a fearful fall for all three of us. Clarissa was a total wreck so far as her habiliments and zouaves was concerned, and her hands and nose was covered with bruises, scratches and blood, while the driver had his nose knocked out of joint by Clarissa's head coming in close contact with it, and my arms was stuck as full of pins as if I had caught a porcupine. We carried her to the carriage and carefully wrapped her in blankets and laid her on the back seat, while I and the driver got on the front seat and drove to the hotel in Colorado Springs as fast as we could. In fifty minutes from the time Clarissa left her "Cla" on the gods' balanced rock, we was in our private room, surrounded with medicine and a doctor, sore from bruises and wounded ambition, and nothing left us but scars and meditation of ruined pride and blasted hopes. It was one day before she had sufficiently recovered from her shock and pain to be able to take the train for Denver, where we stopped over night. The landlord noticed she was powerful weak and considerable lame, and asked her what the matter was. She said she had met with a slight accident—that the climate and other things in Colorado was altogether too high for her health, and she had concluded to leave the next morning, which we did, via the C. C. R. R., arriving in Cheyenne in time to connect with the Union Pacific train west. I succeeded in getting Clarissa a down-stairs bedroom, but I had to take a bed in the loft.

CHAPTER XXVII.

ONCE more on our main line we felt a little at home. It is singular, but nevertheless true, that when one is traveling a long distance, the road that takes him to his objective point is regarded as a sort of home, and when he leaves it for a few days and again returns to it, a home-like feeling seems to possess him. It was so in our case this time. We felt that for at least thirty-six hours we hadn't got to make any changes, as we concluded to not leave this line again until we reached the end of it at Ogden. Pulling out of Cheyenne, we made rapid time for about four or five miles, when the engine began to puff and snort and roll out the smoke in monstrous great black clouds, as she climbed up the steep grade to Sherman, the highest point on the Union Pacific Railroad. As the train stopped about five minutes, we stepped out on the platform, and filled our lungs with the air that circulates around the highest railroad point on the American continent, which is about 9,000 feet above the level of the sea. Judging from the looks of the half-dozen natives we saw swaggering around the depot with their hands in their pockets, their mouths filled with tobacco, and dirty slouch hats drawn down over their eyes, I cannot say that a close residence to heaven has any great tendency to improve the human race. Looking off to the north we saw a huge pile of rocks they called "The Skulls;" I suppose they are the skulls of them gods that made that garden down in Colorado.

Leaving Sherman we went down a sharp grade about twenty-five miles, passing over Dale Creek on a bridge of iron trestle-work,

130 feet high and 650 long, to Laramie City, the capital of Wyoming Territory. The little city is noted for its rolling-mill, its lonely location, and for its being the home of the famous "Bill Nye," whose writings are like the climate and soil of his home, dry and sandy, sparkling with little gems. Two miles to the east of the city is Fort Laramie, where the government keeps a company of soldiers, when they haint down in the village getting high. After leaving Laramie we settled down into a sort of stupor; everything without was monotonous, cold and uninteresting. In every direction I looked, I could see distant rocky points of the Rocky Mountains. The sun had already dropped behind a range of these rocky points, and his glimmering rays, streaking up the western sky like the framework of a Japanese fan, made me think of the dying fire in our old fireplace in the kitchen, before we lit the candle, when I was a innocent boy.

The brakeman come in and lit the lamps in our car. Presently a card party was organized, composed of three wholesale drummers and a newspaper man. I discovered this by their talk. I have learned one thing on my travels, that if you take the advice that Clarissa gives me, viz., keep your eyes and ears wide open and your mouth shut a reasonable part of the time, it wont take long to find out who nine-tenths of the passengers are, where they are from and where they are going to, and what the drift of their business is. Somehow or other, about nine out of ten, when they get on a train, get very talkative, and they grow confidential and tell more than they think they are doing, just as I did the first day we started out, and about one-tenth are close mouthed and keep a keen eye on the rest. Well, I know I haint smart, but since I adopted Clarissa's advice, I have learned lots.

They proposed a game of whist. After deciding on their co-partnership, they went at it. The first round was won by a Chicago groceryman and a Boston clothing man. They claimed three points. The next round was lost by a St. Louis hardware man and the Denver *News* man. They lost four points, and as St. Louis generally does, according to the Chicago *Times*—lost the game. They was a jolly set of fellows, and real smart, but they was troubled with the same weakness that drummers in general, are ; they tell their business to most everybody. In less than ten minutes I found out that the Chicago man represented Sprague, Warner & Co., and was going to Ogden and Salt Lake. The Boston fellow was traveling on commission and represented half a dozen concerns—his name was Tom Ticklefeller. The St. Louis man they called Simmons Hardware Co., and t'other fellow, by the very gimlet and corkscrew combination countenance—couldn't be mistaken for anything but a newspaper man.

For right-down smoothness, greasy slickness, oleomargarine smearing over of things, the Sprague-Warner combination took the cake ; for swell and lofty self-estimation, the Boston combination had the bulge on the pot of beans; for hard luck and hard kicking, the Simmons hardware combination took the *hard-tack*; but for brass, volubility of words and fly-specks of ideas, combined with masterly lying, the Denver *News* machine took the whole *Dutch oven*. By the time they had finished the game and exchanged the usual amount of funny jokes, ready-made witty speeches—somewhat stale—and soap, hard-tack and concentrated lye, the train stopped at Rock Creek for supper, and we was glad of it, as we was real hungry.

We missed our magnificent dining car, which was left at Omaha. The pleasure of sitting as long as you please in an elegant car, with a delightful meal spread before you, and any quantity of time to eat it, with "not a wave of trouble to roll across your peaceful breast"—compared with making a mad rush for a hotel dining-room table, keeping your hat on your head for fear of having it stolen, and bolting your victuals down on express time, swallowing a cup of hot coffee to one gulp for fear you can't get another cup in time, and then, with a feeling of uncomfortableness hear the cry of "All aboard!"

while you make a rush for the train, being interrupted on the way by the landlord, who wants a dollar apiece from you—is true happiness.

After returning to our car I called Clarissa's attention to the difference between taking our meals this way and the dining car system. She said, "Yes; but Benjamin, we ought to be satisfied, when we think how delightful this is compared with the first rail-

"A DOLLAR, IF YOU PLEASE."

roading that was done about fifty years ago in the United States. I was just reading in the Philadelphia *Press* I have here, about the wonderful growth of railroads. I'll read it to you; it is this: ' Early Railroading. The marvelous growth of the railroad interest of the country in such a short time is illustrated by the fact that old men are still living in Baltimore who took the first ride with Peter Cooper in the first steam locomotive in America. The locomotive was simply an old stationary engine, about the size of a barrel, mounted on a truck, and connected with the wheels by a crank.

It pulled an old-fashioned coach, loaded with forty-two passengers, thirteen miles in fifty-seven minutes. On the return trip it raced with two fast horses. The contest was nip and tuck, when the band slipped off the fly wheel. Peter Cooper, the engineer, in attempting to replace it, lacerated his hand. The horses won the race. The first engine of really serviceable qualities was manufactured at York, Pennsylvania, by Phineas Davis. It made a mile in three minutes, drawing forty persons, and it took the prize offered by the Baltimore & Ohio Road. Davis became the road's chief constructor of engines.'"

The gentlemen resumed their card playing and funny talk, while Clarissa and I got acquainted with an elderly lady and gentleman who was sitting right in front of us. They was from New Jersey and was on their way to Honolulu to visit their son, who, they said, was Secretary of State in King Kalakaua's Cabinet. We found them real interesting folks to talk to, and the old gentleman had been to Honolulu before, and could talk the language of the natives of the Sandwich Islands quite well. He was telling us something in that language so we could see how it sounded, when a man that was sitting in a seat front of him, hearing him talk in the Sandwich language, spoke to him in the same tongue, and then came over and set down beside the old gentleman and went right into a conversation with him. We all got well acquainted in a short time. This man was a sea captain sent out by a New Bedford whaling company to take charge of a fleet of whaling vessels that was to sail from San Francisco up into the North Seas. He had been in that business for the past thirty years, and had spent a good many winters at Honolulu. They could all tell very interesting incidents in real life that they had experienced, except Clarissa and me. We was as barren of interesting experiences with which we could make up a marvelous story as an apple tree is of fruit in winter. However, we was good listeners, and considering that good listeners are as necessary to the interest of story telling as the narrator, we felt that we filled an important part in the sleeping car drama after all.

The evening passed away so pleasantly that time had stolen itself from us unawares, and we was forced to disband, by the porter making up the beds. A half hour later we was in bed, and the rattle and hum of the train was a lullaby song that sent us to the dream land of forgetfulness. Strange visions of snorting whales, savage sharks, barking sea lions, howling walruses, bare-legged and bareheaded dusky natives, wonderful sugar plantations, intermingled with coffee, spices, oleomargarine and oily stories hammered with Simmons, Hardware Co.'s hard tack, clothed with Boston garments and papered with Denver *News* sheets, was playing hide and seek through my brain a good share of the night.

When the morning light came peeking into my loft through the windows in the sides of the chamber story of our car, I stretched the usual morning stretch and got my pantaloons on with considerable trouble, threw myself down to the floor, woke Clarissa up and proceeded to toilet myself, after which I went into the front car and got a seat, where I remained until the sleeper was made up. We was approaching Green River Station, and the scenery was wonderfully grand. At Green River we took breakfast, and had plenty of time to eat a good meal, and we had a glorious meal to eat. After breakfast was paid for, which was $1.00 per head, we walked out on the platform and took a good view of the great cliffs that rise up behind the village several hundred feet. They are wonderful mountains of limestone shell formations, slate deposits and other kinds of stones in regular layers, alternating one above the other like a huge layer cake. We was told that the cliffs was full of fossil fish and reptiles. I bought several specimens they had for sale at the lunch counter.

As we pulled out of the station, our train hugged the base of monstrous cliffs to the left of us, while to our right, bending in graceful curves, following close to our track, was the placid waters of Green River. Some of the rocks that attract the traveler's attention in this vicinity are Castle Rock, the Giants' Club, the Giants' Teapot, and the Twin Sisters. As my purpose is not to write descriptions of country, but rather to give a few glimpses of human nature as it is revealed to me in different places, and as every foot of the country over which we have and may yet pass has been so oft described by able writers, I shall omit all references to scen-

STRANGE VISIONS.

ery except incidentally, for the purposes of showing what effect the surrounding country has upon the people. I was informed that the people in the village of Green River, like the cliffs surrounding 'em, are scaly, fishy, and considerable mixed—that their motto is, when you meet a stranger, take him in. I am fully satisfied that the feller that runs the lunch counter and curiosity shop at the depot lives up to the motto strictly. Passing through a countless number of snow sheds and over about 150 miles of country that was entirely unnecessary to have been traversed by this railroad—as it could have been made that much shorter with less work and expense than the way it is built—but which would have cut out 150 miles of stealings at the average rate per mile figured on by the projectors and constructors of the gigantic Union Pacific Railroad scheme—we arrived at Evanston, where we took dinner at the Mountain Trout House. The name of the hotel indicates the principal characteristic of the dinner you are to get, namely, fresh mountain trout, which, to lovers of the finny tribe, is a great treat. Beside this, the table is abundantly supplied with venison and bear meat. You are waited upon by grinning, goring-eyed Chinamen, who wear their shirts outside of their pantaloons, and in reply to any question you put to them not directly connected with the victuals before you, are always ready with the same speech, "Ah! Ah! Me no savvee, Mellikee manne. Me Chinee! Yum!" After we have had all the dinner we want, and taken the last look at the human puzzle in the form of the "Me no savvee" Chinee waiter, we stepped aboard, and left the little town with its 1,500 inhabitants, about 300 of which are Chinamen, just where it belongs on the geography, just half way between Omaha and San Francisco, 957 miles from each city. Twenty miles from Evanston we enter the most sublime and wonderful scenery on the entire length of the Union Pacific, Echo Canyon. From the time we enter this canyon at Castle Rock until we pass out of Weber River Canyon, a distance of sixty miles, we are constantly met with new surprises. It must have been the masters of the gods that built the Colorado gardens, that arranged these two canyons. The gigantic walls, reaching in many places the height of 2,000 feet, are so varied in color and shape as to claim the attention of the tourist every moment. Echo Station, a little town at the mouth of Echo Creek, is famous for the echoes which gave it its name. Here is to be seen the remarkable monument, a square column of red sandstone, 50 feet thick and 250 feet high. Four miles below Echo we pass a lone *fir* tree, called the 1,000 Mile Tree, as it is just 1,000 miles from Omaha. Then comes that wonderful crevice between two sharp rocks, extending down the side of the mountains, where it is said that Brigham Young and the Mormon elders that was with him during his memorable exploring trip hunting for the promised land, slid down the mountain side into the little stream below, when they all got out of the water and brushed the dirt off themselves. It is said that Brigham stretched himself up as far as his one unbroken suspender permitted, and exclaimed, "Well, I be d——d ! That is a devil of a slide," and ever since then it has been known as *The Devil's Slide.*

We are now fairly in the country where the Devil ought not to be—Utah, the land of the "Latter-day Saints of Jesus Christ," and certainly his Satanic majesty ought to keep out of this land. However, we are all more or less painfully aware that the Devil is quite apt to crowd himself in where he has no business to.

At 5:30 we arrived at Ogden, the terminus of the Union Pacific Railroad, and where we took the train for the Great Salt Lake City, thirty-seven miles to the south.

We had become so well acquainted with each other in our sleeping car, that to leave it and part company was a good deal like breaking up housekeeping. Our jolly, good-natured Sprague, Warner & Co.'s drummer had become so genial and kind, and our St. Louis hardware man had made so many pleasant hits; our Honolulu-bound friends was so kind and interesting ; our big-hearted sea captain so noble and generous; our Denver *News* man was so clever with his questions and lies ; Clarissa was so philosophizing and motherly in her many remarks, while I done the best I knew how to in my country style and with my farm speeches to make all things smooth and agreable, and even the Boston swell uncorked himself once in a while with some concession that there **was** some things worth seeing outside of Boston, so that by the time we got to the end of our road we had become so free with each other in conversation that we felt like a family, and the separation was the breaking up of the household.

> Rattling o'er the mountains, and running through the sheds,
> While setting in our seats or lying in our beds,
> It was amusement combined with learning and song,
> While our toiling engine was pulling us along.
> Our Chicago drummer, selling taffy and tolu,
> And our elder couple bound for Honolulu;
> With our whaling captain headed for the North Sea,
> Was just the kind of folks that suited Clarissa.
> The thing that on dry land—in his eyes—makes a swell
> By coming all the way from Boston, clothes to sell;
> And the St. Louis traveler and the Denver *News*
> Was good company for Uncle Ben and his muse.
> But when the time drew nigh for us all to depart,
> There was shaking hands and good-byes that come from the heart.

CHAPTER XXVIII.

TEN days among the Mormons ought to give a close observer of folks and things a little insight to their ways of living and their religious notions, especially if the sole purpose of his visit is to that end. I think, to use a watchmaker's term and speak figuratively, I saw the cap taken off, and the mainspring, as well as a good share of the wheels in their machine. The first night we staid at Ogden, stopping at a little hotel close to the depot. I wanted to go down to Salt Lake City by daylight. It was dark when we got to Ogden, and as we was quite fat-i-gued, we didn't leave the hotel that night, but we had a good night with the landlord. He was a great, fat, good-natured man, and was a Gentile, and we got a good many pointers from him that helped us considerable. (Gentile means any and everybody that isn't a Mormon.)

The next morning we took the train on the Utah Central Railroad, and whizzed along down the narrow valley lying between the foot of the Wasatch Mountains and the Great Salt Lake, thirty-seven miles south to the "Holy City," the Mecca of the Saints. The scenery is grand in the extreme; the mountains rise so abruptly and present such sharp, rugged outlines and peaks that they seem higher, and come nigher to the pictures I used to see in Olney's geography, when I went to school, than any we had yet seen. The overbearing Wasatch humps his back up and puts on high airs, on our left, while on our right is the Great Salt Lake, its quiet bosom glistening in the morning sunlight just breaking over the rocky peaks, like a vast sheet of silver. And the valley, running from two to seven miles wide, dotted with small farmhouses and villages, all surrounded by orchards and shade-trees, even with a light covering of snow on the ground, formed a beautiful picture.

I know of no spot where Nature has put her choice bits together in a more pleasing and harmonious manner than all through this wonderful valley. Even in the winter, when the beauty of nature is concealed by an icy overcoat, one is charmed by its appearance, and in spring and summer it must be delightful indeed. Just before I arrived at the Mormon paradise, I was reminded of the Clark Street museum in Chicago, where Clarissa and I saw them play Hell, by the strong smell of sulphur, and, looking out of the car window on the left side, there I saw a stream of water boiling out of a rock so that a heavy cloud of steam was continually rising from it. And off to the right of the track there was acres and acres covered with this hot sulphur-water, and the cloud of steam rising from it looked like fog lifting off the meadow in autumn.

This curious spring impressed Clarissa in a peculiar manner. She said, "Benjamin, don't you think it is a singular coincident that the headquarters of the Mormon Church and the big sulphur works down below should be so close together?" I told her "Perhaps it was, but the impression I got of Joe Smith and the organization of their church, when I was a young man, and read a good deal about it was, that it originated in that big sulphur factory, and had worked its way up to the top of the ground, but I was perfectly surprised at its spreading and growing so rapidly."

"Well, Benjamin," she replied, "you know that pussly, Canada thistles, and every other mean and vile weed, when it gets a start on a man's farm, will spread all over it mighty quick, and it grows so fast that it will ruin it in a short time; and, if what I've read about the Mormons is true, they are the pussly and thistle to the morals of this lovely country. and in time they will be the destruction of it in a moral point of view; but we will know more about it in a few days."

We had now arrived at the depot. We took a street car for the Walker House, where I met an old friend, Mr. C. M. Henderson, from New York City, who was representing a blank book manufactory. He used to know me and Clarissa a good many years ago. He introduced us to Mr. Erb, the landlord, and told him where we was from. Mr. Erb was very nice to us, and gave us a very fine private bedroom on the parlor floor, right next to Mr. Henderson's sample-room, fronting on the principal street in the city—Temple Street. The Walker House is one of the best taverns we have seen since we left Chicago—in fact, it is the best. They set a splendid table, and give you five meals a day, and everything is done to make the stranger that stops there feel at home.

After we was settled in regard to room, etc., Mr. Henderson volunteered to go with us to what places he was familiar with. We walked up Temple Street slowly, so we could have a good chance to see what we viewed on the way. The first large building on our left was the White House; across the street was the large mercantile institution of Walker Brothers, the largest Gentile store in Utah. These gentlemen was originally Mormons, but perceiving a ray of light piercing the misty cloud of Mormonism in an early day, they abandoned the church, and was branded by the hierarchy as apostates, a title of which they were proud. Further up the street, and on the opposite side, he showed us the first hotel built in the city—the old Salt Lake House; it is one of Brigham's landmarks. Next, we passed the Z. C. M. drugstore, and next door to it the drygoods store of the Mormon elder, Jennings. On the opposite corner was the drugstore of Godbe, Pitts & Co. Godbe was a seceder from the polygamous church, and the head of a branch known as the Godbeites. As we proceeded up the street, we passed the great bookstore of one of the Mormon bishops. We crossed the street to the corner, where stands the exponent of the controlling power behind and under the Mormon throne, the Deseret Bank. The next building of importance was the mammoth Zion Co-operative

Mercantile Institution. This is the largest general store I ever saw. The building is eighty feet wide and over three hundred feet deep, three stories high, and basement. We went into it, and was introduced to Mr. Eldridge, the general manager. He was very polite, and showed us all through this monstrous establishment. It is a marvel of neatness and system; everything is in perfect order, and a separate department for each kind of goods. The floor is as white and clean as soap, water and scrubbing-brush can make it. Mr. Eldridge, understanding who we was and where we was from, and where we was bound for, and our desire to see and learn all we could about his city, called a young man, and told him to go with us to the Tithing House, the *Deseret News* office, through Temple Square, the Main Tabernacle, Winter Tabernacle, the Museum, and also to ask the president if he would receive a call from us.

As Mr. Eldridge wished to see Mr. Henderson on business, we excused him and went on in company with the young man. We first visited the office of the *Deseret News*, the principal Mormon newspaper; was introduced to several, among the rest Brigham Young, Jr., who told us in a very pompous way what a wonderful people they was, how they was the chosen people of God, and they had been led by the prophets of God into this beautiful land, how God had protected and prospered them, and had been on their side all the time, and how mean the United States government had been to them; how they had persecuted them on every hand, how they threatened to destroy them in days past, how the government had all the big cannons up at Camp Douglas pointed right down on their sacred city, so that in an hour's time they could destroy the entire city; how, at one time, the Mormons had combustible material so arranged in every house, that they would have the whole city reduced to ashes in an hour, had the government troops moved upon 'em; but how the hand of God had stayed the power of the government; how the Gentiles was lying about them all the time, and working themselves into the country, trying to undermine them;

EXPERIENCE WITH HYPOCRITES. 301

continually meddling with that which was none of their business; how Congress was passing laws that was wicked and unjust, and wasn't satisfied with persecuting them by taking away their right to vote, but now they wanted to take their wives away from them, and make their children orphans, and their wives nameless things, to be thrown on to the cold and uncharitable world, and not even satisfied with that damnable work, was trying to confiscate all their

BRIGHAM YOUNG, JR., TELLS US TERRIBLE THINGS.

property; but they had gone as far as they could go, and if they was interfered with any more, the Saints would rise up in a body and destroy the government.

I fairly trembled in the presence of this wonderful big piece of human clay, and Clarissa spoke up and advised Mr. Young not to do such a rash act, as he might scare some one; that Uncle Sam was pretty nigh as big as he was, and there might be some trouble if he and the rest of the Saints got so mad. Her remarks had a quieting effect upon him, and he softened up some, and asked us to call again before we left the city, if we had time.

We then went into the Tithing House, and was showed all through it. We saw great bins of wheat, and oats and flour, and all kinds of produce; and out in the yards was cattle and hogs, sheep and horses, hens, geese and turkeys of all kinds, that people had brought in as their gift to the church.

"You see," said a big Scotchman, who, we was told, was a bishop, and who had charge of the house and yards, "every good Mormon brings into this place one-tenth of all he produces, or of all his income, as his gift for the support of the church;" and then he went on, quoting Scripture to prove that that was the way they done in Christ's time; and he talked for more'n an hour to show us how Joe Smith was the prophet of God, and that the Mormon Church was the only true and authorized church of Jesus Christ on earth.

We left the Tithing House and walked out of the high wall inclosure, crossing the street to the great eastern gate to Temple Square. As we passed through the gate we was requested to step into the little house close to the gate and write our names in the big register book where every visitor's name appears. We shall always have the satisfaction of knowing that the names of Benjamin Morgan and his one, single, solitary wife, Clarissa Snodgrass Morgan, are written on the Saints' book in their New Jerusalem. After signing the book, a carroty colored haired gentleman proceeded ahead of us as a guide. In front of us a few feet, stands the great Temple that has already been over twenty-five years in process of construction, and which, according to our guide, will not be completed for thirty years or more to come. This building, he said, is built of the hardest gray granite taken from the mountains about twenty-five miles from here. The walls are fifteen feet down in the ground and fifteen feet thick at the base, tapering up to the surface of the ground, where it is nine feet thick. **The walls are now up to the top** of the second story. When the building is completed, it will be two hundred feet long, one hundred feet wide, and one hundred feet high to the roof, and the top of the steeple will be two hundred feet above the ground. This building is to be arranged for the use of the church in the administration of its rites and ceremonies until Christ comes to earth again to reign a thousand years, when he is to occupy it as his official mansion while here below. (This is one of the ideas they teach, and which most of them believe.) For the construction of this temple, every year all the Mormons are required to pay a tithing of their income. This money is called the Temple fund. In the basement of this temple is constructed a huge stone washbowl, called the baptismal font, where all the dead generations of the glorious and inglorious past are to be baptized by proxy in order to be restored to the kingdom of the Saints in the endless future.

Passing by the Temple, we come to one of the wonders of the nineteenth century, the great Tabernacle. Its wonder consists in its plan of architecture, which was given to the great prophet, Brigham Young, by the Almighty, in a dream. It is the largest auditorium in America, capable of seating 15,000 people, if necessary. The roof is oblong oval shape, like a dish cover, and is supported by stone and brick piers nine feet thick. Between each pier are wide folding doors, so that when thrown open, the room, if crowded, can be entirely emptied in three minutes. A deep gallery extends three-fourths of the way around the room. The west quarter of the room is occupied by the officials of the church, so distributed and arranged as to represent the complete organization and power of the church. In the center, the lower front seat, behind the communion table, is occupied by twelve elders. Behind them and a step higher up, is a seat occupied by priests; behind them and another step higher up, is a seat occupied by high priests; and behind them and another step higher up, is the seat occupied by the twelve apostles; and behind them, and another step higher up, is the seat occupied by the president and his advisory council. This is the last and highest seat. On the one side are the seats occupied by the bishops, while on the other side sit the deacons and teachers.

Behind all these and on raised seats sit the great choir of singers, while back of them is the monstrous pipe organ, forty-two feet wide. This organ was built within the room, our guide told us, by one of their members, a Swede.

The guide called our attention to the wonderful acoustic (as he called it, I don't know what it means) properties of the room, by having us go up in the gallery at the further end of the room while he stood by the side of the organ and whispered to us. We could hear him as plain as if his mouth was within an inch of our ear. We were perfectly astonished, and wondered if after all it was not true that God did give the plan of this great Tabernacle to Brigham.

We was telling about it when we got back to the hotel, when we was informed by truthful persons that if we set in the seats on the floor anywhere in the middle of the house, we could not hear a single word distinctly; and for hearing, it was a failure everywhere except in the gallery and under it. Then the story of God having anything to do with the plan appeared as false to us as the idea is apparent, that He has nothing to do with their church, in any manner whatever. But the great mass of Mormons no doubt believe implicitly what their shrewd and crafty leaders teach them.

After leaving this building we went through the Winter Tabernacle or Assembly Hall, on the south side of the square inclosure. It is called the Winter Tabernacle, as it is used in the winter and during cold weather, as the great Tabernacle is used only in the warm weather, there being no means of warming or lighting it.

Coming out of the Winter Tabernacle we noticed a smaller house over in the northwest corner of the square, and asked our guide what it was. He said it was the Endowment House. We asked him to show us through it, but he very firmly declined; and told us that none but Saints was ever permitted to enter there.

Clarissa cast a look at me with a meaning visibly upon her countenance, that she wished I was a Saint; while for the purpose of satisfying my curiosity at the time, I wished she was a saintess and I a sainter, but from what I have since learned about it, I am glad we are neither one of which.

As we left Temple Square by the same gate we entered, we thanked our guide, and give him fifty cents. It being one o'clock, we told the young man we would not trouble him more that day, and thanking him for his kindness, walked down to our hotel. We had rode, walked and talked and seen enough in this half day to tire younger and stronger persons, and we felt quite weary. We ate a hearty lunch and went to our room, where I took a little nap, while Clarissa was reading her "Shadows of the Future."

In a couple of hours I woke up, feeling much refreshed. Mr. Henderson called at our room, and suggested our taking a ride; we expressed our thanks for his kindness and a desire to accept, and he ordered a carriage and driver. The day was pleasant and quite mild and springlike. We rode all over the city, and went up to Camp Douglas. The ride was delightful. The streets are all wide, smooth and hard, with a clear stream of mountain water running on each side. The evidence of prosperity and quietness was abundant on every hand. We saw the Lion House, where Brigham and several of his wives used to live, and across the street the magnificent palace he had erected for his nineteenth wife, who was generally called his favorite, in honor of whom he gave it the name of Amelia. It is said that she was quite beautiful, but I can't understand how any woman possessed of either beauty or brains, with self-respect, could for gold or palaces consent to be the nineteenth wife of a great animal in human form; but the strangest of all strange things in this world, I believe, are the freaks of human nature.

We returned to the hotel at six o'clock, and had an excellent meal, after which by invitation we visited Mr. Henderson in his sample room. He told us he had an engagement with Mr. ——

(whose name I purposely omit), the Mormon Bishop, who owns the big bookstore, at 7 o'clock, and if we would remain he would introduce him to us, and we would find him a jolly, bright fellow, full of Irish wit which he inherited from his Irish parents. Mr. H. said his customer stuttered terribly, and might make us laugh.

While we was talking about the bishop, there was a rap on the door, and as Mr. Henderson opened it, there he stood; a tall, sandy complected man with a twinkle about his eyes. As he took Mr. Henderson's hand in response to a good-evening welcome from Mr H., he bowed and said, " Go-go-go-go-go-good-e-e-e-e-e-evenin', good-evenin'."

Mr. H. turned and said "Mr. ————, let me make you acquainted with some old friends, Mr. and Mrs. Morgan, of New York, who have stopped here for a few days."

"Ho-ho-ho-how d-d-d-de d-d-do. How de do. I-I-I-I'm g-g-g-g glad—glad t-t-t-to me-me-me-meet you. Glad to meet you. It's a f-f-f-f-f-fine d-day. D-d-d-do yo-you come to s-s-s-s-s-see the wi-wi wicked M-M-M-Mormons?" he said.

We saw he was of a happy nature, and we felt free to ask him some questions, which he as freely answered. We talked considerable about the Mormons. Finally Clarissa said:

"I understand you are a Bishop, which I presume is an important office in your institution. Now I want to ask you a plain question, and would like a plain reply. Are you a Mormon from conviction as to its being right and true, or for fun, or for the money you can make out of it?"

In reply, he said, "T-t-t-to b-be p-p-p-p-plain, i-i-it's f-f-f-f-for all th-th-th-th-three re-re-re-reasons, b-b-b-b-but p-p-p-p-p-principally the la-la-latter. Y-y-you s-s-s-s-see I-I-I-I am c-c-c-convicted in m-m-my o-o-o-own m-m-m-mind tha-tha-tha-that to m-m-m-make m-m-money is ri-ri-ri-right, tha-tha-therefore, therefore my c-c-c-c-convictions is a-a-a-a-all right; and i-i-it's f-f-f-fun t-t-t-t-to m-m-m-make m-m-m-m-money. So you s-s-s-see I-I-I am a M-M-M-Mormon f-f-f-for all th-th three re-re-reasons, and-and-and I m-m-make l-l-l-lots of m-m-money out o-o-of it. Wouldn't y-y-y-you l-l-like to b-b-be one?"

Clarissa very emphatically told him No; she didn't believe in trading principles for money.

"B-b-but m-m-m-my d-d-dear m-m-madam, if-if-if y-y-y-you c-can ex-ex-ex-exchange p-p-p-poor p-p-p-p-principles f-f-f-f-for g-g-good m-m-m-mon-money, th-th-the m-m-m-money b-b-b-becomes g-g-good p-p-p-principle; a-a-and y-y-y-you c-c-c-can af-af-af-afford t-t-t-t-to th-th-th-throw a-a-away y-y-your p-p-p-poor p-p-p-principle. D-don't y-y-y-you s-s-see ho-ho-how it is?"

I could see how it was from his standpoint, and I can understand how a couple of dozen shrewd and deceiving men organized and promoted the growth of that whole institution, and became the hierarchy themselves, for money, and that money is the mainspring to the whole Mormon machine. The Deseret Bank, an institution managed by this hierarchy, is the main wheel into which all the smaller wheels fit, and play their necessary part. Honest convictions of conscience have led many to embrace the strange religious doctrines and belief, while a desire to better their condition has led thousands and thousands in Europe to leave homes of poverty with the prospects of beautiful homes in a land flowing with milk and honey, and come to this country only to be made slaves, to contribute to the insatiable greed for money that has been and is the controlling spirit of the leaders of this institution; and while this Bishop spoke half in jest, he revealed the true spirit and reasoning of these leaders.

There is a good side and there is a bad side to this institution. The good side is the practical results that have given thousands and thousands of poor people homes to live in, if not paid for, and the conversion of a vast desert into a garden of fruit, flowers, and abundance of grain. But the motive of the organizers, leaders and contractors of the church is one of fraud and swindle. Hypocrisy of the deepest and darkest kind stamps the whole concern. The incorporating of the church as a business institution under the Territorial laws, establishing the tithing scheme under pretense of giving to the Lord for the support of the Church—the building of the Temple under the hypocritical pretense of providing an executive mansion for Christ to dwell in, but the real purpose of which is to extort from its devotees large sums of money to go into their hands;

POLYGAMOUS MORMON.

a temple that will never be completed—stamps the origination and perpetuation of the scheme with fraud and wickedness.

And then, the most infamous of all, where the animal shows itself superior to the spiritual among these leaders, is polygamy. That they are a quiet, well disposed, peaceable class of people, as a rule, does not for a moment lessen the moral degradation of the leaders and teachers of this infamous doctrine. To give an idea why I speak in such strong terms, I will tell you what Clarissa and I saw. We was walking up Temple street one day, and a gentleman called our attention to a man about thirty years old with a woman on one side of him about forty years old, with a baby in her arms, probably six weeks old. On the other side of him was a woman about twenty years old, with a baby about the age of the other baby in her arms. He said, "Both of them women are that man's wives, and one of them is the mother of the other, while each of them are mothers to his babies." If such practical results of the teachings and practices of this Church are not enough to damn it, then cease to censure any other actions of the human race. Under this monstrous doctrine human convenience is substituted for human love. As Shakespeare wrote to a friend once:

> "Call it not love, since love to heaven hath fled;
> And passion, base usurper, hath taken its throne instead."

A condition of society that creates large families without being able to establish the relationship existing among them, must have a tendency to destroy all the finer sentiments of the human heart.

We remained in Salt Lake City a few days, and while we was well treated, and saw a great deal to interest us, the more I saw of some of the leading men, including President Taylor and George Q. Cannon, representatives who was acting for them while they was off hiding from the officers of the government, the more I read in their papers, and the stuff I heard them preach the Sunday I was there, the more I was convinced that there was the biggest lot of contemptible hypocrites connected with the Mormon Church that can be found alive in America out of jail.

There are a great many Mormons that are pleasant people, and there are also a good many pleasant fellers that have been unfortunate enough to get into prison. Pleasantness, prosperity and peaceableness don't make the principles of the institution right. Its founders were frauds of the worst type, and its managers have been apt scholars, guarding well their precious treasure and all the avenues leading to it. The play they make upon the ignorant religious superstitions and prejudices of its followers is their gold mine.

Their institution has left its filthy tracks on every foot of soil over which it has passed, from Palmyra, New York, to Independence, Missouri, to Nauvoo, to Council Bluffs, and thence across the plains and over the mountains to this lovely valley where, taking advantage of the natural barriers surrounding them, it flourished and

"HOLINESS UNTO THE LORD."

spread with magic speed, so that from the few that landed there forty years ago next July, it has reached to nearly, if not quite, 200,000, which is more followers than the Saviour had 300 years after his birth, so I am told.

There are a great many laughable things in Salt Lake City.

One is a large signboard with an open eye painted on it, and over and under the eye the words, "Holiness unto the Lord," put up over the door of a whisky saloon. Profanity does not seem to be out of order by officers and members of the church. The cheating of a Gentile is strictly in order. A quarrel between two Saints generally ends in both Saints taking something to drink at the other's expense in the nearest saloon. A quarrel between a Mormon and a Gentile generally ends in one of the parties getting an overcoat.

I understand that Senator Edmunds has got up a bill he is going to paste up all over Utah next year. He'll have quite a job of bill-posting, for Utah is a larger country than most folks are aware, and it's alive with people.

After taking a bath in their famous hot sulphur springs bathhouse, we said good-by to Mr. Erb and some friends we had formed there, and left for Ogden, where we remained over one day to take a drive up some of the beautiful canyons and around where we could get views of the grand mountains which rise so abruptly and reach enormous heights. Clarissa is captured by the loveliness of this country, and says if it wasn't for Mormonism she would want to move here, but as it is she will take the old farm in Morganville and be contented, for there, unlike Utah life, by her own fireside she can realize what the poet said of human love when he wrote:

> " There is a story told
> In Eastern tents, when autumn nights grow cold,
> And round the fire the Mongol shepherds sit,
> With grave responses listening unto it:
> Once, on the errands of his mercy bent,
> Buddha, the holy and benevolent,
> Met a fell monster, huge and fierce of look,
> Whose awful voice the hills and forests shook.
> 'O, son of peace,' the giant cried, 'thy fate
> Is sealed at last, and love shall yield to hate.'
> The unarmed Buddha, looking, with no trace
> Of fear or anger, into the monster's face,
> In pity said, 'Even thee I love.
> Lo! as he spake, the sky-tall terror sank
> To hand-breadth size—the huge abhorrence shrank

> Into the form and fashion of a dove,
> And where the thunder of its rage was heard,
> Circling above him sweetly sang the bird—
> 'Hate hath no charm for love,' so ran the song,
> 'And peace, unweaponed, conquers every wrong.'"

I am aware that the country is flooded with books and newspaper articles on Mormonism, therefore I'll say no more about them. I only envy them on account of their lovely country and healthful climate, a climate that is free from any germs of disease. I don't envy them for their numerous wives, for while I think one wife, if she is a good, true and smart one, like my Clarissa, is the greatest boon to man, two would be bad luck, and a multitude would be his everlasting damnation, morally and socially, and ought to brand the man who enters into such business with a curse that should make his name a hissing and byword as long as the memory of him exists. God pity the poor innocent believers and supporters of such a horrible doctrine as polygamous Mormonism!

CHAPTER XXIX.

I THOUGHT we would go from Ogden up to Helena, Montana Territory, and visit the National Park, see the spouting geysers and other curious things we had read so much about, but Clarissa said that while she would like to take the trip, she thought it was prudent not to do so, as our finances was working down considerably fast. She had counted over the money last night and found that we had paid out pretty nigh $300 since we had arrived at Chicago. and in case we should fail to get any drawback in San Francisco, we would need all we had got with us. This decided the case, and we took the train the next morning on the Central Pacific Railroad for the West.

We was lucky in getting down stair beds for both of us in the sleeping car. The scenery from Ogden to Sacramento is in the main monotonous, but in places very wild, picturesque, and interesting. Nearly every one who reads English has read so much about it that I will not take your time, or punish you with such exaggerated stories in regard to it as have been so often told. I found out one thing to be true, by actual observation, and that is, most all the descriptions of the entire route over which we have traveled, are overdrawn and exaggerated. A mountain that is about 1,000 feet high is put down anywhere from 1,500 to 5,000 feet high, and so in regard to everything else that is described. To keep within the limits of the exact truth, seems to be about the hardest thing for a traveler to do. The longer he has traveled, the harder the task becomes, and when they tell their stories in print for the public to read, the higher color they can gild them with the more interesting they think they will be to the reader.

Commercial travelers are noted for being liars; the longer they have been on the road the more accomplished liars they become. Why! what little time I've been traveling I feel I'm getting to be "somewhat of a liar myself;" and still I intend to confine myself as close to the truth as I can.

There is something in the air of a car, stage coach and steamboat, that is catching when it comes to telling stories and relating

SANDY BOWERS, AN UNEDUCATED IRISHMAN.

what a person has seen, gone through and experienced, that gives it a balloon appearance.

The fellows that get up geographies and histories are troubled with the same complaint to quite an extent. Somehow or other distance seems to add greatness to scenery as it does to noted politicians; they haint nowhere nigh as great when you are at home with 'em, or if they be, you see so many of the little things that stick out all around 'em, that their greatness is very materially lessened.

The first place we stopped off at was Reno, near the middle of the Truckee Valley, at the base of the Sierra Nevada Mountains, and fifty miles from their summit. We took the train on the Virginia and Truckee Railroad for Virginia City, which is only sixteen miles from Reno, as a crow flies, but which is fifty-two miles by this railroad. I think it must be the crookedest railroad in the world; it is stated that if all its curves was put together they would make seventeen complete circles. They never allow very long trains to run over the road, for fear the engine might run into the hind end of its own train.

We went thirty-one miles south to Carson City, the capital of

SANDY BOWERS AFTER HE GOT HIS WEALTH.

Nevada, where we rested for the night, and listened to marvelous stories of immense fortunes that had been made and lost in that vicinity in the palmy days of the glorious past. Gulliver can't hold a candle to some of them Carson City shams. There are a class of fellows that loaf around these Western hotels that I believe the landlord hires to entertain the strangers that stop within his gates, with lies; the bigger liars the more entertaining they are, generally.

We passed through Washoe, a once busy but now a played out town, sixteen miles south of Reno. We was shown the Bowers' mansion, a magnificent dwelling built by Sandy Bowers, an uneducated Irishman, a miner who, when the rich deposit of gold-bearing quartz was discovered at Gold Hill, in 1860, owned a good share of the vein, and he soon became worth millions. He erected this mansion, bought the furniture, carpets, etc., for it in France at an enormous expense, filled the spacious grounds with beautiful shrubbery and had the most costly and elegant home in the whole State. Like as it is with thousands of people, his great misfortune was his sudden fortune, for while it come to him swiftly it as swiftly left him, left him worse than before he had a dollar of it; and now, having dissolved all connection with earth and its fleeting scenes, he leaves a widow in poverty. The magnificent gardens have disappeared, and the great mansion stands there as a curiosity.

The next morning we left Carson City for Virginia City, stopping at Mound House, about half way between the two cities, near Sutro, the outlet of the Sutro Tunnel. This tunnel strikes the great Comstock mine, 1,898 feet below the surface croppings of the Gould & Curry mine. It is 19,790 feet long, and cost $4,500,000 for construction. It drains and ventilates the mines.

An hour after leaving Mound House we was in the far-famed Virginia City, noted the world over for the marvelous fortunes that have been made there in mining and mining speculation.

One of the wealthiest if not *the* richest man in America is Mr. J. W. Mackay, who has made millions of dollars at this place. It is not a difficult thing to hear and read about the fortunes made at this and in other places, nor to ascertain the names of the parties who have had their pockets tickled by the goddess fortune, but of the fortunes lost, of the thousands upon thousands that have chased her deceiving figure to this and hundreds of other places, with bright hopes and great expectations, and dropped every nickel they possessed and walked away hungry paupers, nothing is said; and it is a very difficult task to find them all out, and still more difficult to trace out the dark and damnable tricks and schemes that have been resorted to to swindle and rob the unfortunates. "You can safely calculate that for every dollar that has been taken out of the wonderful mines here—the richest mining camp in the world in days gone by—there has been a dollar dropped by some one." An old miner who told me he had lived and worked there for more than twenty years, said: "Stranger, if you want to see the tallest hypocrites, the biggest liars, under pretense of telling the truth, you go into a gold or silver mining camp and live there for six months." While I listened to his remarks, I could not help seeing Geo. Waddles and Jim Teeters right in front of me.

Virginia City, with Gold Hill, has about 7,000 population, and is built on the side of a steep hill. The entire 7,000 souls depend upon the Comstock Lode for their existence. The Comstock Lode is composed of twenty mines, namely: Utah, Sierra-Nevada, Union, Mexican, Ophir, California, Consolidated Virginia, Savage, Best & Belcher, Gould & Curry, Hale & Norcross, Chollar, Bullion, Exchequer, Alpha, Imperial, Yellow Jacket, Kentuck, Crown Point, Belcher. The deepest workings are 3,000 feet below the surface. The total yield since 1860, has been $350,000,000.

I heard so much about gold and silver and great fortunes, that I was all fuzzed up; I didn't know but what I might run right into a big fortune in spite of myself, before I got out of that part of the universe. I knew one thing, and that was that I wouldn't get caught in any swindling speculation that would involve the loss of more'n fifty cents, as that was the limit of my visible pile of cash at that time, and so long as Clarissa carried the money, I didn't have a particle of fear of getting caught in any schemes. After eating a hearty supper, and listening for three hours to tall stories, every one of which was tipped and trimmed with gold, and heavily lined with silver, I went to bed. It was not long before sleep stole away consciousness. Soon, however, I was suddenly transcontinentalized— to use the fashionable language of this winter's congress—to my father's old farm. There I was cleaning out the cow stable, and milking with freezing fingers, coming in to a late supper, going to an early and cold bed in the chamber attic, getting up by candlelight in the morning, doing all the chores, and then walking over a mile over the snowdrifts to the little schoolhouse, getting hold of a book that one of the boys at school let me have, telling about the wonderful gold fields of California, and the fun there was in getting it, and how anybody with pluck in their heart and sand in their gizzard, could be worth a million in a few years; how tired I got of the cold and hard life I was having on the farm, when an eagle fly-

DOING CHORES AT 4 O'CLOCK IN THE MORNING.

ing over the barnyard, while I was watering the horse, flew down and grabbed me in her claws and carried me with lightning speed over the great States of Ohio, Indiana, Illinois, Iowa, Nebraska, Colorado, the Rocky Mountains, and the great Tabernacle in Salt Lake City, and dropped me down in Virginia City, and before I had time to thank her for the wonderful trip, two little angels as sweet as sweet could be, flew down from the clouds into my lap.

EXPERIENCE WITH HYPOCRITES. 319

One had rosy cheeks and crimson lips, and golden wings, and said, "Young man from Samuel Morgan's cow barn, in Morganville, Blank County, New York, ain't you tired of those coarse, dirty boots?" I was muchly agitated as I tremblingly said I guessed I was, when suddenly my boots by some magic power flew off and out of sight, and the rosy cheeked angel stooped and put on my feet a pair of elegant, eighteen-karat solid gold slippers. The other angel had light blue eyes, blonde curly hair and the loveliest freckled cheeks that ever adorned a face, and silver wings; and as he stroked my

THE GRAND MASTER OF THE FIREWORKS.

hair so softly, he said, "Young man from the rural districts of the Empire State, your clothes smell a little fresh of the bovine kine and the fruits of the udder; wouldn't you like to change them for new robes?" I was so surprised I couldn't speak, but with a consenting wink of my left eye, I nodded, "Yes." Immediately my clothes left me, and the angel put a beautiful robe, woven of pure silver onto me, and then both angels put a crown, made of gold and studded with diamonds and rubies, on my head, and said to me: "With this crown we make you this day, King of the Big Bonanza. Ask for what you may, and it shall be yours, except one thing, which you cannot have, by accepting this crown." I asked them what that was, and they said, "The crown of everlasting life." And in the twinkling of an eye the angels had flown out of sight. I was dizzy with the thought of being so suddenly the possessor of such vast wealth. What to do with it, puzzled me; and then the thought of losing my chance in the crown of everlasting life annoyed me terribly, and while I still sat there with my crown of jewels, and silver robe and golden slippers on, turning the wheel of thought in my mind, and wondering one minute and trembling the next, a horrid monster, with huge ears and fiery eyes, holding in his hand a fork of red hot iron, rose up out of the earth in front of me, and with a voice that seemed to shake the mountains that echoed back from their rocky sides his awful command, said, "Come! You are mine. I have bought you with these glittering trinkets with which you are clothed and crowned, and they, together with your soul, belong to me; and I want you to go with me!" I was so scared, my hair stood erect, and I stammered out, "Who be you?" He said, "I am the Devil, the grand master of the fireworks down below. Come with me; you must go." In horror I shrank, and cried, "How and when did you buy me?" "I sent my gold and silver imps in the guise of angels, and they gave you the things with which I purchase more souls than with any other price I pay."

> "Say what you will,
> Think what you may,
> The truth is still,
> Gold is the pay
> For which a man,
> Tho' sick or well,
> Does all he can
> His soul to sell."

I tried to reason how I had of my own will, sold myself to even these angels, but even reason forsook her throne, and I was his property. He reached his bony fingers out to take my arm, when suddenly I awoke. Oh, what a sigh of relief I heaved. A reliefer sigh was never heaved by mortal man, and I just hollered out, "Thank God, it's nothing but a dream." My hollering awoke Clarissa, who wanted to know what ailed me. I told her to wait a minute and I'd tell her. I got up and lit the gas, and of all the lookin' sights our room was the worst. Usually I am pretty orderly and have a good deal of system. When I go to bed and retire, I lay my coat in the chair first, then my vest, then my pantaloons, and then I draw the chair up side of the head of my bed, and put my shoes and socks down on the floor in front of the chair, and that was the way I done when I went to bed and retired this time.

When I lit the gas one of my shoes was in the washbowl, and t'other was in the slopjar; one sock was lodged in the transom over the door, and one was under the back side of the bed. The pants was in the middle of the floor, and the chair was bottom side up on top of my coat and vest, and the pillow-case was pulled onto my head. I didn't notice it until I went in front of the looking-glass on top of the bureau—(they had regular sleeping-car pillows in this hotel). I explained to Clarissa my dream, and told her how scared I was after I got through.

She said, "Benjamin, that is either a prophetic dream, or else you have had a nightmare. I told you not to eat them twelve big pancakes for supper, if you expected to sleep." "Well," says I, "pancakes never affected me that way before, but them dumb stories about fortune, etc., is what has set hard on my stomach, and I believe the dream is a warning for us not to love money more'n life and our fellow men, and above all, not to stay in Virginia City another day, if I value your and my eternal happiness, for it's as catching here as the measles, and we'll take the first train for Reno."

CHAPTER XXX.

AFTER a light breakfast, we took the 8 o'clock train, and was in Reno in time to catch our west-bound train. Once more on our regular journey, and nearing its latter end, we felt better. I did, especially. This time we was unfortunate about the sleeping-car arrangements, as we couldn't get a down-stairs bed for either one of us, and we had to take what the porter calls *uppers*.

We wanted to stop at Truckee, and take the stage for Lake Tahoe—we had heard so much about it; but it was a little too cold, and we was somewhat tired. So we was content to listen to the stories of some of the passengers who got on there that had visited the wonderful lake, twenty-two miles long by ten wide, and 1,800 feet deep, whose waters are so clear that they say you can see the bottom, where it is sixty feet deep.

At Truckee we strike the steep grade reaching from there to the summit, which averages seventy-nine feet to the mile. At Summit we are 7,020 feet above the sea level, and are surrounded with very wild and interesting scenery. We go through a 1,659-feet tunnel, and begin the descent of the mountains to Emigrant Gap.

A person that is a lover of romantic scenery can spend a couple of days in this vicinity very pleasantly; can climb to the summit of Castle Peak, and Fremont Peak, if he is a good climber, and with a good glass can take in an immense scope of country, both in Nevada and California. We made no more stop offs until we arrived in Sacramento, the capital of the *paradise* of the old forty-niners, California, a lively business city of 20,000 souls. From this city the traveler can take the trains for Los Angeles and San Diego.

EXPERIENCE WITH HYPOCRITES. 323

The change we experienced in arriving in California was pleasing indeed. Passing out of winter into mild spring, from cold, dead and desolate mountains, clad in snow, into green valleys, where flowers bloom and fruit trees bud for the coming harvest, is as delightful as going from the cheerless woods in New York, where the farmer has been chopping wood all day, with cold feet, into a warm and cheerful house to be entertained by young and mirthful friends, and

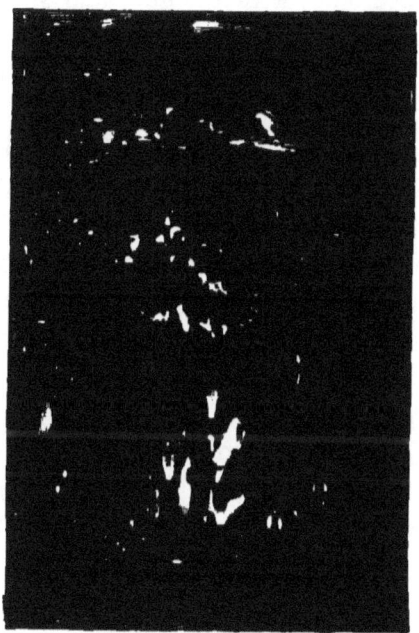

A REGULAR OLD '49ER.

a bounteous table, loaded with choice fruits and flowers. In his enjoyment he soon forgets the cold without. A few days' living in the delightful California climate causes one almost to forget the winter he has left behind.

Again we was on board the cars and rolling on to the destination of our great excursion ride across the American continent. We took a regular passenger instead of the sleeping-car, and was pleased with the change, for we saw a much greater variety of people coming in and going out than we did in the sleeper. In the front seat set a couple of pigeyed Celestials, while on the opposite side was one of the old settlers, a regular old forty-niner, whose brindled locks fell upon his shoulders like a Piute squaw, while under the shade of his broad-brimmed hat and heavy, shaggy eyebrows sparkled a couple of black eyes that seemed to tell a story of a long and hard experience with the gold and silver-winged angels and his Satanic majesty. There was an air about him that seemed to say that the latter had been his master, and that he had been in hard luck.

Most every nation seemed to be represented in that car—Spain, France, Italy, Germany, Russia, Austria, Ireland, Scotland, England, New York, Chicago, and Missouri.

To walk slowly through the car and hear them all talk, one would think they had been ordered by King Babel to some city to erect another tower. We didn't pretend to understand what they was talking about, but by their actions I knew they was talking about something or other.

Clarissa, in remarking about the confusion of tongues with which we was surrounded, said, "If Sarah Smuggins and Betsy Teeters was here, the thing would be complete, and the car itself would be a good first story to start a tower with."

At Benicia, thirty-three miles from San Francisco, we crossed the Strait of Carquinez on the largest ferry-boat ever built—the Solano, 424 feet long, and 116 feet wide. Our whole train ran right onto the boat, and when we got across our engine pulled us on land again. We whizzed along at a rapid rate until we reached the western rim of the city of Oakland, by which we slowly passed, running out on a mole one and a half miles beyond, to a large station-house on the bay.

We changed to an elegant ferry-boat, and soon started to cross the four-miles wide bay. We went on deck. It was evening, and the sight before us was grand. To our right was quietly sleeping Goat, Angel, and Alcatraz Islands; to our left, glistening in the moonlight, was the Golden Gate, while in front was the City of a Hundred Hills, the successor of two old villages, San Francisco, named by Franciscan friars who settled there in 1776,

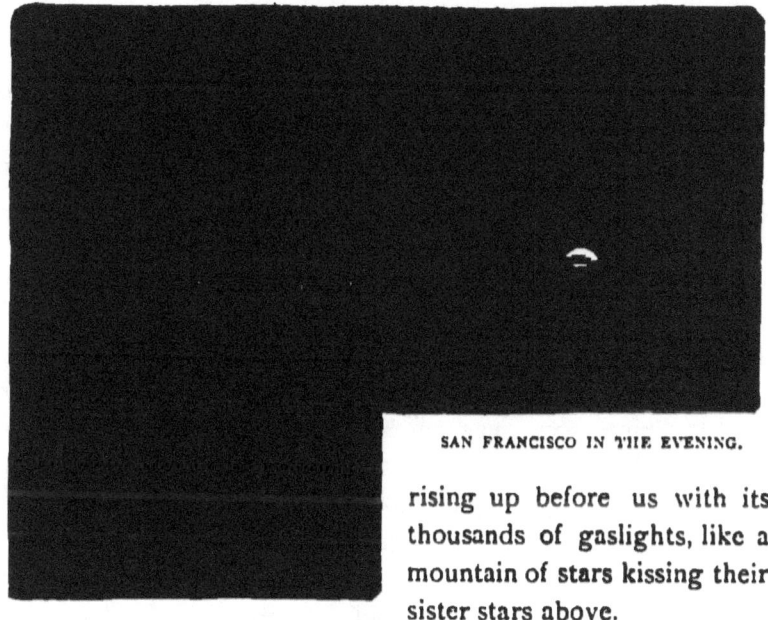

SAN FRANCISCO IN THE EVENING.

rising up before us with its thousands of gaslights, like a mountain of stars kissing their sister stars above.

In twenty minutes we landed and took a carriage for the Baldwin Tavern, where we secured an elegant private bedroom and settled down for the night with a feeling of rest and satisfaction to know we had reached the end of our journey, and Clarissa and I could pillow our heads on the great Pacific shore. I had already dreamed my dream, and Clarissa was entitled to have her dream now.

CHAPTER XXXI.

THE next morning the noise of the newsboys and rattling wagons awoke us, and looking out onto Market street we thought we was in Chicago, but the fact that the atmosphere was so different dispelled that idea.

I asked Clarissa what she dreamed. She said she was so tired and sleepy when she went to bed she never thought a word about dreaming, but she felt young and strong, and ready to put in the day sight-seeing.

We had a splendid breakfast, and enjoyed the hour we was in the big dining room very much. There was lots of fine dressed women and men eating breakfast, and we heard some women sitting at the next table to us talking a good deal like them women in Mr. Palmer's dining room in Chicago, and Clarissa said she guessed the women was pretty much alike the world over—them that wants to be good are good and kind, and them that wants to be mean and hypocritical are as mean as they know how to be—regular slandering hypocrites. I was so biling mad to hear 'em slandering folks that according to their own talk had been friends to 'em, that I was just going to wheel round and give 'em a piece of my mind when Clarissa, perceiving my mind (she is an awful perceiver, and can tell what a person is thinking about before they speak a word), said:

"Benjamin, stop! don't you do it. It's no use for us to undertake to make folks true and honest by talking to 'em. We'll find, if we undertake it, that we've got a bigger task on our hands by two thousand times than General Grant had in driving the rebels out of Vicksburg."

Clarissa was right, and I knew she was, so I finished my breakfast and let the rest of 'em alone.

After breakfast Clarissa and I went down to the office and inquired for the office of Dodgem, Skipem & Oppenheimer. The smart young fellow behind the counter twisted his red moustache several times in a meditative manner as though he didn't know whether 'twas best to answer our questions or not, and turning so as to get the most sparkle possible on the big sign for a glass factory he had deposited on his shirt bosom, finally condescended to tell us that he didn't know any such persons in the city.

I told him if it wasn't too much trouble I'd be much obliged to him if he'd show me some one that wouldn't spoil by answering a few civil questions. Just then a middle-aged gentleman, standing near the counter, overhearing my remarks, says, "Mr.—what is it you want to know? Perhaps I can tell you." This man, I found out, was the proprietor of the tavern, and it didn't hurt him a mite to talk like a gentleman, which he was. I asked him about the agents of Ketchem, Holdem & Skinem, and handed him the card of Dodgem, Skipem & Oppenheimer. He said he would send a boy with me to the street and number indicated on the card, but he had never heard of the firm. I told him about the excursion, and showed him the advertisement, and then told him how I had to pay for everything, and received the promise of a rebate to be paid to me for all these extra charges at this office, and showed him the checks.

The landlord shook his head in a doubtful manner, and said the names of the parties didn't inspire much confidence in his mind that the thing was very honest.

The boy started, while Clarissa and I followed until we found the place, which was a small, dingy room in a dirty-looking part of the city, not far from the wharf where our ferry boat landed us. We went into the office and found a fellow behind a desk. As we went in he got up and come up to us. He weighed about 140 pounds, had a horrible big nose shaped like a parrot's bill, a little low forehead, short, kinky black hair, and black eyes that could look right through you.

There was something about our manner and looks that told him what we was there for.

I said, "Is Mr. Dodgem in?"

"Ah, mein frent, you vants to see Mr. Dodgem, doen't you? Yis. Vell, I am reely sorry, but Mr. Dodgem dodged onto a train for Ní Yark last Vendsday, and ve haf not heard von word from him sense."

"Well," said I, "is Mr. Skipem in?"

"Vell, now, mein frent, it vas reely too bad agin! You see, mein frent, Mr. Skipem vas a vary nice shentleman, and from a vary respectable family, but the poor feller had the consumption ven he come oud here from Boston. He thought this climate vud cure him, but effry sense he vas here he has had a horwyble cough, und last Saturday night, ven all vas still, the poor feller skipped the country."

"Where did he skip to?" I asked.

"Oh, mein frent, he must haf skipped right up to Heften! Oh, it's too bad; Sharley vas such a nice feller. I am reely sorry he isn't here for you to meet him."

"Well," said I, "I suppose your name must be Oppenheimer, as I don't see anybody else in."

"Yis, that vas mein name. Vas there anything I can do for you, mein frent?"

I said, "Yes," and immediately produced my tickets, rebate checks, receipts, and the company's advertisement, and the card of Dodgem, Skipem & Oppenheimer, and told him my story, which was backed up by the testimony of my beloved Clarissa.

He looked the papers and checks all over, and then, with a holy grin on his dirty yellow countenance, that looked as though it had been handed to him by Jacob and his forefathers (for certainly it was an old grin) said, as he wrung his hands together:

"Ah! mein frent, I am not the Oppenheimer you vas looking for. I don't belong in that firm. I vas a broker in diamonds. It is mein pruther, Moses Oppenheimer, what is the member of that firm. Reely I vas vary sorry for you, but mein pruther Moses sailed for Europe last Sunday, the day we all luf to observe on account of the Holy Shesus. I don't know vat can pe done for you."

Said I, "Haven't they left any one here to attend to their business, and hasn't the company made any arrangements for doing as they agreed?"

MOSES OPPENHEIMER.

"Vell, now, mein frent, I don't know nudding at all apout that company or any of their arrangements. Only I know mein pruther paid lots of money to Eastern passengers coming in here on a big excursion, but I spose the firm haf vound up their peeziness."

While we was talking to this son of Abraham, a fine, healthy-looking young fellow come in through the back door, smoking a cigar, and threw some papers on the desk; at the same time a fine-dressed young man come into the front door, and approaching the young man that come in from the back door, hollered out:

"Well, well! Charley Skipem, old boy, how do you do?"

"My dear Ben, by George, I'm glad to see you; when did you leave Boston? and how are the folks? did you see my father and mother before you left? Come in Ben and have a seat, and tell me all the news, and everything about yourself."

During this short conversation between Charley Skipem (who died last Saturday night) and his old friend Ben, Mr. Oppenheimer's face had turned ashy pale. Mr. Skipem, upon noticing it, hollered out, "Moses Oppenheimer, what in the devil ails you?" Moses sank into a chair as limp as a dish rag, and cried out:

"Oh! mein Shesus, mein Shesus! You vos proke us all up in peezness, and our hull tam shanty vill pe arrested;" and the Jew fainted, while I took advantage of the situation and asked Charley if he was Mr. Skipem of the firm of Dodgem, Skipem & Oppenheimer.

He replied that he was.

I asked him if that sick Jew was his partner. He said he was.

Then I told him who I was, where I was from, and produced the advertisement, my tickets, checks, rebate receipts, etc., and demanded a settlement.

He began to hem and haw, and said he was very sorry that he could not do anything for me. "The fact is," said he, "the funds deposited with us for rebates on those excursion tickets have all been exhausted, and I can't pay any more rebates until the company advance more funds."

"Well," said I, "I have already paid an extra price on tickets, and sleeping car fares and meals, to say nothing about the enormous railroad fare in Colorado, Utah and Nevada, over $380, and I want my pay; and if you don't settle this at once I'll have you arrested in less than five minutes." I got hopping mad when I discovered their scheme, through their lying son of Abraham, and I thought I'd scare them if I couldn't do any more.

"Well," said Skipem, "I haint got any of the company's money, and I don't see how I can pay you."

"Well," said I, "I'll see how you can." So I asked Clarissa to write a note to the landlord of the Baldwin Tavern, to send an officer right down here, and I'd send it right up to him by the boy, who was still here. Then Mr. Skipem said, " Look here; rather than have any trouble, I'll pay you the $200 extra that you paid for your tickets in Syracuse, and will write to Ketchem, Holdem and Skinem, and state the case and tell them to send me the funds, and you come here before you leave the State, and I'll have it all fixed up for you."

"YOU VOS PROKE US ALL UP IN PEEZNESS."

I said, "Very well, I'll take it that way."

Then he sat down and wrote out a check for $200 on a bank (that had been busted for more'n four years) and handed it to me. I asked him what he wanted me to do with that? "Why," said he, "take it around to the bank on Montgomery Street, and get your money."

"Yes!" said I, "well, I'll do nothing of the kind. I want the cash."

"Well, then," said he, "I'll go around and get it for you. You just stay right here till I come back."

Said I, "I guess not; you died last Saturday night, and your Moses, there, sailed for Europe Sunday. I guess I'd better go right along with you, for fear you may die on the way."

"Why, what do you mean?" said he.

Said I, "I mean that you are a confounded hypocritical set of swindlers, and I wouldn't trust you out of my sight."

He grew red in the face and finally went to his safe and got the money and gave me $200, and handed me a receipt for the money for me to sign, which I did.

As we left the office I said to Clarissa, "That is $200 more than I really expected to get." Said she, "I wouldn't be a bit surprised if the money is counterfeit."

We returned to the Baldwin and I got the landlord to give me directions for finding the principal points of interest in the city. I went to the postoffice and got some letters that was sent to us by mail and returned to the tavern, went to our room, where Clarissa and I read the letters. The first one we read was from Mary, and was as follows:

"THE VILLAGE, BLANK CO., N. Y.,
"December 6, 1886.

"DEAR MA:

"I have been expecting a letter from you every day, but have not received but the one you wrote in Chicago. I was so glad you consented to my request. I showed your letter to Ebenezer, and it tickled him so that he forgot what he was doing when he waited on the next customer, which was a woman from up north of the village, who called for fifty cents worth of granulated sugar, and he weighed out and wrapped up twelve pounds of salt ; and then a boy that came in after a quart of white vinegar, got a quart of kerosene. Eb said you was a darling good old lady, and he was going to kiss you when you got home.

"Well, we was married last Sunday night, in the front room, where he and I was sitting the night you come home from Smuggins'. We had to get Elder Danberry to marry us as the Baptist minister was away from home. I invited our old neighbors in, and they all had a good time except Sarah Smuggins, who seemed to be out of sorts all the evening. Abe behaved real nice, and hitched up the horse for us to take a sleigh ride. After it was all over, we drove down to the village and staid all night at Brown's tavern. We have just commenced housekeeping up stairs over the store where Teeters used to live. Oh! ma, you don't know how much fun we are having. Eb is up stairs two-thirds of the time, and he wants to kiss me all the time. Say, ma ; can you tell me what is good for sore and chapped lips? My lips are dreadful sore. I think it was from taking cold in them when Abe brought us down here Sunday night. Ebenezer has had to hire a clerk since we got married, as he don't get time to wait on all his customers. He says that I draw trade wonderfully ; that although I have not been in the store an hour altogether since we was married, yet every one of our old neighbors and friends are trading with him. Say, ma ; can you tell me what is good to make me sleep? I haven't slept scarcely a wink for the last five nights, and I feel just as tired as though I had done a big washing. Oh ! Eb is a perfect darling, he is so good to me ; but ma, he is troubled with an awful headache. What had I better give him for it ? He has got our rooms all furnished up just as nice and pretty as they can be. He is such a dear good darling ; and the cook stove is splendid. He is as neat as wax. The carpet on the front room is three ply. He helps me get the meals and wash the dishes and says it is fun, and then winds up by kissing me a dozen times. The curtains are buff and have got a brass ring on the bottom of them. He brings up all the wood and water, and stops to kiss me each trip. I brought the organ from home, and have got it in the front room. He carries all the slops down stairs for me, and says it's fun. The bedstead and bureau are black walnut, and are real nice. He made up the bed this morning, and the looking-glass is a large nice one ; the carpet is rag, and was presented to me by Abby Standish. He shuts the store up real early so as to be with me during the evening. Our dining-room table is a ten foot ash extension. Aint he awful nice? We have got a room all fixed up nice for you and pa to sleep in when you get home. Oh ! he is just too sweet for anything. Now ma, write me just as soon as you get this, and let me know when you are coming home. I hope it will be soon. He is hollering for me to come down to the store to sell some candy, as he is awful busy and hasn't time to come up stairs to see me. So I'll have to go, and bid you good-by.

"Your loving daughter, MARY."

"Well," said I, "she's got it bad, haint she?"

"Well," said Clarissa, "it looks that way; but, Benjamin, you know they always have it worse the first part than any other time, but generally, when they have a severe attack the first week, it aint apt to last very long"

"Is that so?" said I. "Well, it will be a good thing for Eb's business if it don't, for if it does, his business won't be apt to last very long." It was my turn to read my letter now, so I tore open the envelope, and read out loud my letter, which was from Abe, and is as follows, to-wit:

"DEER DAD. mary has got marreD. and I'm golldarned glad on't, i never got so sick uv enny thing in mi life as i hav uv hur. she haz ackted like a golldarned fule fur the last munth, until she got marred. she wuld go around the house like a kat with fits, and I had tu hitch up the old mare and taker down to the villege every forenoon, and every nite i'd hav tu take care uv plunkits Horse. i didnt git ennything tu eat haf the time, After she got your letter, she jest went krazy she cum up tu me and kissed me. and kissed the hired man an kissed the pump and kissed the old brindled kow. She ackted like a fule, until the nite she got marred—Then she behaved sweet, and I wuz glad ont, and sence then she has ben down to the villege, and dolly dulittle has bin keeping house fur us, and we hav plenty tu eat now and dolly iz az allfired nice az she can be, and she luks kinder sweet on me every time

i cum in the house, say pa, The old mare slipt down tother day and spraned hur back, and i'm frade she wont git well and missis boyles iz sick with morbus kolick and dave Kirk wuz sude fur cheatin the baptist minister in a hoss trade. and george waddles haz had to sell his farm to git monney enuff tu pay fur his swindlin and keep from goin to Jale—and he and hiz wife hav packed up thayer goods and are goin to go to Chicago and pa and ma, i wish you would hurry home i want you to take kare uv the cows and help milk, so good by,
"Your dutiful Abra Ham."

Clarissa said, "Well, there haint any deceit about Abe. What he thinks, he says." "Yes, just like his dad," I replied.

There was another letter I had not yet opened, so I tore it open and read it, viz.:

'THE VILLAGE, BLANK CO., N. Y.,
"Dec. 7, '86.

"MR. BENJAMIN MORGAN, San Francisco, Cal.

Dear Sir :—We regret being obliged to ask you to make your visit to the Pacific Coast short and hasten home, but certain things have recently developed in relation to the Waddles difficulty, and other things, that we deem it to your interest to be here before the next term of court, which commences four weeks from to-morrow. If you can arrange to be here within two and a half weeks, or three at the outside, from now, we should like to have you do so. It will be to our mutual interest for you to do so.
"Very respectfully yours,
"BARKLY & EVANS, *Bankers.*"

I was perfectly surprised at the contents of this letter, and could not possibly imagine what was up. We talked the matter over, and concluded to look around San Francisco for two or three days, then go down to Los Angeles, stay there one day, and then take the Southern Pacific Railroad home.

After we had dinner we started out to take the whole city in, and know all we could about it in the short time we had allowed ourselves. We went through the new City Hall, the United States Mint, taking some specimens from the mint with us, the National Treasury, the Palace Tavern, the Standard Theater, the Panorama Hall, the Vienna Garden, the Mercantile Library, the Mechanics' Institute, the Mechanics' Pavilion, the Hammam Baths, the Art School, the California Market, the Fish Market, Leland Stanford's residence, Saint Patrick's Church, the Hop Wo Joss House, the Ning Wong Joss House, the Kong Chow Joss House, the Dan San

Fung Theater, the Anu Quai Yuen Theater, the Chinese Merchants' Exchange, and the Cliff House, and Fort Point Narrows of Golden Gate.

Considering that we took all these and some other points that was interesting in, and got an idea of them in three days, we think we done pretty well for green farmers. Nothing escaped our notice that we saw, and we wasn't afraid to ask all kinds of questions.

I was most interested in Chinatown, as there I met a class of people that don't grow in Morganville or anywhere nigh there. Their pigeyes and pigtails, greasy, yellow faces and heathenish countenances; their funny shoes, and pantalet breeches, with their shirts hanging outside, was so different from any other kind of folks that I couldn't keep from looking at them as I would a menagerie, and the way they lived, ate, slept, and done business was so peculiar that I come to the conclusion that they must have been dropped down onto the earth from some of the planets. I presumed they fell from Jupiter, as they look as though they might be a cross between a Jew and the original Peter, for the way they live, move and have their being, is strongly suggestive that they came from some celestial climate, and are bound for the place to which it is said Peter carries the keys, and have stopped temporarily on the surface of old earth to pick up what they can, like flies in summer, and carry it along with them. Like the bothersome flies, they are content with a little at a time, but they are all the time after that little, and when I found out there was about 25,000 of them in this city I could readily see how they managed to get pretty much all the subsistence away from the respectable white laborers.

I had read in the papers during the past ten years more or less about the persecution of the poor Chinaman on the Pacific Coast, and naturally, I come to the same conclusion that most of the Eastern people have—that they was a innocent and honest class of folks, being imposed upon and persecuted by a lawless set of Irish vagabonds. But my ideas have undergone a radical change, for I find the honest laborers, including Irish and all other kinds, have been driven almost to want and poverty by these pesky transient heathen, who, by their low wages and miserable living, serve to fatten the pockets of the avaricious capitalists of the Pacific Slope, and rob the honest, respectable white laborer of his livelihood; and I ask my Eastern friends, in justice to humanity and the facts in the case, not to waste their sympathetic brine and spoil their lovely countenances with red eyes for the poor, persecuted heathen in California. If these are true representatives of that Celestial country, I'll pray to the Creator to keep Jupiter on t'other side of the earth, and under no circumstances let him roll through the heavens over the Empire State, and fill its domains with any of its windfalls.

Hypocrisy crops out all along the sunny Pacific's slope, as thoroughly, and in some instances, more so, as it does on the Atlantic side of this great country. I would like to refer to many instances where I met it in all its grandeur and submitted to its tricks in being swindled to the extent of what little loose change I had in my pockets, but I haint got time to do it.

I am, every day of my life, convinced that the wisest thing that Benjamin Morgan ever done in his whole life, was to make his wife Clarissa, the banker and general financial manager of the firm of B. Morgan & Wife. Ever since he done that deed, the swindling hypocrites have had mighty poor picking in his patch; and my advice to the male sex in general is this: First, wait before you marry a female, until you are old enough to know what you want to marry her for; then pick out a level headed, smart woman of the female sex and marry her. Don't, under any circumstances marry a fool because she is pretty, nor a male woman, because she can talk and argue, but take a genuine, sweet-tempered, but firm female, and then make her what the name of her sex indicates she ought to be—a fee-male, and give her the fees that you receive from your business, and let her take care of it, and you'll be surprised in ten years to know how much she has saved for you, and how many chances of

EXPERIENCE WITH HYPOCRITES. 337

being swindled you have escaped. In case she doesn't prove to be a good financial manager, you'll have the satisfaction, at least, of having some one else beside yourself to blame for your lack of prosperity.

Of course, I am aware that circumstances alter cases. You might not have any money for her to take care of. In such cases, you needn't pay any attention to this piece of gratuitous advice, and you needn't bother her with the responsible duties of being your cashier.

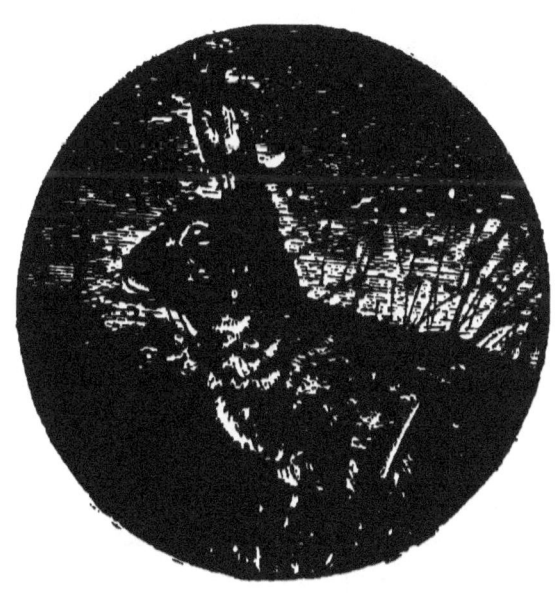

CHAPTER XXXII.

THREE days of San Francisco life has crowded my head with many pleasant things that may be profitable for me to keep there, until such time as I want to draw them out.

We took the morning train for Los Angeles, stopping on our way to visit some of those mammoth trees whose wonderful proportions have been described by every press in the world, and no one thinks of visiting California without writing a full description of them, even if they haven't been within a hundred miles of them, and generally they will manage to lie all they dare to about them. They are all-fired big trees, anyhow, and it makes you dizzy to try and watch a mosquito light on one of the top branches. I mean one of the branches on the top of the trees—these big tall trees I'm talking about, is what I mean. I saw the biggest one in California, and walked around it. I was tired when I got around to the point I started from, I acknowledge, but what of that? I've been pretty tired at times when I hadn't walked half as far, but that's no sign that it's necessary for them to build a horse railroad around it, so the visitor can see the tree on all sides the same day, and save the expense of five dollars for staying over night, in order to finish his tour of inspection.

I went into the hollow place inside, and I know now by my own observation, that it haint half large enough to accommodate a crowd at a *World's Fair* as the Californians have been hinting about. As I said before, it is an all-fired big tree, but there has been a tremendous big lot of lies told about it. Out of respect to this king of

THE DEAD GIANT.

the forests and his cousins, and his sisters and his aunts (I wish I knew who rung that bell in my ears, then?) I guess I'll let 'em stand there, and go on to Los Angeles.

The ride to this city, made famous by its fruits and wines, is delightful. The cars are well filled with natives and tenderfeet—the latter being in the majority. The train talk differs from what you hear on the Eastern railroads, as it consists largely of expressions of surprise and wonderment, such as, "Oh, oh! Isn't that grand!" "Say, Jennie, haint that pretty?" "Yes; and George, do you see that mountain peak off yonder?" "Oh, do you mean that one that glistens in the sunlight?" "Yes; it looks like the Bartholdi statue when the torch is blazing." "Oh, say! what are those pretty trees?" "Why, those are orange trees; that is an orange grove. Don't you see that farmhouse almost hid in their shade?" "Oh, yes; now I do.," etc., etc.

The talk of the natives, instead of being on the topic of hogs and cattle, is about mines and orange plantations, with an occasional story of some San Francisco scandal, in which some United States Senator, or banker, or big gun of some kind, or a common preacher is mixed up with some woman of the female sex.

The average Californian that one meets in traveling through the country, seems to live and grow fat on sensation. It makes but little odds what it is; anything, from the torturing of a pigeyed heathen to the killing of an editor; from kissing another man's wife, to the real, genuine domestic happiness and purity of a family (considered a rarity by some), so long as the news is *fresh*, and likely to create a little breeze, it is a good meal, and seems to be relished.

Of course, I don't mean to apply this remark to the general run of residents in the Golden State, but to the average of them that you meet on the trains and boats, and at the taverns. And for that reason, I understand that a first class liar that can swing the quill in good shape, has no difficulty in getting a good paying job as a reporter for the press in the Golden State. There is not any more difficulty in finding first class liars in California, than there is in Nevada, Chicago, Omaha, Denver, or even New York, but to get one that can use the pen in a smooth and rapid manner, and can wrap up his stories in Webster's choicest words, is not so easy a task, consequently good reporters get good pay. A reporter that can tell both sides of a lie in good shape at the same time, can get double pay by working for two opposition papers at once. He wants to possess the qualities of that reptile that has the power to change his color at will. Most good liars get in the habit of telling their lies in the same style, consequently they are unfit for newspaper use as double-barreled reporters, and have to content themselves in lying for small papers at moderate pay. A reporter that confines himself strictly to the truth has no commercial value, and consequently, is out of the market. Even tract publication concerns have no use for them! When I was in Chicago, Clarissa tried to get such a situation, but they wouldn't give her enough to board her at a free lunch counter. One would think females would make good reporters, but there haint a newspaper in the country, not even a temperance journal, that will hire them. I know no other reason for it than that they are too truthful. I find I have pretty nigh forgot to tell what I started out to, which was about our arrival at Los Angeles.

We got into "The City of the Angels," Los Angeles, in the evening. The sun had crossed the Pacific, or had sailed over its pacific bosom out of sight, but had left his rays of gold, crimson and purple on the sky, and scattering clouds that seemed to spread over the great ocean like a huge crazy quilt, and looked like a sublime picture, set in a dark navy blue velvet frame, the surrounding shades of night furnishing the velvet. We took a omnibus to the principal tavern. I was going to mention the name of this house, and speak well of it, but the landlord charged us for everything we had, just as if he never expected to meet us again on earth or in heaven, and considered it his last chance to shear us lambs, and I wont say a word about his tavern, for I don't want to do either him or the traveling public any harm.

We didn't intend remaining but one day, but there was so much to be seen, and something so enchanting about the place, that we staid there two days, and then hated to leave. We felt almost bound to it, and had it not been for them letters we received in San Francisco I wouldn't be surprised if we had staid there until now.

"A LITTLE FOR THY STOMACH'S SAKE."

When the Spaniards founded this place in 1781, they named it the "Los Angeles," which means the city of the angels. Judging from its lovely location in one of the finest valleys in the world, fourteen miles from the great Pacific, divine inspiration must have caused them to give it that name. If the angels ever occupied the city, they have long since flown away. I have no doubt that the avaricious speculator and land grabber put up a *deal* with them and froze them out. At any rate, there are no angels there, but the land-grabber and lot speculator is there in all the glory and strength of his prime, and is pretty nigh monarch of all he surveys.

This is one of the beauty spots of nature. Nature and art seem to have joined hands here and received the approving compliment of the Infinite: "It is good; Yea, very good. I'll bless thee with sunshine and dew; thy fields shall yield abundance."

The orange groves, orchards and vineyards are wonderful, and furnish millions of people throughout the United States with delicacies for the table.

I had to lay aside my scruples on the drinking question, and take some of their elegant wine. The force of St. Paul's suggestion to Timothy, "Take a little wine for thy stomach's sake and thine oft infirmities," seemed to appeal to my conscience and settled the question in favor of the wine, which I imbibed several times while I was there. Clarissa told me she was afraid Saint Paul would have a tremendous accouut to settle if he had to father all the drunkards in the world. She said there was more hypocrites sailing under Saint Paul's advice to Timothy, than under all other banners in the world, "And now," said she, "you have joined the band."

Her remarks was cutting, and I found I had got to lie if I explained it under that old sham. So I up and said, "Well, Clarissa, I wont lie. I drank the first glass of the wine to see what it tasted like, and I have drunk the rest of them 'cause I like it."

I haven't got any headache, toothache, stomach ache, weak lungs, liver complaint, rheumatism nor scaldhead, to offer as an excuse for drinking that wine; and I haint Timothy nor any relation to him; so I've either got to lie for an excuse, or tell the truth, and I prefer to maintain the purity of my standard of principle, and own up to the real reason why I drank the fluid extract of grapes manufactured in the City of the Angels. I have firmly resolved not to drink any more of it for fear I shall like it muchly, and I advise my friends to quit drinking just before you take the first drink.

CHAPTER XXXIII.

WITH regret we leave the angelic city of delicious fruit and sparkling wine, California's rosy-cheeked joy, but the time comes when the best of good things must separate. There is no such thing in this world as permanency in union; the bonds will and must break in time, and then separation follows. We turned our faces eastward. A bright star shining in the heavens over the Empire State, marked the exact location of Morganville, Blank County, and henceforth was to be our guide. What its beauteous rays foretold, we could not understand, as the missives we received in San Francisco seemed to cloud affairs in that locality with a veil of mystery.

Although we had for two days been dwellers in the City of the Angels, 'nary an angel condescended to tell us whether to joy or sorrow we was urged to return by the banker's letter, and the feeling of uncertainty and doubt was more annoying than the real facts, however unpleasant, could have been.

Right here let me ask some of our learned men in the school of metaphysics why it is that men and women can't be honest and frank enough to write about plain facts in a plain, straightforward manner, and not go to work and make a great mystery out of a simple fact, and if it is unpleasant news they have to communicate put their hand on an honest pen and make it say the words plainly, that its recipient may know the worst as it really is, instead of torturing him with cruel and hypocritical ambiguous phrases of uncertainty? If it is joyous news they have to impart, why mix the wormwood of doubt with the sugar of bliss in store, thereby destroying the delectable dish, and converting it into stale grapes? I don't suppose any of them will be able to give any better explanation than the one Clarissa gave me just now, as she looked over my two shoulders while I was asking this question. She said,—

"Benjamin, that is simple enough; it's because the folks that write that way can't help it, they have so much *sham* in their make up. They couldn't be plain *yes* and *no* kind of folks if they tried to."

I believe Clarissa is right. That banker, Brown, down to the village, could just as well have wrote me plain just what was up, as to have done as he did, if he hadn't been born a sort of hypocrite.

Here I am chasing after a figure that hasn't any business figuring in this book, and I am sorry, patient reader (if you have read the book so far) that I have inflicted this trip after a figure onto you; but if you haven't read the book I am glad I have done the inflicting, for you deserve it. If you allow all the other cranks to stuff their books into your head, you ought to give me an equal show with the other idiots that think they can write something. I will invite you to "get on board" the Southern Pacific train and go East with us.

"Some great writer has said, "There is a limit to all good things." Much as I regret the discovery was ever made, I have always found it out to be a fact. Even that beautiful suggestion of the immortal Horace G., "*Go West, young man;* GO WEST," good as it seems to be, has a limit, for you finally arrive at a point where you can't go west unless you are a good swimmer. Clarissa and I had reached that point, and as we started out to travel for a period of what Julia Spear in her essay, called, "Tempus fugiting," but which being translated from the Turkeyses language, means "flying time," we would have been obliged to go East about now, if banker Brown hadn't urged me to come home.

Clarissa and I have talked it over and we have concluded to not let that letter worry us at all, and take our time in going home.

Life is too short to perspire it all out, and if we keep cool we will last longer. And now if you'll go East with us, we will have a good time, but if you wont, just you watch us while we go, and see what nice things we pick up on our way between the wine cup of California and the pleasant meadows of Uncle Ben Morgan's farm in Morganville, Blank County, New York, and look out for "Tidings of Comfort and Joy."

A STREET SCENE IN LOS ANGELES.

We took the train leaving Los Angeles, of the Southern Pacific Railroad, at seven o'clock Tuesday morning. The usual performance was undergone in securing our bedrooms. This time Clarissa and I concluded we would take a box room pretty nigh one end of the car so she could lay down during the day if she felt tired. We found this to be an improvement over the up and down-stair arrangement, as we could be a little more secluded, and then it was higher toned, and gave us an appearance to the rest of the passengers of being millionaires, and you know there is a little satisfaction in being considered wealthy where you aint known.

We paid our respects to the colored lord of the car in the shape of a fifty-cent piece in order to secure civility on his part.

It is surprising how much colored respect and attention you can buy for fifty cents. I lost my identity as a Morganville cow-stripper, and was taken for Spreckles; whether it was because of my wealthy appearance or because of Clarissa, who looked as sweet as a hogshead of Sandwich Island sugar, I couldn't tell, but I suppose it was on account of that box room and the fifty cents.

The common passengers looked up to me with a sort of reverential air, and was very polite to us. Clarissa had on the black crow grain silk dress she bought in Field's store in Chicago, and which she intended to give to the poor busted speculator's wife, for whom it was made, but which she didn't do on account of not having time to hunt her up; and of course she made an impression that money with us was plenty.

I was frequently called "Mr. Spreckles." I couldn't understand what they meant, at first; but when a gentleman approached me with a pencil and book in his hand and said,—

"Excuse me, Mr. Spreckles, for taking the liberty to ask you a few questions. I am the traveling correspondent of the *New York World*, and am getting all the points of interest I can in this country for its columns, and as I have been informed you are the great sugar man of the Pacific coast, I should like to have a brief outline of your history, and an account of your immense possessions, and the *modus operandi* of conducting your mammoth business," I laughed at the anxious reporter, and said:

"Young man of the *World*, I have suffered a great many inflictions in the course of my life; I have had the *measles* and the *mumps*, the *yellow jaundice* and the *rheumatism;* I have had my left leg broke and set, and a crick in my side; I have lost more or less property, have been fearfully deceived in men, and swindled besides, but the worse inflicticated I ever was in my life, was by a newspaper reporter, and you will please excuse me if I turn you over to my sugar plantation, the only one I possess at the present time, or ever did possess, my wife Clarissa, and maybe she can entertain you."

I took a paper, borrowed Clarissa's specs, and set down in the seat next to the one she and the reporter occupied. I pretended to be reading, but really was listening to their talk. I wanted to see how she would handle him, and the joke that that porter had evidently started. It run about as follows:

"Mrs. Spreckles, I beg pardon for disturbing you, but if it will not be asking too great a favor, I would like an outline of your husband's history, and his great business interests. The world has been wanting to know all about him for a long time, and this is the first opportunity I have had to meet him."

"Well," said she, "are you the world? and are you the *whole* world? and is it possible that everybody lives and moves in you?"

"No, no! Madam, you don't understand me. There is a newspaper published in New York City called the *World*, and I am its correspondent, and that newspaper desires the information I ask."

Clarissa heaved a sigh of comfort, and seemed to feel easier, and after wiping her eyes and taking a peppermint, she said:

"Well, Mr. Man of the World, I am glad I understand you. Now, as a general rule, I do not allow myself to be interviewed by newspaper reporters. I don't like them. I have found them to be meddlesome, and as a rule, inclined in a large degree to prevaricate. And furthermore, I am by natural build opposed to giving away family secrets, and if I have the correct idea of what you are after, it is my husband's life—"

"I beg your pardon, Madam," said the correspondent, "I am no murderer."

"Well, I didn't say you was. I don't suppose you intend to kill him, although, nine times out of ten, when you fellows get a chance to write up a person's history, you manage to kill them—either socially, religiously, politically, or financially, and I suppose you want me to tell you all about him that I know, so that the world may know it, and put its approving, or otherwise, stamp upon it?"

"Yes, yes! you catch my idea."

"Well, as we have got a long ride before us, and as I see nothing of interest in the country through which we are passing, I had just as soon kill time in accommodating you with what information I possess. In the first place, I am unable to give you his early history—I mean from the time he first received the kiss of woman down to the period when manhood seemed to rest upon his shoulders. Whether he came from highly respectable and honorable parentage, or, to use a lawyer's term, *versus*, I know not, as I never saw them; but I have strong suspicions that they was the former, and not *versus*, as he bears the earmarks (so to speak) of respectability and honor, and I know he is strictly honest, and in the main, truthful. How do you think that description of my husband will suit the *World?*"

"Oh, splendidly; but please go on."

"Oh, certainly, I intend to go on, as I have only just begun. When he first met me, it was at a prayer-meeting, at the Giddings schoolhouse. I was introduced to him by his aunt, who seemed to take a strong liking to me. I can tell you enough that happened during our courtship and early marriage to fill the *World* three or four times, if you will only leave the advertisements in."

"Please excuse me, Madam, but I do not wish to enter into your private life, or know anything about your family relations. I do not wish to enter the secret domains of family privacy."

Clarissa threw her hands up in perfect astonishment, and the spectacles fell off from my nose onto the floor, breaking the left-hand glass into three pieces. I never saw a more astonished person in my whole life, and in a loud voice she exclaimed,—

"Young man, do you mean to say that the *World* don't want to know all about our family affairs—that it don't want to tear down the curtains of our private apartment—that it don't want to even enter into the Holy of Holies of everybody's private life and trample its sacredness into the dust, in its eager desire to find food for the scandalmongers—do you mean to tell me this?"

"Madam, that is just what I wish you to understand."

"Well, then, all I've got to say on that point is, that you are not of this *world*. I want to know what kind of a *world* your *World* is. I want to go to it. I long for a world where the sacred rights of an individual may be considered safe, and where the scandalmonger has no place or vocation."

"Madam, I am not surprised at your remark, or your desire for a fair world; but my *World* will afford you little, if any, comfort, as it is nothing but *a paper world*—not a real world. So, please lay aside your astonishment, and proceed to give me the general points of your husband's public career."

"Well, I can't tell you much about how he has careered in the public, as he has been around home on the old farm, ever since we was married, until we started out on this excursion train. He and I own a good, nice farm down in Morganville, Blank County, New York, about ten miles from the village, and it is all paid for; and what time we have lived there, which is going on to a quarter of a century, he has careered pretty decent. Once in awhile he has acted real foolish, and got swindled to pay for it; but that is nobody's business but his'n. I guess almost every man acts foolish, some time or other, during their lives."

It was the correspondent's turn, this time. He dropped his pencil, and looked up in perfect astonishment, and exclaimed, "Isn't this Mrs. Spreckles, of San Francisco?"

Clarissa seemed to enjoy his bewilderment, and in a laughing manner said, "Well, she was not, unless she had changed her name unconsciously."

With a sort of fox-and-geese puzzle running all over his countenance, he said, "Is not that gentleman (pointing to me) Mr. Spreckles, the great sugar man of the Pacific Coast?"

"Well," she replied, "he is a great hand for sugar and all sorts of sweet things, but his name is not Spreckles, but Mr. Benjamin Morgan—generally called around home and down to the village, 'Uncle Ben.'"

The correspondent said, "I must confess that I have been mistaken, or rather, misinformed. That colored porter told me that your husband must be Mr. Spreckles. I asked how he knew, and he said, ''Cause he was a mighty rich man, and give him a fifty-cent lump of sugar,' and here I have been bothering you on the supposition that it was Spreckles, and I beg your pardon for taking your time."

Clarissa said she was real glad to have her time occupied, and that she had enjoyed the conversation. "But," said she, "appearances are deceiving. If wealth seems to gild the outside, the world is ready to take off its hat and bow to the appearance, not stopping to see whether the inside be emptiness, or still worse. If rags clothe the appearance, the world passes it by cold and stiffly, not caring to take the pains to see whether or not

An angel fair,
Bedecked with jewels rare,
Is there enthroned.

"The SHAM appearance commands the SHAM respect of the SHAM part of the world. But I suppose your *World*, being a *Sham World*, readily detects the world of SHAMS?"

"Yes," said he, "you are quite right. Although I have made a mistake, I am quite well pleased in my good fortune in meeting Uncle Ben Morgan and his excellent wife Clarissa, and I am sure the *World* will be much more interested in knowing about them than

Spreckles, and I hope, at no distant day, to make you acquainted with the world, and make the world, including 'BILL NYE,' acquainted with you."

Clarissa took his *taffy* in a professional manner, the same as Grant, Blaine, Sherman, and Cleveland and all the rest of the big men of the world do and have done, easy and graceful-like, with a matter-of-course air onto her complexion, and said:

"I thank you for your kind intention, but you needn't put yourself out to introduce us, as we have already got pretty well acquainted with part of it; and if our money holds out and life continues in partnership with us long enough, we will become better acquainted with some more of it."

I had by this time joined them in the occupation of the double seat, and shook hands with the Young Man of the *World*, and we fell into conversation very easy like. He wanted our address, so I gave it to him as he wrote it down—"Benjamin Morgan, Morganville, Blank Co., New York, care of The Village." He wanted to know the name of the village. I told him it hadn't got a name. He was surprised, and desired to know the reason for a nameless village of 1,000 souls. I told him that it happened this way: "There was three men got together in a beautiful little valley in our county, through which perambulated (which means a sort o' saloon-reel-homeward at four o'clock in the morning) a charming stream. It swaggered from one bank to the other, stepping up high in some places to get over some big rocks, and then pitching headlong into the mud on t'other side. It was going up and down, and ziggerty-zaggerty all day long, in order to keep up its perambulate through that lovely valley, while them three men was concluding on a plan to establish a town at that particular spot. Mr. Givemall, a farmer, owned all the land, and proposed to stake out 100 acres into lots, streets and alleys, and give every odd numbered lot. Mr. Takemall, a civil engineer, proposed to do the surveying and laying the land off into lots, and establish and define the boundary of each, and to *take* every odd numbered lot for his trouble. Mr. Runemall, who had been an alderman in Albany a number of years, said he would organize the village after there was enough people there, and run the town. They drew up a contract and signed it with a stick dipped into some elderberry juice (as they had forgot to bring any ink with them), after which they all lay down on their front side and took a drink out of the creek. The Albany ex-alderman, after regaining his normal standing, and wiping his mouth on his shirt sleeve, said he hadn't tasted anything like that since he was first elected as a member of the water board in Albany, thirty-odd years before. After their *free* drinks they each lit a *cob* pipe and smoked the emblematical pipe of peace as a guarantee of their bond of union, and their faithful efforts to build there a *city*.

"In time there was 200 people there and a town organized, and the question of name came up. Mr. Givemall insisted that as he had given the land, that it should be named Givemallburg. Mr. Takemall insisted that as he had took it all, by rights it should be named Takemallburg, and Mr. Runemall demanded that, as it become his business to Run 'em all, the city should bear the name Runemallville. The spirit of rivalry run high, and the question is not yet settled, and probably will not be for twenty-five years to come. I have got a private petition in the hands of Tom Conners to take to Albany with him to the Assembly, to have the place named Hypocritsburgh."

The man of the world listened patiently to my lengthy answer to his question, and said he would take that as an item for the *World*.

While we was rattling along through a dry and uninteresting country the passengers in our car got pretty well acquainted, and the day didn't seem half as long as it would have, had it not been for that. The man of the *World* and Clarissa and me seemed to attract more attention than any other corresponding number of gentlemen on the train. I couldn't understand it, for there was a number of men of notable names on the train, as you will readily see by the following schedule:

Prince Kingokangokoko, the heir apparent of the Whaicki-Wooicki Islands, and his wife, Bridget O'McGinnis Kingokangokoko; Rising Grand Duke Van Haltren, the celebrated baseball twirler; Moxic Jim Bludsore, the inventor of a ginger and molasses compound solution that is being drunk all over the United States as a substitute for beer, and "Mr. O'Reilly, they speak of so highly, that keeps a hotel." There was a number of others of minor importance on board, but we three seemed to be the pivotal point of attraction.

It was getting along toward nine o'clock P. M., and I got tired of attracting, and Clarissa had already gone into our box, so I said to my friend that if he would excuse me, I guessed I'd bid him and the world good-night and go to bed and retire, which I did in less than five minutes.

We had a refreshing rest and sleep. The gentle swaying and rocking of the magnificent sleeper, supplied with the finest kind of beds, seemed to act like a charm, conveying us to dreamland in less time than a mother can rock her baby to sleep when she has company waiting for her in the front room, and the next morning found us fresh and ready for anything.

As we looked out of the window a dreary, desolate country, stretching its dry, sand-and-fine-pebble covered surface off into space beyond the reach of our eyesight, dotted here and there with various kinds of cactus, met our gaze, and it seemed as though a day of monotonous scenery was before us; but we was happily disappointed before two hours had elapsed.

We was in New Mexico. When I was at home on the farm, about all I knew about New Mexico was from the map I used to see in the children's geography. I didn't suppose it amounted to much. I didn't have the least idea that it was to the history of the United States what a rare specimen is to a museum; that it was a mine of wealth to the botany-maker, the geologer, and the builder of *an-ti-que* history. I use the word, AN-ti-*que* to satisfy Clarissa. She insists upon it, and says it is proper to put it in my book just at this place, and that I may not have another chance to use it, and she says, "A book without the word An-ti-que in it haint of much account nohow."

All along this trip, from the time I left home until now, I am finding out what a ignorant old fool I have been; but when I look out of the car-window and see a native New Mexican, or, as they call them here, *Greasers*, trying to plow a patch of ground with a

GREASER PLOWING.

crooked stick, with a steer's horn on the ground end of it, drawn by two oxen hitched to it with rawhide straps (as I did just now), I conclude there are others in the world that are ignoranter fools than I am. And when I see women out in the hot sun, standing around a clay hut about six feet high by five or six feet or more in diameter, just outside of an old adobe wall surrounding a lot of low, flat-roofed, one-story adobe buildings, baking bread for their hungry families, while the perspiration rolls down their greasy, dirty, brown faces, as we saw them just then while passing, I conclude that it will be a pretty tough job to find a ignoranter set.

It seems to me as though that old man that is pictured in

the almanacs with long shaggy hair and whiskers, and carrying a scythe on his shoulder, has mowed a swath of one hundred years out of time's calendar in this country, and left them that much behind the rest of the world. I do not make my calculations merely from their ways of plowing, baking and grinding corn by rubbing it between two big flat stones, operated by hand, but because what work there is done seems to be largely done by women. So far as the outside world is concerned, the majority, I am told, are in complete ignorance.

Everywhere you look, primitiveness seems to reign. What the Creator done, seems to remain. The native evidently is contented with its being so, and cares not, if possessed of the ability, to improve thereon. If he can succeed in finding enough mud, gravel, water and straw, or 'dead grass, to tread into mass by driving his ox over and through it, he will cut it into blocks about a foot square by one-half a foot thick, and spread them around on the ground for the sun to dry and bake. When his adobe bricks are hard, he will build him a little one story flat-roofed room, and feel proud to think he has a house. This much of improvement on nature, fills his cup of ambition, but the way the *adobe* brick was made by the first manufacturer of the article, is the way they make it now. If ignorance is bliss, their cup of bliss is running over. —

CHAPTER XXXIV.

THE scenery had suddenly changed, and from the dull monotony of arid plains, we was surrounded by the picturesque landscape in and around Albuquerque, and from here on to Lamy, where we changed cars for Santa Fe, eighteen miles north, and on to that city, the scenery is very interesting.

At noon we rolled into the oldest city in America. When I was a boy, and up to the time I was married, I supposed New York was the oldest place in this country, and that the Dutch was our grandparents on both our sides. At that time Clarissa up and made me believe that the Spanishers was the first to lay claim to us as posteritors; however she didn't know any more'n I did that there was a city away out west, in a country that neither one of us didn't know nothing about, that was a dumb sight older than New York City. But here we was—both of us ignoramuses—right in the heart of the oldest city in America, so far as anybody in this world had any knowledge of, Santa Fe.

We entered a hotel, the walls of which was laid up by hands that for three centuries or more had been sweeping the strings of golden lyres, in paradise, or poking up the fires down in Hades & Co.'s sulphur factory, and wrote our names in a register that bore visible signs of a corresponding an-ti-que-i-ty.

Somewhat weary from our long ride, we was glad to rest ourselves on the splint bottom chairs in the low, but spacions dining-room. The dinner was Spanish in its general architecture and build. The first thing on the printed programme was Chili soup,

SCENE ON THE ATCHISON, TOPEKA & SANTA FE RAILROAD.

It being a hot day, we thought something Chili would go first-rate. Since we left home we have drank all sorts of *chilly* drinks, and eat icecream and frozen puddings. but Chili soup was a thing we had never heard of before. So Clarissa and I called for a plate of it. I took a heaping tablespoonful to one swallow, and I thought the whole upper story of my physical mortality was on fire. I called for ice water while I held a towel to my burning tongue. After smothering the conflagration, I said to the greasy waiter,—

"Young Spanisher, if such be your ancestral character, what do you mean by playing such a trick on your honest and unsuspecting customers?"

"What trick for you mean?" said he.

"Why," said I, "palming that goll-darned hot stuff on us for ice-cold soup."

"Oh!" he replied, "that is Chili soupeo."

"It's a dumb lie," said I, "it's hot enough to scald hogs in."

"Oh, Noeo! Noeo! You no savveo; the soupeo be made of chilio, which is Mexicano red peppero, and is a heap goodo."

"Oh, I see; it is red pepper soup, is it, with a sham name to deceive folks? Well, I don't want any more of it."

Clarissa said, "Ben, it is no deception. All there is about it, you don't understand the Mexican, or Spanish, language."

"I know it. I know I am no Spanisho Mexicanero Greasero, and consequentlyo am not supposed to knowo what to cato and be safo, buto one thingo I do knowo, and that iso, they don't geto any moreo confounded Chili stuffo into my moutho."

Clarissa said, "Wello, Ben, don't make such a fusso about that soup, or they'll all find out what a greenhorno you areo; but eat your victuals and let them stop your mouth."

The next things on the catalogue was Chili con-corne, Chili colorow, Chili baked beans, and one or two other Chilies, roast beef, roast chicken, and a few other roasted and boiled American animals.

After a fashion, I managed to make out a pretty good meal. I asked the waiter if they was cannibals?

"What be they?" he asked.

Said I, "You poor, benighted heathen, be you so ignorant that you don't know what a cannibal be? Well, I am sorry for you; you ought to be converted. A cannibal, my poor fellow, is a savage brute of a man, that will slay his brother man and cook and eat his body."

The waiter started in surprise and said, "Why, me no hear of such a horriblo thingo. No! me no cannibal."

"Well, but according to this here dinner catalogue, you must be," said I. "Look there—right there (pointing it out to him), do you see what it says—don't it say meats for dinner there?"

"Yes."

"Well, now, put your two black Spanish eyes on that sentence, don't it say *Chili Colorow?*"

"Yes."

"Well, that Chili Colorow is to be eaten, isn't it?"

"Yes."

"Well, you ignoramus, don't you know that Old Colorow was an Indian chief of national reputation, living up in Colorado, and the Coloradoans have been trying a long time to get rid of him, but couldn't, because they was all afraid of him? And now they have evidently killed him and sent his carcass down here to destroy all traces of his murder, and you have got hold of his cold, dead remains, and are disgracing the proud name of America, as well as the name of its oldest city, by Mexican red peppering it, cooking and serving it to your boarders," and I turned to Clarissa and said, "Come, let's get out of this hotel; it aint safe to be here."

The waiter turned from horrifying surprisedness into violent laughter, and said, "Stranger, wait a minuto; that be no dead Indiano. That is a very fine Mexicano dish, made of potatoes, cabbage, turnips, and any other good, fresh vegetables we can get in the marketo, mixed with Chili and cooked in plenty of lardo, and it be a very nice disho. You just try someo."

I found I was the "benighted heathen ignoramus" this time. I have resolved not to make another break of that kind as long as I live. I wonder if all the heathen think the same of the missionaries we smart people send to 'em to convert and enlighten them, as that Greaser thought of me? If they do, I pity the poor missionaries.

MR. JUAN FERNANDEZ-MARACILLO-ROMEO MARTINEZO.

I eat that colorow, and found it a little hot, but very pleasant.

After dinner I had a very pleasant chat with the landlord; told him who we was and where we was from, and stated also that, as our time was limited, we desired to see and learn all we could of Santa Fe in our allotted time, and asked how we could do it.

He informed me that my best way was to get a competent guide, one that knew all about the city and its history, to go with us.

Said I, "That is a capital idea, and I am much obliged to you; but how is a fellow going to find such a man, when he is a total stranger?"

"Oh, that is easy enough. That old porter of mine has lived here 117 years, and knows all about Santa Fe, from its infancy, and you give him a couple of dollars, and he will tell you all you want to know—and more, too."

I was pleased with our good fortune, and Clarissa was fairly tickled. If anything on earth can tickle that noble, good woman, it is a opportunity to learn, and she has been infatuated (I believe I've got the right word) for the past fifty-three hours, coming five o'clock this afternoon, with a desire to learn all about Santa Fe.

Said I, "Will you please produce the porter, and get us acquainted, for I'd like to get a early start."

The porter was called and introduced to us as Mr. Juan Fernandez-Maracillo-Romeo Martinezo. We bowed a very polite bow in recognition of his lengthy title and his extreme old age. He received us with equal cordiality, and said he was proud to serve us. We found him to be a remarkably smart man, quite vigorous, and that he spoke United States perfectly, without any Spanish brogue.

We started out, and after walking a long distance through a narrow street lined on either side with low, flat-topped houses, with overhanging balconies that afford shade to their fronts, and following our guide a short distance out, we came to a hill back of the city, on whose top were the crumbling ruins of an old fort. We climbed up to the summit of this hill, whose color resembled a crazy-quilt, with brown and yellow predominating, and set down on some rocks.

Our old guide commenced his description of the city by giving us the following history:

"You must know, in the first place, that this is a very old town, and you will, no doubt, be surprised when I tell its age, so far as we have any reliable information."

I interrupted him, and said, "Well, never mind our being surprised. You can tell us as big a whopper as you are a mind to. You can put its age anywhere from 100 to 100,000 years. We are used to whopping tall stories. We have heard all sorts of big yarns about all sorts of things, ever since we crossed the Missouri at Omaha, and we have got over being surprised at anything. This

HEADWATERS OF THE RIO GRANDE.

whole Western country is so full of surprises that they have got to be quite common to us, and we run onto a dozen or more of them every day. So, just go ahead, and tell us about it."

While we was admiring the scenery he went on:

"In 1540, Coronado, a Spanish adventurer, while on a tour of exploration, with a large force of Spaniards, marched up the Colorado River from its mouth, where they landed, to the confluence of the Green and Grande, which form the Colorado. Here he divided his forces, sending part up the Green, while he with the remainder came up the Rio Grande.

"Arriving at this place, he found a large and important city, occupied by the most intelligent race of Indians that there is any historical evidence of, as having been the inhabitants of North America—the Aztecs.

"Coronado was seized with a desire to obtain it. His forces were camped upon this hill, which you see commanded a view of the entire city. At his command they marched down and leveled its walls, and laid the city in ruins, driving its inhabitants to the mountains.

"The present city was erected upon its site. Although many changes have occurred during the past 350 years, yet I am able to show you some of the landmarks of 1540 that still exist.

"The world has been cheated out of the history of this stronghold of the Aztecs by the cruel and inhuman treatment of this wonderful race. With Coronado's conquest, every vestige of history of the city was destroyed. The tyrannical treatment of the Indians so embittered them that in 1680, after more than a century of humiliation and grinding servitude, they arose and drove the Spanish invaders out of the land. The example set by the Spaniards was followed, and they, in turn, destroyed everything they could. Churches and public buildings were burned, and all the documentary records of Coronado's discovery of the place, served as a fire in the plaza, by the light of whose flame the angry Indians pushed on their work of destruction. Time did not serve them to complete the destruction, for in 1693, DeVarque, at the head of the Spaniards, reconquered the city. From then until now it has been undisturbed, and as a rule, quietness and laziness have lingered around and through it.

"Were it not for its place in the history of America, and its picturesque appearance, it would receive but little attention from the travelers that are daily visiting it, but as it is, it commands the attention of every one passing through New Mexico.

"You will find the city, outside of the modern structures, is emphatically Spanish. You will see its streets are narrow and crooked, and lined on both sides with low, one-story, quaint old adobe buildings. The balconies give us the shade that is necessary in this warm, sunny climate. The flowery *placitas* add much to the picturesque appearance, and give the place a charm."

I spoke up and said, "I'll be dumbed if it aint so."

"Everywhere you go, you will see the Spanish origin of the town.

"Lieut. Pike, of Pike's Peak notoriety, is supposed to be the first live, genuine *Yankee* to visit this city. In 1806 he run the risk of registering his arrival in our hotel, and I waited on him. Forty years later General Kearney captured Santa Fe from the Greasers. He and his bold soldiers marched to victory without any opposition. Not even a pin was pointed toward them by us wicked Spaniards.

"He built Fort Marcy on this hill top, and we are now sitting on its old ruins. I brought you up here so you could get the best view of the old city and the surrounding country that can be obtained."

"Well, I'm glad you did," I said. "You are a dumb good fellow, if you be a Greaser, and know your business first-rate, but excuse me for breaking in on your story. You know where you left off, don't you?"

"Oh, that is all right; it don't bother me any. I am used to being interrupted. That is part of my everyday experience.

"You see this view overlooks the plateau on which the city is built and the country stretching off toward Old Mexico. Right off to the north you notice a range of foot hills, and back of them a number of mountain peaks whose summits are covered with perpetual snow; while over there, reaching off southward, are the blue Cerrillos. You see they are partially hid by wreaths of clouds hanging around their summits. The distance gives them a dim and smoky appearance. You will observe that the constant shifting of the clouds produces a succession of lights and shades, and heightens the interest in the scene."

Clarissa spoke up and said,—

"Isn't it beautiful? I could sit here a month and look at this wonderful picture and not grow weary." I couldn't help saying—

"I'll bet you'd get goll-dumb hungry before the month would be up, and want something to eat. I don't know of but one fellow that could set in one place for a whole month and live on shadows, and he is a lunatic."

"Who is that?" asked Juan A-mile-and-a-half-long-name.

"Why, I don't know his right name, but by occupation he was a Tanner; but don't stop; go right on with your story."

"Now turn your attention to the city lying at your feet. I don't suppose you care for the modern buildings and improvements, but will be more interested in the antique portion of the city."

"Yes, you are just right; an-ti-que is the thing we are after. You can give us all the an-ti-que. I like it pretty well, and Clarissa can live on it, almost."

"Benjamin!" ejaculated Clarissa. You will notice if you have read the book so far, that this is the first time I have used "ejaculated." I had it ready to use more'n two weeks ago, but something or other happened so that I lost it. I had it writ down on a slip of paper and stuck it in my vest pocket, and two or three times when I was in San Francisco I tried to find that slip of paper, but missed it, and just now I went to light a cigar that Juan —— ——'o gave me, and stuck my fingers in my vest pocket, after a match, and pulled out that slip, and for fear I may lose it again, I just put it in now. As I started to say, she just ejaculated, " Benjamin, don't interrupt the gentleman ; I am anxious for this description."

Mr. Juan —— —— —— ——'o proceeded as follows, to-wit:

"Those old flat-roofed houses you see along the Santa Fe Creek, that little stream that divides the city, are among the first that were constructed after Coronado captured the town. You notice the color of the children playing around the doors is about the same as the houses—dark-brown, bordering on the red. The adobe houses, when newly built, are brown, or the same color of the ground ; but age acts upon these as it does upon men—it gives them a darker shade, and deep furrows are made in their walls by the action of weather and time, as wrinkles come upon the aged human being.

"The streets are narrow and crooked, winding and twisting among the buildings like huge serpents. Over there, a little to the right as you are sitting, is the broken facade of San Miguel, the oldest church in the United States. It is nearly in its original condition, barring the inroads of natural decay worn by time. Over there stands the Church San Francisco. There is but little of its exterior but what is modern, having received a new painted roof and new stone walls; but by carefully examining the interior, you will discover some of its original make-up.

"Out yonder you see the spire of the great Church Guadaloupe. There, in the center of the town, is the plaza, or what you folks in the East call a common. On that side of the plaza, almost hid by the trees, whose rich foliage in spring and summer produces a pleasing contrast with the somber, brown walls and yellow, drab streets, is the palacio del Gobernador. Now," said he, " we will descend, and take a walk through the city."

We was loth to leave the spot, as the beauty of the scene seemed to speak right out and say, " Don't be in a hurry; just lay off your things and stay a spell. You can have your old friends and neighbors with you back in your Eastern home all the time, but it will be but once in your lifetime that you will, in all probability, visit us." The broad, open country to our left seemed to say, "Come and see us before you go home, and we will do our best to entertain you." The peaks, with their foot-hills, to our right, beckoned to us, and seemed to whisper in our ear, "Don't forget to come up and stay all night with us, before you go home. We will give you lots of good fun, catching trout in our crystal streams, and will treat you to ice-cream in abundance." The blue Cerrillos and their snow-capped neighbors behind them, who seemed to be disputing with the sky above for the possession of the clouds, called to us in imagination, and said, "Don't fail to come over and stay with us a couple of weeks, before you start on your homeward journey. We will show you wonders that few in this world know about. We have plenty of rare and pretty things locked up where none but our invited guests can see them. We will show you the ancient homes of the Cliff Dwellers, and let you climb a ladder and sleep in one of the places where the grand old Aztec Indian dwelt. We can charm you, if you will only come."

The historic Rio Grande, that moves majestically toward the sea twenty miles west of us, seemed to sing to us in pensive tones, "Come! come, come, see me."

Even the smoke that twirled and circled from hundreds of chimneys below us, up into the clear blue vault above, seemed to say, " Stay a little longer, and I will paint you some fancy scenes,

"Wreaths, clouds, and castles fair,
For you I'll build in the air."

But to all these pressing invitations we had to say, "No, we thank you, for old Mr. Juan —— —— —— ——'o is waiting for us to join him, and he is half-way down the hill now." After we had caught up with him, he says:

"Now we will enter the city Santa Fe, or, as the name means in your language, Holy Faith, and we will go to the *Plaza*, passing by the Bishop's Garden on our way."

As we proceeded, every little while he would call our attention to this and to that church. I said, "It looks to me that the Fathers that founded this darned old town got awfully stuck on religion, or else they was afraid the Devil would steal their young ones, and built these churches for places of refuge, should that old cuss with big ears and a hot pitchfork attack the place. I don't think the old men needed to be afraid of that, for there couldn't have been money enough here in them days to have induced him to raid the place. It's money men he's after and he gets 'em, too."

He asked me what made me think that.

I told him that I knew it, for I had a personal interview with the old cuss up in Virginia City, and he told me all about it. Said he:

"I can't say how that is; but it seems to have been the Spanish custom to have plenty of churches. Perhaps their idea was to keep the people moneyless, by taking every penny they had to spare, to support the priests, thereby removing all temptation for the Devil to attack them. I can't say what the reason is for so many churches here; but one thing I can say, and that is this: For over one hundred years they got all the money I could save. As fast as I could get it they called for it, and I either had to hand it over to them, or go to purgatory when I died. But about ten years ago I concluded I would take care of my money myself, and run the risk of old purgatory. I have quit being under the priesthood's control, and I intend to run the remainder of my days on my own hook, try and do what I know to be right, and do my own thinking."

I grabbed the old man by the hand, and gave him a regular old New York shake, and said, "Good for you, young man; them is my sentiments. Stick to 'em, and by golly, I hope you will live to a good ripe old age."

He was visibly affected by my congratulating him, and said, "Thank you," and as we was passing a saloon at the time, he further remarked, "Let's go in and take a drink."

Alas! alas! the noble character he had already created for himself in my mind began to drop down to the level of the ordinary human being, as I discovered the regular Chicago taste was formed in his gullet. I swelled up with my old-fashioned farmer honesty and purity, and in the dignity of a man that has the consciousness of knowing he isn't a dumb hypocrite, and said, "No, sir; I don't drink, and I don't like to trot around with them that does."

He looked at me with utter amazement, and seemed glued to the spot where he stood for five minutes, looking at me from feet to head, and back again, and exclaimed, "Please give me your photograph."

"What for?' I replied.

"Because, for 117 years that I have lived in Holy Faith Town I have never known of a stranger coming within our borders that didn't drink something for the 'stomach's sake' and his oft infirmities, if not because he loved it, and I want your picture to look upon and show to my posterity by the woman I expect to marry next July, as a living curiosity."

Said I, "When I get home I'll get some pictures took, and I'll be glad to exchange with you, for I assure you it will be as big a curiosity for me and Clarissa and the posterity we have got raised up down home, to look upon the picture of a man that is well along in the second century of his life who is going to raising posterity, as it will be for you to gaze on the picture of an honest, sober, and temperate man, that isn't a Biblical Timothyan hypocrite, always looking, for his stomach's sake, in the bottom of a whisky-glass or beer-mug. But, as we are losing time standing here, if it will be any accommodation to you, I'll go in and take a glass of ice-cold lemonade, and Clarissa can eat a dish of icecream while I am drinking the lemonade. She is powerful fond of it."

We agreed on the picture exchange, got our drinks and icecream, and proceeded on our way.

Soon we came to a place inclosed by a high adobe wall, and Mr. Juan —— —— —— ——'o began—

"This is the beauty spot of Santa Fe, the Garden, owned by Bishop Lamy." Gaining admission, we found therein a beautiful garden indeed. The guide said, "The Bishop has labored a great many years in making this lovely garden, and you have no idea of the amount of *purgatory* money that has gone into it. Neither have I."

We walked all through the grounds, and found them indeed delightful. A small fish-pond, beautiful trees and flowers in great

PALACIO DEL GOBERNADOR.

abundance, and rustic seats, where we could sit down and look over the walls and see the tops of cities over in the sea of sky.

We went on until we reached the Plaza. Passing on to the farther side, we were in front of a long, one-story adobe building, in front of which was a wide portico, held up by a number of wooden columns.

"This," said Juan, "is one of the oldest and most important structures in our city. It is the *Palacio del Gobernador*, or the Governor's Palace.

"We all take a great deal of pride in this old palace, as the history of Santa Fe is closely allied with it, and if its walls could give up their secrets, stories of pathos and thrilling incident could fill many a volume. This was the palace of the Pueblo chiefs, long before the Franciscan friars gave the town its present name. The Spanish generals issued their orders and proclamations from its rooms for nearly three centuries. It is now occupied as an official residence by the Territorial Governor."

We was indeed interested, alike in his story and in the examination of the palace, some rooms of which we entered.

It was time for us to return to our hotel for supper, and the long walk we had taken made us tired and hungry.

A good meal and an hour's sitting under the portico in front of our hotel rested us. The soft, cool air of evening was very refreshing. We talked with the landlord considerably, and also with a number of the business men that was sitting around in front of the house. After we went to our room Clarissa and I talked about what we had seen. She said it was the strangest place she ever saw. Says she:

"Strange things meet us in nearly every direction we travel. Strange incidents seem to pop up in the road right in front of us wherever we go; but about the strangest thing we have run across in looking around this famous city, musty with age, resembling an old coat, tattered, torn, and patched with many-colored cloths, is that old palace—not so strange because of its long and lingering existence, nor for its having been the executive mansion of noble Indian chiefs and hot-headed Spanish usurpers and rulers, but because the man that everybody supposed was over in Judea visiting with the natives of that country, while he was writing the story of the three white camels and their riders from three different nations meeting upon the desert on their way to discover the Saviour—Lew Wallace, was secluded in one of its dingy rooms while he was writing the interesting story of Ben Hur.

"Strange, also, is the fact that so great a man as Wallace is should play sham by trying to make folks think he was in the Holy Land, a-discovering, when he hadn't left the United States. Now, I read that book through last summer, and enjoyed it, and many was the time I wished I could join company with his party in that old land of ancient story, and see some genuine Judeans, and enter Jerusalem with him, and see those things so sacred because of their connection with the New Testament and its principal characters. And

BLOWING OUT THE ELECTRIC LIGHT.

now, to come away out here and find out he wasn't in Jerusalem at all, but secluded in this old palace, making up that story, has opened to my eyes a new sham. I wonder if any of that New Testament was written in such a way?" And she concluded her remarks by heaving a heavy sigh upon whose ebb tide were the words, "Woe unto ye, Scribes and Pharisees—Hypocrites."

"May be," said I, "he sketched the book over in Palestine and polished it off here in this Holy Faith town. Don't be too severe in your remarks on an author; you may be doing him a wrong."

"Well," says she, "I don't mean to. But I am tired; let's go to bed and retire." I agreed to the proposition.

The bedroom we slept in had a musty smell of old time lingering about its walls. It was lighted up with new-fashioned lightning, in little glass-covered contrivances, just the same as the Denver tavern had, and for the second time I got fooled in trying to blow it out. After trying to blow all the wind I could muster at it, I happened to remember that the Denver porter turned a little brass thing to put it out. I found it and turned off the lightning just as easy as could be, and got into bed.

The next morning after breakfast our guide met us in the office, ready to take us through the town. I told him we had concluded to leave on the noon train, and we couldn't be out but an hour or two; and as we had got a pretty general idea of the place, we would be satisfied if he would take us into one of them old, moldy churches.

"All right. Then we will go and see Old San Miguel."

As we approached it I was not struck to the heart with the idea that it was beautiful, in any sense of the word, on the outside. Its broad, squatty tower, century-stained, surmounted by a wooden cross that time did not intend should remain another century, on account of its feebleness, had no pleasing proportions, but the anti-que-ity of the thing made it look like some old picture. It was evidently built for solidity and durability, rather than beauty.

Our Juan —— —— ——'o called our attention to the empty belfry, and said, "In early days, when the church was completed, the Spanish parishioners hung a heavy bell there that was cast in Mexico in 1356, but the walls being rendered unsafe, the bell was removed and placed in a niche that has been made for it within the church."

We entered through the wide doorway, and as the heavy doors swung together behind us, shutting out most of the light, at first we felt as though we was in a vault, as we couldn't see very plain, but a soft light struggled through the small windows, and assisted us to see the interior quite well.

The room is long and narrow, and the windows are set into

deep-cut openings. In the further end stands the altar, decorated with high-colored ornaments and emblems, and dressed up with a whole lot of candlesticks and candles, and a lot of stuff that looked as if it had been bought cheap at some second-hand store.

Right up over the front doorway is the gallery, supported by massive beams, on whose brown surface can be seen some carvings made by the builders. There is nothing in it of any interest to the practical world, and only that crank that is hunting after old, worn-out, musty things to put into his collection of an-ti-que-ities, could see anything here that he would want to take away with him. I asked Mr. Juan —— —— —— ——'o if he knew when this church was built.

Said he, "It was originally built about the year 1600, when Oñate was the Governor, but during the Indian revolution, in 1680, it was mostly destroyed by the enraged Indians, who for 140 years had been cheated out of their homes and liberty, and there was only a small portion of its walls left standing. After the Spaniards reconquered the city they rebuilt this church, completing it in 1710, since which time it has remained undisturbed by aught but time."

We told Juan that we guessed we had seen about all of this old place we had time to, and Clarissa paid him and expressed our thanks for his kindness, and asked him to come and visit us after he got a little older. He walked back to the hotel with us, and after waiting on us very politely, urged us to come again.

We took the noon train and rolled out of America's oldest city with a feeling of pleasure we had received in going over and through it. It was a chapter in geography and history that neither one of us had ever studied in school, and one we shall always remember.

Whether in point of greatness Santa Fe will have a future history that will compare with the past, remains to be seen, and we will let it remain, while we take our homeward journey.

We was told that we would not do New Mexico nor ourselves justice if we did not stop at the celebrated Las Vegas, and take a bath in the hot springs. So, when the train stopped for supper, I told the conductor we would stop there a day. He fixed our tickets for us, and we took a 'bus for the Phœnix Hotel, where we staid all night. We had a fine private bedroom. The bed was so soft and springy, the air so cool and delightful, we had a rest and sleep that thousands (locked up in prisons) would have given a good deal to have enjoyed. Clarissa said she dreamed of God's Garden—and she saw me and her and the driver standing a-looking at that Balanced Rock. She tried to find her CLA but couldn't see it, and while the driver was pointing it out to her, she woke up. I am glad we stopped there, as it gave us a good opportunity to see another of Nature's beauty-spots. The hotel is a magnificent building, put up for man's comfort. While in its outside and inside appearance it is handsome and grand, in its construction the comfort and happiness of its guests was not for a single moment lost sight of. In every detail the ease and pleasure of its customers was studied. The location could not have been excelled if they had sent old Coronado with his exploring party all over the world hunting a spot for it, for here is a beautiful dell, surrounded on three sides by mountains, and its other side open toward the broad meadows, where, six miles distant, is the town of Las Vegas. It enjoys a lovely climate and ever-changing scenery. Everlasting freshness meets the eye, and all the variety one can ask for. The sparkling waters of the Gallinas River tumble along at a short distance from the hotel, while the most delightful wash-water is furnished at any temperature desired in the wonderful springs, whose waters have, no doubt, been boiling and bubbling up for ages past, and will continue to bubble and boil long after Clarissa and I, and a few other good souls, have gone to join the angels.

We took a bath in the springs, and, for making a fellow feel first-rate and getting him real clean, it beats all the places we have come across.

I said to Clarissa, " We have got Las Vegas, and mighty good ones, on our old farm in Morganville, and we have got the Gallinas River. and I wish we had these hot springs there. If we had, I'd open up a summer resort, and see if we couldn't make a lot of money, as well as some other sharp folks."

" How do you make that out, Benjamin?" said she. I'd like

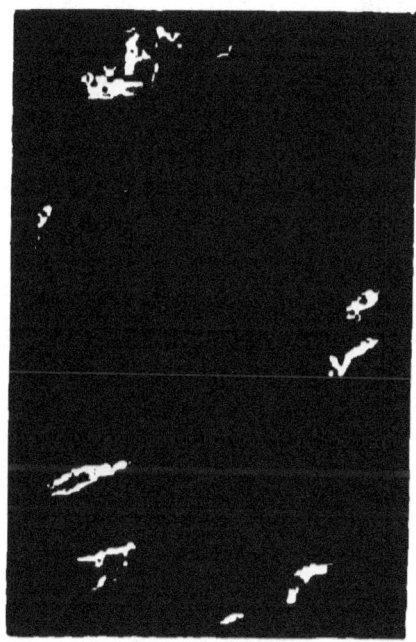

BALANCED ROCK.

to know where we've got Las Vegas and Gallinas River on the old farm!"

" Well," said I, " we have the meadows, haven't we? and mighty fine ones, too."

" Yes, that is so."

" Well, that is what Las Vegas means—the meadows, and we have got old Hen Creek, running down through the west pasture, haint we?"

"Yes, to be sure," she said.

"Well," said I, "that is a Gallinas River, for that's w- i; it means in United States language."

"How did you find that out, I'd like to know?"

"Just the way I find out most everything—by asking what they meant. I asked that young Greaser that scrubbed me in the bathhouse about it, and he told me that them was the meanings of the terms."

Clarissa wanted to stay here another day, but said she couldn't afford it as they wanted a small farm for keeping us a very short time, so we bid *The Meadows* and *Hen Creek* good-by, and took the Atchison, Topeka & Santa Fe Railroad for Kansas City, the nineteenth marvel of the nineteenth century, where we arrived after passing through the magnificent State of rich prairie farms, with their wonderful improvements, and splendid schoolhouses—Kansas.

I would like to have stopped at a dozen places in this glorious State, renowned for its struggles for existence without the dark stains of human slavery blemishing its rich soil, but I hadn't got the time.

Kansas City is one of the wonders of the age. It is wonderful for its push and go-aheadativeness, but its greatest wonder consists in its wanting the whole earth and claiming over half of it. We met several fellows there that could beat the Omaha gentlemen for tall stories about its future prospects, but we didn't meet any one there that was deaf and dumb; we asked several if there was any such a person there, and was informed that there was not one in the city. I told Clarissa that it was a downright pity that the Almighty had failed to bless Kansas City with one. What the city would come to, nobody could tell.

We was entertained one day by the Mayor and the leading men, and we found that while they was all good fellows, so far as we could see, they was all dreadfully troubled with the same complaint. —See reference to the Omahaians that boarded our car at their city.

I wouldn't be surprised to hear at almost any time that the sun had quit getting up in the east in the morning, but would hereafter rise in Kansas City and set in Omaha. Well, I believe them is the kind of fellows to make business, and develop all there is in a country. I wish we had some of them down in The Village. As long as we have got to have more or less hypocrites, we had better have live ones that have got snap and vim in 'em—that will do other folks good by giving life and prosperity to a country, than a lot of old close-fisted, penurious, never-dying ones, that will hang on to all they have got, and never give anybody else a chance.

While in Kansas City I discovered a new scheme, a scheme that would just suit Jim Teeters. I wanted to get an idea of what property was worth. So I went into a real estate dealer's office and putting on the appearance of a man that had got more money than he knew what to do with, asked him if he had got any good corner lots to sell.

"Oh, yes sir. I've got some that will just suit you. If you'll wait five minutes, I'll have my private carriage brought around and will take you over the city and show you a number of very desirable lots, any one of which you can double your money on in sixty days, at the rate our city is growing. Please excuse me a moment, while I order my porter to bring up my carriage."

"Oh, certainly," said I. "You go on and get your horse and don't mind me; I'll wait right here, and see that they don't anybody carry anything off."

He slipped out into the next door which was in a barber shop separated from his office by a thin board partition, and I heard the following conversation;

"Tom, will you go down to Jim's livery stable, and tell him I want a good horse and buggy right away, and you bring it up, will you?"

"Yes, boss; but de last time I was down there after a hoss for you, he said dat was de last one he was goin' to let you hab, until you paid up, and I spoze he wont let me bring one up—but I'll go and see."

"Well, you just tell Jim that I have struck a soft snap; that I've got a rich old farmer that I want to show through the city, and I think I can sell him half-a-dozen lots; tell Jim I will try to sell that old hole in the ground, that he calls a residence lot—the one he got off from Bob Green in a game of poker, and which haint worth twenty-five dollars—to the old man, and if I strike him for a deal, I'll come right down and pay him up. Just say to Jim for me that my business has been very dull for a month past; that during that time I haven't sold a single piece of property, but I have got a good many prospects, and now I've got a soft looking old farmer that is no doubt rich, in the office, and I can stuff him the same way we stuff everybody that comes here, with K. C.'s wonderful future, and I will sell him some lots, sure."

"Yes, boss; I'll go."

"Well. Say, Tom, when you drive up to the door, you please act just as though you was my porter, for I want the old man to think I am away up. You know a big impression helps business."

"Yes-sah; I spose it do. Well, all right, boss; I'll be dar in a few minutes."

The gentleman returned to the office with an air on to his countenance of business importance, as much as to say—"I am the heaviest real estate man in the city," and sitting down in his spring cushioned, whirl-around chair at his desk, he pulled out a drawer and took out of it a box of cigars, and passed them to me and very politely said, "Please take a cigar." I don't smoke very often, but on this occasion I thought I would.

He drew his chair up near mine and in a very confidential way, laid bare the tremendous city this place would be within the next ten years; that its million of inhabitants would require so many hundreds of railroads to convey them to and fro. "And, sir," said he, "every lot within fifteen miles in either direction from where we are sitting, will be gobbled up in less than six months from now, and if you want to invest some money where you can clear 500 per cent. profit in less than a year, I can take you to some pieces of property that you can buy, where you can make that much, easy."

"By George! You don't say so?" I exclaimed in surprise.

"Yes, but I do say so, and more than that, I can take you where you can buy a couple of lots that by holding on to 'em four or five years will make you a millionaire."

"How in thunder is that?" I asked.

"Why, the capitol of the State is going to be moved here within that time, and they will have to have those two lots to rest one of its wings on," he replied.

"Look here!" said I. "You don't pretend to tell me that the capitol of the great State of Missouri has got wings, and flies around from one place to another, do you?"

"Yes; she has wings, and she is bound to leave Jefferson City, and she will roost right down by these two lots, sure. Then don't you see they'll have to have 'em, and you can put your own price on them?"

"Yes," said I. "How is business with you? Are you selling a good many lots?"

"Well, I should smile," said he. "Why it's simply marvelous, the amount of business I am doing. I average about a hundred sales a day. Some days my office is just crowded, and I can't get around to wait on them all. It is a little quiet just now, but it will give us a good chance to go out, and here is my carriage at the door."

We stepped into the buggy and drove off. As we rode over hills and through hollows, shaded by an overhanging cliff on our right, while on our left was a yawning chasm one moment, and the next crossing a street that seemed to be running down a ravine, I said, quietly: "You have a very fine horse and buggy; it rides mighty easy. How much do they charge you a day for such a rig here?"

"I don't know how much they would charge for such a turn-out. You see I own this rig. I have several more; I have to have them in my business to take our customers over the city with. I presume that I have five or six out this morning with my clerks, showing property to customers."

By this time we stopped at a corner where there was a deep hole in the ground, about thirty feet wide by one hundred and twenty feet deep, and right next to it, a monstrous high hill.

"Now, look at those two lots," said he. "There is a fortune for you. That corner lot belongs to a poor livery stable man in town. He took it of a man that was unfortunate in a little speculation, and as he needs some money pretty bad, he will sell that lot dirt cheap."

"Why," said I, "you don't call that hole in the ground a lot, do you?"

"My dear sir, that is one of the most desirable lots in the city. You see you have got your cellar dug already. You lay the foundation of your house right on top of the ground, and the man that owns that high lot next to you will give you fifty cents a load for the privilege of shoveling his hill into your lot, and fill it all up even to grade."

"By George! I never thought of that. It looks reasonable, though, don't it? How much do you ask for it?"

"I can sell you that lot, if you should conclude to take it before two o'clock this P. M.—the hour when the Real Estate Exchange meets—for $400 a front foot, but at that hour it is liable to go up another hundred dollars a foot."

"That is very cheap, I must confess, but I don't believe I want it. I would rather have the lot next to it. How much can that be got for?" I inquired.

"Well, the man that owns that lot, holds it at $450 a foot."

"Whew! How's that?"

"Why, he says that the man that owns this low corner lot will give him a dollar a load for his hill to fill up his lot with, and the dirt that he can sell in getting his lot down to grade will more than pay for it."

I could not help saying, "By Gosh!" and I asked him if them two lots was a fair specimen of the balance he had to sell.

He said they was about a fair average.

I was taken with a violent swimming in my head, and asked him if he would please drive me to my hotel. He saw I was as white in the face as a ghost, and took me to the hotel in quick time.

He wanted to know when he could call for me.

I told him not until I had recovered from the first attack.

Of all the doses of rank, genuine hypocrisy that I have swallowed since I left home, this was the worst, and I told Clarissa that it wasn't safe to stay in Kansas City any longer, for if we did, I should be prostrated on a bed of sickness. So we took the evening train, and the next morning arrived in Chicago's great rival city, that stretches its busy arms up and down the meandering Mississippi, while its monstrous body lays back from Sippi's western bank.

CHAPTER XXXV.

WHILE we was in Chicago we got the impression from remarks we frequently heard, and from items we occasionally ran across in their papers, that St. Louis had in former days been a thriving, active small city, but that in the race for business and influence with the great Chicago it had been completely distanced, and consequently had become discouraged, and had laid down, fatigued, and gone to sleep, content with being numbered with the great things of the past. Therefore, we was expecting to see a city of quiet peacefulness, whose large buildings were closed, and upon whose walls we would see posted, "Hands Off. Don't mar these premises, or carry off any splinters for relics," and other indications of sacred silence that usually reigns in abandoned and dead cities and towns.

But we was perfectly surprised, when we rode through the streets from the depot to the Southern Hotel, to find all the activity and stir there was in Chicago. There was not quite so much *rush* and *bustle*, but there was an air of determination resting on the faces of the men we met and passed on the streets, that seemed to say, "We are getting there all the same, if we don't make so much fuss about it."

At the Southern we was treated first-rate, and everything was done to make us feel at home that could be done. They gave us their best spare bedroom, with a bathroom opening out of it, and they took special pains to introduce us to several distinguished persons that was there; among the rest was the mayor of the city.

He was a perfect gentleman, and was very polite, especially to Clarissa. He invited us to take a ride with him in his own private carriage. We was just as polite to him as we knew how to be, and told him we was dreadful glad to go riding with him.

While he was having the carriage hitched up and brought up to the hotel, I went and got a store shave—the first one I ever had, for I always shave myself—and got a nigger to black my boots, while Clarissa changed her dress and put on her crow-grain black silk, so both of us would look real slick and nice.

The carriage had arrived at the front door, and the mayor was waiting for us. As we stepped into the elegant carriage I noticed his driver, like Mayor Harrison's, had on a mourning hat-band.

They took us all over the city, and out to Mr. Shaw's garden. We was surprised almost every minute, for, instead of a dead or abandoned city, we found a great city, chuck-full of enterprise and business, while in the residence portions we found an air of old-fashioned comfort, solidity combined with beauty, that was far ahead of Chicago, and Mr. Shaw's garden was perfectly beautiful. Clarissa said she would like to live in that garden for a month. She is passionately fond of posies.

We drove across the pride and glory of the city—her wonderful bridge—and had a good look at Old Mississippi. The steamboats that lined the bank of the river told the story of her wonderful advantage in reaching the towns up and down the river, that Chicago did not possess. The ride was highly instructive, as well as pleasant.

On our way back to the hotel Clarissa and I and the mayor got quite well acquainted. He went on for a long time, telling us about the advantages St. Louis possessed over Chicago. I asked him if he thought that St. Louis would in course of time be as large and important a city as Chicago was at present. "Of course," said I, "it will never catch up with it, for while your city is growing, Chicago is jumping right ahead all the time."

He said, "Of course it will. While Chicago is a little ahead of us in population, and outstrips us in braggadocio and flapdoodle, we are far ahead of her in solid wealth. Our city is prosperous, and its inhabitants own their places of business, and their homes are paid for, and not plastered all over with mortgages, as two-thirds of the Chicago houses and homes are." I saw there was a spirit of envy sticking out of both ends of his remarks. I spoke up, and said:

"Isn't it an indication of the prosperity and growth of a city, when it is able to borrow all the money it needs on the security of its property? Men of means don't very often loan money to dead folks and take mortgages on their corpses, do they?"

"I want you to understand that St. Louis aint dead, by any means," said he, in a little huffy tone.

"I beg your pardon. I did not say she was,—and by the way she kicks whenever the word Chicago is mentioned, I know she haint dead, nor did I even think she was; but I spoke as I did to show that if Chicago has got some mortgage porous plasters on her back, she is an all-fired smart city, and the business men are making money there, and your folks hadn't ought to be so sensitive whenever there is any mention made of the eighth wonder of the world."

The mayor didn't like my remarks, which I could plainly see, and I said, "If you won't get offended at my suggestion, I think I can put you on the track of rapidly improving your city, and ultimately make it go away ahead of Chicago."

He brightened up, and said, "Certainly not. I shall be very happy to receive any suggestions you have to offer."

"Well, then," said I, "you just enter into an arrangement with Carter Harrison, of Chicago, to give you some pointers, and if he will, and he is not elected mayor this term, he can put you on the right road to success."

"Well! well! well! what makes you think so?"

"Think so? think so?" said I. "There is no think about it. I *know* so, for he told Clarissa and I both that he took hold of Chicago when it was a small city of a couple hundred thousand, and since he had run it as its mayor he had brought it up to nearly 800,000. Why! it's perfectly marvelous what that man can do. You just take my advice, and write to Carter in regard to it."

He said he would think about it.

By this time we had arrived at the hotel. We thanked him for his kind attention, and invited him to come with his family and visit us some time, which he agreed to do. After dinner I went to pay my bill, and the landlord wouldn't take a cent. He said he had noticed our visit in Chicago, and he felt it as much of an honor to him to entertain us as it was to Mr. Palmer.

After expressions of gratitude, and extending him a pressing invitation to visit us, we bid him good-by, and took the Chicago & Alton train for Chicago.

CHAPTER XXXVI.

WE arrived in Chicago Friday morning, and went to the Palmer House. Everything seemed to be alive and stirring. The rustle, bustle, rattle, roar, bang and jam on every side seemed about as it did on our former visit. They was glad to see us back again at the tavern, or at least they said so, and of course, tavern-keepers and their clerks never say anything they don't mean. I thanked them, and said I was glad to return.

Everything around this great palace seemed quite natural. The same general rush in the office, the same mixture of different nationalities, the majority being the descendants of the dwellers in the Holy Land, who seemed to have an eye open to the main chance, the same lot of country merchants, stockmen, and farmers, and the same crowd of swells and dudes, with their one blind eyeglass and cane. And among the general crowd I saw the tall, lean, lank, hawkeyed, cadaverous cuss that belongs to the *reportorial staff* (as he calls it) of the Chicago *Tribune*. I made up my mind I would avoid him if possible, and so I started for my room, and proceeded up the grand stairway. I had only got up to the first broad stair, when that cuss, with a hop, jump and three steps, landed beside me, and with extended hand and a horrible grin, said, "How are you, Mr. Morgan? Glad to see you! When did you return? I'd like to have a little interview with you, if you can spare me a little of your time."

If you ever had a bare spot on top of your head when you have been sitting on the bank of a river under the shade of a tree in the summer, with your hat off, holding a fishpole in your hand, waiting an hour or so for some innocent fool of a fish to invite you to pull him in out of the wet, and realized the peculiar sensation of having the tallest skeeter in the woods light on the clearing in your locks and sink a shaft for blood, you can imagine my feelings just at that moment. I turned to the town tattler, and in the language of Mr. Harrison, said, "I won't be interviewed; I don't want to be interviewed, and dumb me, if I will be interviewed. I haint got nothing to tell; I don't want to tell nothing, and dumb me, if I will tell

SINKING A SHAFT FOR BLOOD.

nothing. I don't want to be lied about, and dumb me, if I will be lied about. I am an honest and upright man; I always was an honest and upright man, and dumb me, I am always going to be an honest and upright man. I am Chicago's best mayor, and dumb me, I always will be Chicago's best mayor—No! no! Excuse me. That last remark didn't apply to me. I was thinking about what he told me, and wasn't thinking what I was saying. No, I haint, nor never will be, mayor of this city. I haint been to breakfast yet, and haint got time to be interviewed, so good-morning." I went up-stairs, and left him on the broad stair in front of the big looking-glass. He had a pencil and paper in his hand, and was scratching like a hen after grubs.

We went into the grand dining room for breakfast. Everything looked as usual, except they had got a new picture over one of the doors. It was off to my left side, and I said to Clarissa:

"Do you see that big picture over there? It's awful nice."

"Where, Benjamin? I don't see it."

"Why, right over there," and I pointed it out with my fork, and she pinched me.

Said I, "What's that for; what have I done now?"

"I thought I told you, when we was here before, that your fork was made to eat with, and not be jabbing things with it," said she.

After breakfast Clarissa and I went down to the mayor's office, to see Mr. Harrison. We was surprised when we was informed that Mr. Harrison wasn't the mayor any longer. That the people had decided at its recent election not to take any more of his valuable time and cause him any more trouble in running the city government, and had elected one of the common people, Mr. Roche, for mayor, and at present Mr. Harrison was out of a job. If lightning had struck the city and shattered it from one end to the other, I wouldn't have been more thunderstruck.

I asked a young man in the office where we would find Mr. Harrison. He said he didn't know. I asked him if he could direct me to Mike McDonald's place of business. He said he could, and after getting our directions we bid him good-by, and went over to Mr. McDonald's place on Clark Street.

We found that gentleman, and after introducing ourselves, told him who we was and what we wanted. He was very pleasant, and invited us into his private room. After we was seated he said, "I have heard Carter speak of you often, and I know he will be glad to see you. At present you'll find him at home—he is not feeling well. The facts are these: He wanted to be mayor of the city, and thought

POINTING OUT WITH MY FORK THE MOST INTERESTING POINTS.

the best way to make sure of it was to announce in the papers that he would under no circumstances run for the office ; that by doing so the people would run after him in a mass, and make him the mayor in spite of his assumed objections ; and in case they did, he could do as he pleased, just as he always has done. But the dumb fools of people thought he was honest, and meant what he said, and they wouldn't—and they didn't elect him, but, on the contrary, they went to work and ignored all of his suggestions, and elected one of the common men, Roche, by the biggest majority that was ever given to any mayor ever elected in the city. When Carter saw the people had misconstrued his real meaning, and took him at his word, he tried to get them to elect a highly respectable anarchist; but the people hadn't got over thinking about a little trouble the city had with the anarchists last spring, and they didn't comply with Carter's desire, and he has been so mad about the way things have gone that he won't come down town any more, only when he is obliged to, and when he does, he is hounded to death by them reporters."

Clarissa spoke up, and with a sigh, said : " Well, I'm awful sorry for Mr. Harrison, for he is such a good man."

"Yes, so am I," said Mr. McDonald; "I am sorry, but I, and four or five of his old chums, drive out to see him most every evening and cheer him up with a few games. The fact is, the city has drifted into the hands of a lot of cranks, and they have got every paper in the city under their influence, and they are just playing —— with the best men we have got. They have gone to work and got all of the old commissioners, and some of the best men we have, indicted for swindling the county and stealing, and a whole lot of other —— nonsense, and now they are going to send them to the State's Prison, if they can hire enough —— liars to prove their charges. Now, there is Dan Wren. Everybody knows that he is the very soul of honor. If he ever gets beat, he pays up like a man. They have a dozen or more crimes charged against him. And Van Pelt, who wouldn't think of doing a wrong—they've got him with the rest. And then, to cap the whole —— scheme, they got the chairman of the board, Mr. Klehm, indicted on the contemptible charge of stealing $5,000 out of the bottom of a well down to the Insane Asylum. That is the dirtiest part of the cranks' work. You see, it was just like this: You know crazy folks drink a pile of water. If they drank good old whisky and beer, they wouldn't be crazy, and they had to have a new well down there, and of course, they wanted a big one. Now, Klehm was working for the interests of the county, and watched everything, and saw that the county got the lowest prices on everything, and that nothing was stole. So, when the well was to be dug, he let the contract to the LOWEST bidder, of course. So he let the job to a feller for 80 cents a foot for the first 300 feet, and for every additional 300 feet a large increase ; and when below 2,000 feet, it was to be $4.50 a foot. When the well was done, Klehm went out and measured it with his own weight and line, and when the weight struck bottom, it broke loose from the line ; but he measured the line, and it was about 2,500 feet deep."

"Oh, what an awful deep well!" said Clarissa.

"Yes, it is; but you must understand, madam, that they are awful crazy out there, and drink lots of water. Well, when this crank jury was hauling the commissioners over, they thought the well was too deep; so the fools all went out there and got Furthmann to measure it, and he went down and measured every foot till he got to the bottom, where he found Klehm's weight, and brought it up with him. He said the well was just 1,500 feet deep. And now they want to raise the devil with Klehm, and send him to the pen, just because he made a mistake in measuring that crazy-house well, of a thousand feet. Don't you see what a mean, pusillanimous piece of work that is? And just so with all the rest of the commissioners. They are being persecuted by these cranks for some little, trivial mistakes or oversights. Why, they have got my little brother, Eddie, who was a poor, hard-working engineer out at the Cook County Hospital, indicted for stealing, on some —— trumped up lies, and poor Eddie feels so sick that he can't say his prayers before he gets into bed in his cool, cool cell. And they indicted Eddie's old playmate, Billy McGarrigle, for being an honest warden, and have locked the boys up in jail."

"Oh, oh! what a pity!" said Clarissa.

"Yes, it is a pity," said Mike. "You see, condemn it, it breaks up all our arrangements. It breaks up our Sunday-school class, and all the nice picnics we had arranged for this coming summer are knocked into a cocked hat by these infernal old cranks. I tell you what it is, I'd rather live in Canada any time, and if I could get the boys together without being watched, we'd all move over there; but there it is, —— it, these —— cranks are right onto us all the time, and we can't breathe but they've got a detective on the spot to catch the lost breath. I am getting disgusted with the city, any way, and I am going to move out, if it goes on this way much longer. We can't act as we would if they would let us alone. As it is, we are forced into a position of hypocrisy which is contrary to our natures, as every one knows that knows us."

Clarissa heaved several sighs, and expressed her sorrow for the persecuted good men of Chicago.

As we left his place, and returned to the Palmer for dinner, I said to Clarissa that she had better keep her briny tears corked up until we heard the dear people's side of the case. Although I know I am chuck-full of shortcomings, yet there is one thing I have always stuck to, and that is to never turn myself loose until I have heard both sides of a story.

We had been so busy traveling and seeing sights ever since we left Chicago for the West, that I had not read very much in the newspapers, so I was ignorant of what had been going on in the city while we was gone; but Clarissa had finished reading her book, and when we went to our room, after dinner, she guessed that Mr. Harrison had anticipated his defeat, as the book, "Shadows of the

Future," was a kind of prophecy pointing to such a result in the coming election. She was sorry for him, as he was such a great man.

"Well," says she, "we'll do our duty, and go to his house this afternoon and see him, and console with him. I know that when folks are in trouble, and are passing under the dark cloud of affliction, they need the sympathy of all their friends and neighbors, and it is the duty of all their friends and neighbors to call on them, and tell them how sorry they are for them."

We went out to Mr. Harrison's house, and rung the door bell. The same servant girl that was there when we was at his house before came to the door, and says, "Och! and ye bees the Morganses as was here last winter, and would ye be after wantin' to see the boss?" Clarissa told her that we came to call on him. "Well, thin, I'll be axin' him if he wants to see ye," and off she went, and in a few minutes he came to the door, and in his pleasant manner invited us into the parlor.

He had changed considerable, and looked much poorer than before. He said he was glad to see us, and Clarissa told him she was glad to see him, but was awful sorry to see him looking so poor. Says she, "I presume it is wearing on you to be disappointed so." Said he, "What do you mean by being disappointed?"

"Why, in not being elected mayor of the city," she replied.

"Oh! no, that isn't wearing on me a mite," said he, "but to think that Chicago has got to get along with a mayor that hasn't had any experience, and is liable at any minute to ruin the city, worries me a great deal, and I can't bear the thought that all the good men I have put into different official positions, and have spent so much time in drilling, so they would do any and everything I told them to do, should be turned out, without a dollar in their pockets, and nothing to do for an honest living."

Clarissa said, as the tears began to wet the left side of her nose— (there is something peculiar about Clarissa—she can't cry out of only one eye), "Mr. Harrison, you are too great and noble a man to sacrifice yourself for the benefit of such an ungrateful city. Why don't you go to St. Louis and be mayor for that city? They need you there!"

"Thank you, Mrs. Morgan, for your kind remarks and your advice. I cannot possibly think of being mayor of any city again, as I intend to sail for Europe very soon," he responded.

We had a very pleasant visit, considering the gloomy conversation, for about two hours, when we bid him good-by, and returned to our hotel.

It may be just possible that Chicago may survive the terrible blow of losing its able Carter and its county commissioners. She survived the greatest fire that ever warmed any city in the world, and in time, I think she will survive this calamity.

CHAPTER XXXVII.

WE remained in Chicago but a few days this time, as we was anxious to get home. I wish I had time to tell the many experiences I had with a host of smooth, highly polished and genteel hypocrites. I met them under the guise of merchants, unfortunate capitalists, heirs of great expectations, but temporarily laborin' under a " Col. Sellers" misfortune of bein' financially embarrassed, missionaries, ministers (that the Lord has no further use for), obliging gentlemen, ready to show a stranger golden opportunities for making a fortune, and a hundred other characters, all seeking one common end, the bottom end of my pocket—but I have not, as the bus is waiting at the door, to take us to the L. S. & M S. R. R. depot, where we take the train for Syracuse. So, good-by to Chicago, the great city of activity, filled with great and good men, who tower like a Pike's Peak above the common mass, and an immense host of hypocrites, who like worms, and snakes, crawl all through it, working their way into every phase of its life.

We left the city on the morning train, and reached Syracuse the next day about noon. Mrs. Buzzbee and her husband met us at the depot, and we went to their house and staid over night with them. The evening passed off so quickly at the house, that before we was aware of it it was midnight. Mr. B. said, "Uncle Ben, how do you and the hypocrites get along? have you reformed them all?" To which I replied, "No! I've given up the job. I thought we had a few up in our neighborhood, but they haint a fly speck compared with what we've met. It's no use, Mr. Buzzbee; to reform one is planting the seeds for a hundred; it's like killing one skeeter in the woods—his body seems to turn into a dozen more. And then there is something so catching about that moral disease, hypocrisy, that while you are trying to reform others that are afflicted with it, you are liable to have an attack of it yourself, and when a professional reformer catches it, it goes awful hard with him, and like leprosy, he never recovers from it. You take these great political reformers, temperance reformers, railroad tariff reformers, financial reformers and even religious reformers, and you'll find that most of 'em get a dreadful severe attack of it. So I've concluded not to undertake the job, but to go home to the old farm, and with Clarissa do my duty as I understand it; be honest and content with what I have, and try to make Clarissa happy as long as we live, and leave the job of correctin' the evil practices of human men in the hands of the great Engineer of the universe, who has His hand upon the lever and can reverse action and shut off steam, whenever, in his judgment, it is necessary. He has done it all along the past. History is but a description of the mysterious workings of the great spiritual engine moving under the guidance of His hand and will."

When I had finished, Mr. B. and his wife both spoke up with an air of surprise pervadin' every lineament of their countenance, and said, "Well, Mr. Morgan, you have changed considerable since you left here on this trip. You talk as though you had been to college, studying."

Clarissa spoke up and said, "Yes, Benjamin has improved considerable. When we first started out, I done most of the talkin', and now he does most of it, but he has taken a good many lessons. His first lesson was here in Syracuse; his next was on the train from Buffalo to Cleveland; then again at Chicago, and again in Virginia City, and then in San Francisco, and all along. I'm glad on't. Our trip has cost us lots of money, but it has been a good school to both of us, and we could, in no other way, have learned so much, to say nothing about the pleasure we have had for the same amount of money, as we have by the swindling scheme of Ketchem, Holdem, Skinem & Co., in running their great transcontinental excursion."

The next day I met the last year's mayor at Buzzbee's store, the same one I met in the club room when I was here before. He was the same polite gentleman he was then, and was very nice to me. I begged his pardon for the abrupt remarks I made when in their clubroom last November. I told him I had just left the farm and was totally ignorant of the ways of the world, and at that

"NOTHIN' STRONGER THAN LEMONADE AND CIGARS."

time supposed that shamming and hypocrisy was an occasional exception to the general rule, but I had, during my travels, learned that it is the general rule; that it is quite fashionable to sham, and I was and still continue to be out of fashion; but I did not intend, in the future, to be a fool by blurtin' out my prejudiced notion of things, and hurting others' feelings without doing any good. He said I was fully pardoned, and he had not thought ill of me, for he knew I was honest, but had not seen the world as it is. His remarks was true.

We arrived at the village at five P. M. We was met at the depot by Eb and Mary, and Abe and Lily, and a whole lot of our old neighbors, all glad to see us home again. And we was glad to see them. They had hired the village brass band to escort us from the depot up into The Village, and as we walked up the sidewalk, the band marched ahead of us with a big banner in front of 'em, saying ; " *This way to the Fat Cattle Show !*"

Of course we had to take it, and I had to stand treat for the whole town. "Nothin' stronger than lemonade and cigars," said I, when we arrived at Ebenezer's store. Eb made a barrel of lemonade, and set out 500 cigars to the crowd. Zolliver Ramsdell stood on the steps in front of the store and delivered a speech of welcome, to which I had to respond. Whether it was the speech of Zolliver or my speech, or the cigars and lemonade that kept the whole village there in a jam for more'n two hours, I can't say, but it was midnight before they all left, and Clarissa and I retired to Ebenezer and Mary Plunket's private spare bedroom, to blissful repose, which we stood in need of.

When we come out to breakfast in the morning, Ebenezer handed me a lot of letters. The first one I opened was from Squire Bigler, containing his Cattle Scheme, showing a statement of the concern he had organized. He had his picture in the center of it representing him in the act of making a speech. Here it is, just as he had it printed :

COLORADO CATTLE COMPANY.

This Company was organized under the laws of the State of Colorado for the purpose of buying, raising, shipping and selling cattle and other live stock, and for the purpose of buying and owning grazing land in said State.

The capital stock is ONE MILLION DOLLARS, divided into TEN THOUSAND SHARES of the par value of ONE HUNDRED DOLLARS each, issued full paid and non-assessible.

The affairs of the company are under the management of not less than five nor more than nine trustees, who are to be elected annually by the stockholders at their meetings to be held on the first Monday in November in each year.

The business of the company, as provided by its charter, is to be carried on in the State of Colorado, with its principal office in the city of Denver and a branch office in the city of New York in the State of New York, where the meetings of the stockholders and board of trustees may be held, and where the books of the company may be kept, and its financial affairs conducted. There may also be established by direction of the board of trustees, if they shall deem it expedient for the interests of the company, branch offices in the cities of Chicago and Baltimore, where certificates of stock may be transferred, and any necessary business of the company transacted.

This company owns one of the largest stock ranges in the State of Colorado. It lies between the Huerfano and Apishipa Rivers in Southern Colorado, and comprises over four hundred thousand acres. The river frontage is more than one hundred miles; the central portion of the range being interspersed with living springs and lakes.

The company derives its title to four hundred thousand acres from the grantees of the Las Animas Grant, a grant made December 9, 1843, by Manuel Armiso, Governor of Mex-

BIGLER MAKING A SPEECH.

ico, to Cornelio Vigil and Ceran St. Vrain, which grant was fully ratified under and by the treaty of Gaudaloupe Hidalgo, in 1848, between the United States and Mexico. The entire grant amounted to about four million acres of the finest grazing land in the world.

The company also owns fourteen thousand acres under government patent and preemption, which controls vast water privileges. The lakes upon this land are inexhaustible and never become frozen to any extent during the winter months. These lakes flow into deep, grassy canyons, which average five hundred feet in width and have natural sandstone walls thirty to fifty feet high, affording an absolute shelter to stock.

This range has a very heavy growth of grass, blue joint, buffalo and gramma, and is ample for the support of at least forty thousand head of cattle. It has all the necessary improvements, such as corrals, buildings, branding pens, water tanks, etc. It has a good, substantial fence—cedar posts and barbed wire, forty miles in length, connecting with the head of Apishipa canyon on the north, and Spring canyon on the south, and inclosing with the deep canyons, about two hundred thousand acres. Waterways are cut, at intervals, down the banks of the canyons and Apishipa River, on the side next to the inclosure. Alfalfa fields are grown at different points upon the range, one field of two thousand acres, closely fenced, now yielding not less than three tons per acre. Groves of cedar and pinon, under which is a heavy growth of grass, are scattered over this vast range, and afford shelter from the summer sun and the winter winds.

The St. Vrain Land and Irrigation Company is constructing a sixty-foot canal across this range, which will afford at all seasons an abundant supply of pure mountain water. The bank of the canal next to the range will be left open to the company's cattle under an arrangement made with the said St. Vrain Company. The company will also be able to irrigate from this ditch or canal a large amount of its land, which can then be cultivated to great advantage and benefit.

The following is a correct statement of the property now owned by the Colorado Cattle Company, together with the cost of the same:

STATEMENT.

400,000 acres of grazing land, part of the Las Animas Grant, at 25 cents..	$100,000
14,000 acres Government Patent and Pre-emption, together with cost of implements, improvements, fences, water rights, etc..	69,000
4,480 cows, 3 years old and over, improved; 200 bulls, Shorthorn, a few bloods; 938 steers, mixed, 3 years old and over; 523 heifers, yearlings, 2 years old Spring '87..............	196,080
67 horses, not including 17 colts.............................	4,200
Total cost to date................................	$369,280

RECEIPTS.

From sale of 3,750 shares of stock at $100....................	$375,000
From sale of 978 steers and 112 fat N. C. cows, net	44,410
Total receipts..	$419,410

DISBURSEMENTS.

Commissions, added to cost of cattle, expenses paid in full to Nov. 1, '86...	$ 6,385
Range...	169,000
Cattle...	196,080
Horses..	4,200
Total disbursements...............................	$375,665
Balance...	$ 43,745

CAPITAL.

Total number shares, 10,000, par value, $100.................	$1,000,000
Number shares sold, 3,750 for........	375,000
Remaining in treasury, 6,250, value......................... $	625,000
Cash in treasury...	43,745
Capital stock and cash on hand................... $	668,745

TAXES.

There are no taxes levied upon the Mexican grant land. The tax on Government patents is merely nominal. Very light on cattle, average about 25 cents per head. The tax for this year will be payable January 1st, to May 1st, 1887.

CATTLE.

Cows, 3 years old and over, improved................................4,347
Bulls, mostly Short-horn, a few high bred........................ 200
Calves, 1886 crop, heifers improved............................2,213
1886 crop steers, improved....................................1,874
Heifers 2 years old in Spring 1887, grade..................... 523

Total number owned by Company January 1, 1887.....9,157
January 1, 1887.

It needs no comments to show the hypocrisy of this swindling scheme, as it carries on the face of it, the same as hundreds of other similar schemes, hypocrisy.

After breakfast I went over to the bank to find what they wanted me to hurry home for. Mr. Brown took me into his private office, and showed me a note for $1,000, signed by me, and said, "Mr. Morgan, did you sign that note?"

I said, "No, I never signed a note in my life."

"Well," said he, "I didn't believe you did. Will you please write your name on this piece of paper, so I can compare it?" I did so and when he compared it he said, "I am now fully satisfied that it is a forgery, and think there will be no trouble whatever in satisfying the court of that fact." Then he went on and told me how George Waddles had been sued by twenty different farmers for various amounts they proved in court he had swindled them out of, and how he had got his criminal case and all the other cases continued to the next term of court; how he had come to them and turned in several notes (this among the rest), and mortgage on his farm, as collateral security for money they loaned him for the purpose of settling these cases of the farmers, and not let them come to trial; and how they had gone on his bail, so he could be let out of jail; how he had skipped to parts unknown since then, and how they would be heavy losers, if the notes was all forged, which they feared was the case.

He said they had found out he had not paid any of these claims, but had taken all the money they had loaned him, and, said he, "We want to know what to do before court meets. We have every confidence in you, and for your sake as well as ours, we felt that you must be here before the time court was called."

I was dumbfounded, for, although I was satisfied he was a big hypocrite, I didn't think he was such an awful big rascal. They have got a detective on his track, and they may catch him. I had just left the bank, when I met Tom Conners, the lawyer that I helped elect to the Legislature. Said he, "Mr. Morgan, I am glad to see you back again. I would like to see you in my office a minute." I went with him. Said he, "I have just received a letter from San Francisco; I'll read it to you." He read as follows, to-wit:

SAN FRANCISCO, CAL., Jan. 25, 1887.

MR. THOMAS CONNERS:

Dear Sir—Inclosed you will find a note for $2,000, given me by one Benjamin Morgan, of your place. Will you proceed to collect the same, and forward the amount, less your fees, to me as soon as collected ?   Very respectfully yours,

CHARLES SKIPEM.

The following, to-wit, was the note:

SAN FRANCISCO, CAL., Dec. 24, 1886.

For the sum of ($2,000) two thousand dollars, received of the firm of Ketchem, Holdem & Skinem, by the hand of their agent, Chas. Skipem, for expenses while in California, the receipt of which I hereby acknowledge, I promise to pay two thousand dollars and interest at the rate of ten per cent. per annum, on demand.

BENJAMIN MORGAN.

"Now, Mr. Morgan, is that correct?"

I was never so surprised in my whole life, and in my excitement I come mighty nigh swearing, when I stood right up like one of them big trees, and said, "It's a goll-dumb lie. I never borrowed a cent from 'em, but the goll-dumb hypocrites owe me more'n two hundred dollars now, and, by thunder, I'll have every goll-dumb one of 'em put in prison, if I can."

"Hold on a minute, Mr. Morgan; look at the signature and tell me whether or not you wrote it yourself?"

I looked at it closely, and said I thought I did, for it looked like my writing. Just then I thought of the receipt I signed for the two hundred dollars. I also remembered signing it in a hurry, and not reading it over carefully, and I related the whole circumstance of our visit to the office of Dodgem, Skipem & Oppenheimer, and said I, "Clarissa was with me every minute I was in that city. I didn't go anywhere without her, and she paid close attention to everything that was done in that office, and I'll go right over to Eb's and bring her over here, and you ask her all about it."

"Very well, Mr. Morgan," he said. I went across the street and up to Eb's store on a run, and took Clarissa back with me in less than five minutes. She told Mr. Conners everything connected with it, just as I had.

Said Mr. Conners, "You will swear to this, will you?"

"Yes," she replied.

"You'll swear to this, will you, Mr. Morgan?" said he.

"Well," said I, "although it's agin my principles to swear, but on this occasion I'll swear a blue streak" and I commenced with geewhilliker dam—when Conners said, "Uncle Ben, hold on! hold on! That haint what I mean." (I did know what he meant, but I felt just like swearing, and I wanted to swear.) "I know you so well, and everybody knows you so well, that if you say a thing is so, I believe it, and now what you say is fully corroborated by your wife's statement. I see that it is a scheme to swindle you. They have converted the receipt you gave 'em for two hundred dollars into a note for $2,000. You needn't give yourself a particle of uneasiness about it, but just leave it to me and I'll see them inside of a penitentiary, and if they are worth it, you'll get all the money back on their advertised agreement that you have paid out. Had it not been that your wife was present, and is a witness that can beat 'em in any court in the United States, you might be caused a great deal of trouble, but she will save you from any trouble in the case."

I again felt she was my garden angel, and every day she becomes more gardener to me, and I feel every day the value of a good wife. God bless the wives! for they prove a blessing to many a poor man.

As we was riding home with Abe and the old mare, and just as we was passing old Smugginses house, Sarah run out to the gate to speak to us. She was dressed up in her best, and she tried to look sweet. After talking with her a few minutes, we drove on. Clarissa said, "Well, Benjamin, I'm glad to get home again, and I

SARAH SMUGGINS.

shall be contented to stay here the remainder of my days, for, after seeing so much of the world, so much grandeur, and style in high life in the large cities and centers of business and fashion, the old home, with its plain and unpretentious air, surrounded by the old orchard, and withal so quiet, seems like a paradise, and I can join the poet in his description of

THE OLD-FASHIONED HOME.

"Of all the tender and comfortable things
That now and then sweet memory brings,
There's nothing dearer that love recalls
Than the old-fashioned house with its whitewashed walls.

"Not a mansion to-day, though a marvel of art
Can ever usurp its place in my heart,
For there my earliest prayers were said,
And I slept at night in a trundle bed.

"'Neath coverlids reaching from feet to chin,
By a mother's hand tucked gently in,
And a good-night kiss on my tired brow—
Oh, earth holds no such blessings now.

"A garden was fragrant in flower-beds,
Where marigolds lifted their velvet heads,
And warmed by sunshine, refreshed by dew,
The bachelor-button and touch-me-not grew.

"In a river that curved like a shepherd's crook
We fished for minnows with a bent pin-hook,
Or with little bare feet oft waded through,
And bravely 'paddled our own canoe.'

"'Twas a home of welcome, no one could doubt,
Whose latchstring hung inevitably out,
And many a stranger supped at its board,
While blazing logs in the chimney roared.

"Oh, this is an age of reform and change!
And things æsthetic, modern and strange—
Improvements that savor of silver and gold
Are superseding the cherished and old.

"But I turn from palaces built for show!
With mansard roof and stories below;
Of frescoed, kalsomined, dadoed halls,
To the old-fashioned house with its whitewashed walls."

Again we are seated in our own big square room, well-lighted by the hanging lamp. Abe is snoring on the lounge; the old dog is stretched out in the corner behind the stove, and the cat is curled up on the rug under the stove-hearth, purring her evening song to feline notes, and everything is peaceful and quiet. Clarissa says, in her old-fashioned way, " Benjamin, it seems just as though we had left a heaven, and taken a trip through the noisy world below, where hypocrisy seems to be superior to plain, simple honesty, and returned again to heaven; it is so quiet here."

"That is just the way it strikes me; but we had a good time, after all, and learned an awful sight of human nature, a knowledge of which we did not possess to any great degree before we went."

"Well," said she, "that is so; but, after all, human nature is human nature the world over, whether on the quiet New York farm, or in the busy cities; whether digging potatoes in Blank County, or digging gold and silver in the old Rockies; whether attending meeting in the Corners' schoolhouse, clad in plain calico, or sitting in cushioned chairs in the great halls and churches in the city, dressed in silks and ornamented with diamonds and bits of sparkling glass; whether in our lyceums at the schoolhouse, or in the great dramas on the stage of the cities' splendid theaters—the feelings and passions of the human heart are alike manifested in daily life. The unscrupulous are continually inventing new schemes to cover up their real natures and keep the public from understanding their true characters, while the careless drift into channels of deception, and in time become stereotyped into the habit of presenting a false self. A few—and what a GLORIOUS few!—are *honest* by birth, by training and education, and how they tower above the hypocrites that surround them! How Mr. So-and-so, in this village and that, in this city and that, on this farm and in that manufactory, occupying this pulpit and sitting on that judicial bench—stands out prominently, and is admired by all, from the simple fact that his *word* is as good as his *note;* that in every act of his life he is *frank, truthful* and *honest.* The Almighty seems to be his guide and governor. It matters not if his education is deficient, or he lacks the [polish that rules of society require for a gentleman. Though he be a diamond in the rough, still he is a gem of greatest value to the world. The polish that education and contact with the world will add, will cause him to sparkle and appear more brilliant, but it is not the education nor polish that gives him value, or singles him out from his fellows, but because his heart and head are *right* and *true* all the way through, but he has got to have that trait born in him."

Clarissa got into one of her regular talking spells, and I said to her, in a sort of mellow tone, a little on the dulcet stop, " Clarissa; now, do—please do."

" Please do what?" she replied.

" Please let up—please shut down a little."

"What do you mean, Benjamin?" she asked.

"I mean to say that this is my first book, and you wondered who'd ' be fool enough to read it.' Now, if you don't let up on this continual philosophizing, and telling what you think, it will kill it, and if ever I should write another, I couldn't *hire* a fool to read it. Now, let's sing the doxology to close your remarks, and let me just tell the dear people, and men and women in general, in closing this volume, what I think. I think that MAN is, after all, partly a product of climate and soil. It is *not* true that *man* is the crowning glory of God's creation, for it depends upon where he is located, and his surroundings, as to the position he occupies in the scale of Glory—in Creation. You go into parts of Africa, where the *palm* and *bread fruit* tree flourish, and man sinks to the level of other brutes that feed upon the bread fruit and sleep under the shade of the palm. *There*, these *trees* are the crowning *Glory* of Creation. Certain impulses lead man in certain directions. Surroundings, climatic and scenic, have very much to do in establishing his tastes and inclinations, while his social surroundings direct his mental habit. Education—broad, liberal and thorough—causes the mental to rise in power above the animal, while idleness and neglect give the animal supremacy over the mental. Neglected fields return the farmer naught but weeds, while cultivation brings him rich grains and grassy meads. So, with the *heart,* the bond of man's mental and animal dispositions, if rightly directed, yields the results of Honesty —if wrongly, Hypocrisy."

www.ingramcontent.com/pod-product-compliance
Lightning Source LLC
Chambersburg PA
CBHW030601300426
44111CB00009B/1065